T0233947

Lecture Notes in Computer Science 12230

More information about this series at http://www.springer.com/series/8183

Marina L. Gavrilova · C. J. Kenneth Tan ·
Jian Chang · Nadia Magnenat Thalmann (Eds.)

Transactions on Computational Science XXXVII

Special Issue on Computer Graphics

 Springer

Editors-in-Chief
Marina L. Gavrilova
University of Calgary
Calgary, AB, Canada

C. J. Kenneth Tan
Sardina Systems OÜ
Tallinn, Estonia

Guest Editors
Jian Chang ⓘ
Bournemouth University
Poole, UK

Nadia Magnenat Thalmann
MiraLab
University of Geneva
Geneva, Switzerland

ISSN 0302-9743   ISSN 1611-3349 (electronic)
Lecture Notes in Computer Science
ISSN 1866-4733   ISSN 1866-4741 (electronic)
Transactions on Computational Science
ISBN 978-3-662-61982-7   ISBN 978-3-662-61983-4 (eBook)
https://doi.org/10.1007/978-3-662-61983-4

This Springer imprint is published by the registered company Springer-Verlag GmbH, DE
part of Springer Nature.
The registered company address is: Heidelberger Platz 3, 14197 Berlin, Germany

LNCS Transactions on Computational Science

Computational science, an emerging and increasingly vital field, is now widely recognized as an integral part of scientific and technical investigations, affecting researchers and practitioners in areas ranging from aerospace and automotive research to biochemistry, electronics, geosciences, mathematics, and physics. Computer systems research and the exploitation of applied research naturally complement each other. The increased complexity of many challenges in computational science demands the use of supercomputing, parallel processing, sophisticated algorithms, and advanced system software and architecture. It is therefore invaluable to have input by systems research experts in applied computational science research.

Transactions on Computational Science focuses on original high-quality research in the realm of computational science in parallel and distributed environments, also encompassing the underlying theoretical foundations and the applications of large-scale computation.

The journal offers practitioners and researchers the opportunity to share computational techniques and solutions in this area, to identify new issues, and to shape future directions for research, and it enables industrial users to apply leading-edge, large-scale, high-performance computational methods.

In addition to addressing various research and application issues, the journal aims to present material that is validated – crucial to the application and advancement of the research conducted in academic and industrial settings. In this spirit, the journal focuses on publications that present results and computational techniques that are verifiable.

Scope

The scope of the journal includes, but is not limited to, the following computational methods and applications:

- Aeronautics and Aerospace
- Astrophysics
- Big Data Analytics
- Bioinformatics
- Biometric Technologies
- Climate and Weather Modeling
- Communication and Data Networks
- Compilers and Operating Systems
- Computer Graphics
- Computational Biology
- Computational Chemistry
- Computational Finance and Econometrics
- Computational Fluid Dynamics

- Computational Geometry
- Computational Number Theory
- Data Representation and Storage
- Data Mining and Data Warehousing
- Information and Online Security
- Grid Computing
- Hardware/Software Co-design
- High-Performance Computing
- Image and Video Processing
- Information Systems
- Information Retrieval
- Modeling and Simulations
- Mobile Computing
- Numerical and Scientific Computing
- Parallel and Distributed Computing
- Robotics and Navigation
- Supercomputing
- System-on-Chip Design and Engineering
- Virtual Reality and Cyberworlds
- Visualization

Editorial

The *Transactions on Computational Science* journal is part of the Springer series *Lecture Notes in Computer Science*, and is devoted to the gamut of computational science issues, from theoretical aspects to application-dependent studies and the validation of emerging technologies.

The journal focuses on original high-quality research in the realm of computational science in parallel and distributed environments, encompassing the facilitating theoretical foundations and the applications of large-scale computations and massive data processing. Practitioners and researchers share computational techniques and solutions in the area, identify new issues, and shape future directions for research, as well as enable industrial users to apply the presented techniques.

The current volume is devoted to the area of computer graphics. The volume is comprised of nine papers selected following the 36th installment of the Computer Graphics International Conference (CGI 2019), one of the oldest international annual conferences in computer graphics founded by the Computer Graphics Society (CGS). The conference was held in Calgary, Alberta, in June 2019 at the University of Calgary. This special issue is edited by CGI 2019 conference co-chairs: Prof. Jian Chang and Prof. Marina Gavrilova. All the accepted papers have been peer-reviewed.

We would like to extend our sincere appreciation to the special issue guest editors for their continuous dedication and insights in preparing this special issue. We would also like to thank all of the authors for submitting their papers to the journal and the associate editors and referees for their valuable work.

We do hope that the fine collection of papers presented in this special issue will be a valuable resource for *Transactions on Computational Science* readers and will stimulate further research into the vibrant area of computational science applications.

May 2020

Marina L. Gavrilova
C. J. Kenneth Tan

Guest Editor Preface

The Computer Graphics International (CGI) conference is one of the oldest international conferences on computer graphics in the world. It is the official conference of the Computer Graphics Society (CGS), a long-standing international computer graphics organization.

The 36th CGI conference was held in Calgary, Alberta, Canada, from June 17–20, 2019. It was organized by CGS, the University of Calgary, and the Alberta Innovates, and was in cooperation with ACM and EUROGRAPHICS. Various topics of computer graphics and related applications have been discussed at CGI 2019. Some of the top papers with extended and revised articles were invited to this issue of the *Transactions on Computational Science Journal*, Springer.

The paper "Do Distant or Colocated Audiences Affect User Activity in VR?" by Romain Terrier, Nicolas Martin, Jérémy Lacoche, Valérie Gouranton, and Bruno Arnaldi presents an experimental study on location and interactions with the audience through virtual reality.

The paper "Physical Environment Reconstruction Beyond Light Polarization for Coherent Augmented Reality Scene on Mobile Devices" by A'aeshah Alhakamy and Mihran Tuceryan provides geometric reconstruction for improved photo-realism of virtual objects in augmented reality.

The paper "Integrated Analysis and Hypothesis Testing for Complex Spatio-Temporal Data" by Kresimir Matkovic, Dieter W. Fellner, and Torsten Ullrich uses a deep learning method to analyze bird song features.

The paper "Action Sequencing in VR, a No-Code Approach" by Flavien Lécuyer, Valérie Gouranton, Adrien Reuzeau, Ronan Gaugne, and Bruno Arnaldi proposes to create scenarios in virtual reality without coding.

The paper "Single Color Sketch-Based Image Retrieval in HSV Color Space" by Yu Xia, Shuangbu Wang, Yanran Li, Lihua You, Xiaosong Yang, and Jian Jun Zhang introduces a fine-grained color sketch-based image retrieval method with deep leaning network.

The paper "Integral-Based Material Point Method and Peridynamics Model for Animating Elastoplastic Material" by Yao Lyu, Jinglu Zhang, Ari Sarafopoulos, Jian Chang, Shihui Guo, and Jian Jun Zhang develops a physically based approach for modeling deformation with peridynamics.

The paper "A Perceptually Coherent TMO for Visualization of 360° HDR Images on HMD" by Ific Goudé Rémi Cozot, and Olivier Le Meur suggests a tone mapping operator (TMO) to enhance visualization of 360° high-dynamic-range images on head mounted displays.

The paper "Simulating Crowds and Autonomous Vehicles" by John Charlton, Luis Montana Gonzalez, Steve Maddock, and Paul Richmond simulates large-scale scenes of crowds and vehicles with GPU acceleration.

The paper "MagiPlay: An Augmented Reality Serious Game Allowing Children to Program Intelligent Environments" by Evropi Stefanidi, Dimitrios Arampatzis, Asterios Leonidis, Maria Korozi, Margherita Antona, and George Papagiannakis defines an intelligent environment through a specially tailored user interface.

The organizers of the conference are very grateful to Prof. Marina Gavrilova, Editor in Chief of the *Transactions on Computational Science*, for her continuing support and assistance. We deeply thank the reviewers for their diligent work which helped improve the papers.

May 2020
Jian Chang
Nadia Magnenat Thalmann

LNCS Transactions on Computational Science – Editorial Board

Contents

Do Distant or Colocated Audiences Affect User Activity in VR? 1
Romain Terrier, Nicolas Martin, Jeremy Lacoche, Valerie Gouranton,
and Bruno Arnaldi

Physical Environment Reconstruction Beyond Light Polarization
for Coherent Augmented Reality Scene on Mobile Devices 19
A'aeshah Alhakamy and Mihran Tuceryan

Integrated Analysis and Hypothesis Testing for Complex
Spatio-Temporal Data 39
Krešimir Matković, Denis Gračanin, Michael Beham, Rainer Splechtna,
Miriah Meyer, and Elena Ginina

Action Sequencing in VR, a No-Code Approach. 57
Flavien Lécuyer, Valérie Gouranton, Adrien Reuzeau, Ronan Gaugne,
and Bruno Arnaldi

Single Color Sketch-Based Image Retrieval in HSV Color Space 77
Yu Xia, Shuangbu Wang, Yanran Li, Lihua You, Xiaosong Yang,
and Jian Jun Zhang

Integral-Based Material Point Method and Peridynamics Model
for Animating Elastoplastic Material 91
Yao Lyu, Jinglu Zhang, Ari Sarafopoulos, Jian Chang, Shihui Guo,
and Jian Jun Zhang

A Perceptually Coherent TMO for Visualization of 360° HDR Images
on HMD 109
Ific Goudé, Rémi Cozot, and Olivier Le Meur

Simulating Crowds and Autonomous Vehicles 129
John Charlton, Luis Rene Montana Gonzalez, Steve Maddock,
and Paul Richmond

MagiPlay: An Augmented Reality Serious Game Allowing Children
to Program Intelligent Environments 144
Evropi Stefanidi, Dimitrios Arampatzis, Asterios Leonidis,
Maria Korozi, Margherita Antona, and George Papagiannakis

Author Index 171

Do Distant or Colocated Audiences Affect User Activity in VR?

Romain Terrier[1,2]([⊠]), Nicolas Martin[1], Jeremy Lacoche[3], Valerie Gouranton[1,2],
and Bruno Arnaldi[1,2]

[1] IRT b-com, Rennes, France
`romain.terrier@b-com.com`
[2] Univ Rennes, INSA Rennes, Inria, CNRS, IRISA, Rennes, France
[3] Orange Labs, Rennes, France

Abstract. We explore the impact of distant or colocated real audiences
on social inhibition through a user study in virtual reality (VR). The
study investigates, in an application, the differences among two multi-
user configurations (i.e., the local and distant conditions) and one control
condition where the user is alone (i.e., the alone condition). In the local
condition, a single user and a real audience share the same real room.
Conversely, in the distant condition, the user and the audience are separated into two different real rooms. The user performed a categorization
of numbers task in VR, for which the users' performance results (i.e.,
type and answering time) are extracted as subjective feelings and perceptions (i.e., perceptions of others, stress, cognitive workload, presence).
The differences between the local and distant configurations are explored.
Furthermore, we investigate any gender biases in the objective and subjective results. During the local and distant conditions, the presence of
a real audience affects the user's performance due to social inhibition.
The users are even more influenced when the audience does not share
the same room, despite the audience being less directly perceived in this
condition.

Keywords: Virtual reality · Social influence · Audience

1 Introduction

In virtual reality (VR), the new trend is toward multi-users [43]. People are able
to share, in real time, the same virtual Environment (VE) and their experience
causing social mechanisms [6] (e.g., social anxiety, social inhibition, empathy,
group effects, leadership). Moreover, social VR applications allow people to share
the same VE in different ways. On the one hand, they can be colocated when
each user is in the same location. On the other hand, when each user is in a
different, remote location, they are distant. This differentiation can affect the
user's possible degree of social inhibition; indeed, neither the effects nor the
appearance of social inhibition are currently well understood in VR. Therefore,

© Springer-Verlag GmbH Germany, part of Springer Nature 2020
M. L. Gavrilova et al. (Eds.): Trans. on Comput. Sci. XXXVII, LNCS 12230, pp. 1–18, 2020.
https://doi.org/10.1007/978-3-662-61983-4_1

one question remains: does our behavior change in VR depending on whether our audience is physically present or remotely located? Using previous experimental studies in psychology, we designed an experiment in which one user must perform a new and unknown task in front of distant or colocated others. In each condition, this audience shares the same VE as the user (see Fig. 1). The goal of this study is to analyze the differences in social inhibition depending on the location of the audience. This is an extended version of the paper invited to SI on CGI 2019 [41].

Fig. 1. User: red dashes. Audience: blue dots. A single shared virtual environment (VE) (middle) for two different conditions: distant (right) and colocated (left). (Color figure online)

2   Related Work

2.1   Social Influence and Audience Effects in the Real World

In the real world, everyday tasks are often done in the presence of other people or in cooperation with them. The perception an individual has of these other people affects his or her actions and behaviors [14] by imitation effects [11] or by a priming effect [37].

First, the mere presence of other people (an *audience*) is enough to influence individual behaviors [47] and to cause social facilitation [13] or social inhibition. The audience acts like an amplifier: it increases the dominant response, which is task complexity-dependent, of the user. Consequently, the realization of an easy or well-known task will be facilitated by the mere presence of an audience, a concept known as facilitation [20]. In contrast, the realization of a complex or new task requiring a learning phase will be impaired by the presence of an audience [46], an effect known as social inhibition.

However, social inhibition or facilitation are not only generated by the mere presence of an audience [21]. How the audience is perceived or interpreted also affects the user, whose performance varies depending on the audience's status (i.e., as an evaluative or non-evaluative audience) [24]. Indeed, the user performs worse when facing an evaluative audience [26] than when alone because of the "evaluation apprehension" effect. A user may perceive an experimenter as an expert, and thus as an evaluative auditor, even if the experimenter is just an observer [39]. Moreover, knowing the identity of the audience (e.g., an audience composed of the user's friends or colleagues) reduces users' accuracy and answering time [45]. Social norm effects can also influence other behaviors: in a risky situation and in the presence of an audience users tend to diminish their "risk-taking" actions (e.g., in poker gambling) [30].

Thus, many studies have been published on the social effects of an audience on a user, including those generated by the mere presence of the audience, the user's perception of the audience, and the predictability of the audience, along with other effects relating to evaluation apprehension, social norms, and distraction. All such studies refer to social facilitation or inhibition. Moreover, the social influence of a virtual audience on a user could be different when compared to the influence of a real audience due to the particularities of VR.

2.2 VR: A Medium for Social Interaction Studies

Multiple users can share the same VE in real time [15] and can be physically situated either in the same room (i.e., colocated) or at a remote location (i.e., distant). In shared virtual environments (SVEs), each user is represented by an avatar. Avatars are distinguished from embodied agents "which are models driven by computer algorithms" [5].

By sharing the same VE, the use of avatars supports social interactions through non-verbal communication (e.g., head movements [3], gaze tracking [18]) and copresence (i.e., "being there together" [32]). For this reason, researchers have used SVEs to study users' behaviors in VR (e.g., paranoia, phobia, stress, anxiety) [31]. For example, the VE is able to induce anxiety in people suffering from social phobia [22]. In such contexts, the user is able to calm down by visualizing their doppelganger (i.e., a virtual copy of themselves) [4] speaking in front of others in the VE [2].

The aim of these studies is to reproduce real-life situations in VR (e.g., sport training [1]) or to analyze real interaction [33] and communication in VR. Other studies have replicated psychological results obtained in real environments in VEs (e.g., the Milgram experiment [35]).

In this way, VR is a valid tool for mirroring real social processes in the VE [10] and for studying social effects.

2.3 Social Inhibition in VR

Since SVEs induce co-presence, they have been used to support studies on users' behavior. Participants are either physically in the same room (i.e., colocated) or in a remote location (i.e., distant). Several studies [16, 44] on social influence focus on analyzing social inhibition in VR. Social inhibition occurs when one performs a new or unknown task in front of an audience, resulting in a decrease in performance (e.g., slower performance and poorer qualitative and quantitative results) [8].

Many VR studies specialize in researching the type of audience (e.g., real versus virtual in 2D or 3D, close versus far). The first studies on social inhibition of return (e.g., increase in answering time in front of a co-actor) found that the presence of an agent in the VE caused a longer response time (e.g., ~20 ms) [44]. A previous study found that only the presence of a real co-actor caused this effect compared to a 2D-agent displayed on TV [34]. Moreover, a user study [25] focused on the difference of impact among three types of audience condition: alone, with avatars, and with agents. The study is based on the previous works of Blascovich et al. [7], who found that users provided fewer correct answers when executing the unlearned task in the presence of an audience. Blascovich et al. also discovered a correlation between physiological patterns and social inhibition: when a participant was performing the task in the presence of others, measurements of the participant's cardiovascular reactivity could be associated with a threat pattern of physiological reactivity. In the Hoyt et al. study [25], social inhibition occurred in VR but not social facilitation, and only in the presence of avatars. Indeed, if agents are judged and perceived as non-evaluative, the emergence of such inhibition can be prevented [13]. Moreover, virtual agents exert less social influence than avatars on user feelings and behaviors [40], resulting in non-existent or low social inhibition. In the Hoyt et al. study [25], lower performance (e.g., a lower number of correct answers during a novel task) was caused by social inhibition. However, given that the assistant stayed in the room even if the condition was without an audience, their presence could have had an impact on results.

There is still uncertainty regarding the effect of the audience type on users. Some results have shown social inhibition in the presence of an agent, while others have indicated social inhibition only in the presence of an avatar in a VE. One limitation of these previous studies is that the effect of co-presence is often not measured, reducing data obtained on the possible effects of the perception of others in a VE. Given that an audience in a VE can induce evaluation apprehension and self-evaluation effects on users, it can influence users' perceived stress [29] and workload [12] during the task accomplishment.

In summary, studies have demonstrated the impact of a virtual audience on a user depending on its type (i.e., avatar, agent) and the user's perception of it (i.e., as evaluative or non-evaluative). However, there is a lack of studies that consider the location of the audience, although the issue of physical distance has always been confronted [28]. Today, applications can be shared and users can be located remotely (i.e., distant) or in the same room (i.e., colocated). Therefore, our study proposes to address this topic through analyzing how different audience locations affect the impact of social inhibition.

3   Our Social Inhibition Experiment

The aim of this experiment is to evaluate the impact of an audience's location (i.e., colocated, distant) on users in a VE. The audience takes the form of two examiners in the VE to establish the social inhibition of the participant.

This paper does not focus on social facilitation because past studies have only found results on inhibition [25]. The study is a between-subjects design with one independent variable: the presence of examiners. The participant performs the task according to three conditions: (1) alone, with no audience present (ALONE); (2) with the examiners present as a colocated audience, sharing the VE and the same real room as the participant (IN), (3) with the examiners as a distant audience, sharing the VE but not the same real room (OUT) (see Fig. 2). In conditions 2 and 3, the examiners and the user wear a head-mounted display (HMD) that enables them to share the same 3D environment.

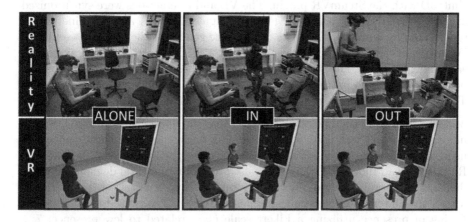

Fig. 2. Setup. User: alone (left), audience colocated (middle) or distant (right).

The evaluation concerns the user's performance (the objective measures are completion time, and type of answer), stress, cognitive workload, and perception of others (the subjective measures are based on questionnaires). Our hypothesis is that the distant audience has less impact on users than the colocated audience because the avatars of the distant audience can be perceived as agents by the user. Co-presence is lower with agents [25], reducing evaluation apprehension and self-awareness. Consistent with the experimental design and limitations of previous studies, our hypotheses are as follows:

H1. In the presence of an audience (i.e., IN, OUT), the performance (i.e., types and time of answers) of users will be diminished in comparison to the condition without an audience (i.e., ALONE).
H2. In the presence of an audience (i.e., IN, OUT), the stress and cognitive workload of users will be higher in comparison to without an audience (i.e., ALONE).
H3. Participants will feel the presence of others and their influence more when examiners are physically present in the same room (IN) rather than located in a remote room (OUT).

H4. When examiners and users are physically present in the same room (IN) rather than physically located in a remote room (OUT) the effects of the audience will be stronger (i.e., poorer performance, higher stress and cognitive workload).

3.1   Technical Details and Material

Technical Details. Participants were equipped with an HTC Vive and its two controllers. The VE was a virtual office with a table, a blackboard and chairs (see Fig. 2). Only three people shared the same VE. The application was built in Unity3D with the SteamVR plugin. The VE and interactions were synchronized using a software layer based on Photon Engine 4. Users and examiners were represented by human-like avatars of the same gender as themselves (see Fig. 2). We used a T-pose-based calibration to adjust the proportion of the avatar for each different user. The avatar animation was based on the rotation and the positions of the two controllers and the HMD using the plugin FinalIK (VRIK)[1]. The skeleton positions were inferred using inverse kinematics.

Material. Four questionnaires were used. First, the Short Stress State Questionnaire (SSSQ) [23] was used to measure task engagement, distress, and worry using a Likert scale (1 = not at all; 5 = extremely; 34 questions). Second, the Raw Task Load Index (RTLX) [9] was used to evaluate mental demand, physical demand, temporal demand, effort, performance, and frustration (6 questions). Third, the Slater-Usoh-Steed questionnaire (SUS) [42] was used to measure the feeling of presence utilizing a Likert scale (1 = related to low presence; 7 = related to high presence; 6 questions). Finally, the questionnaire regarding the perception of others (QPO) was used only for assessing the conditions IN and OUT. The QPO was based on multiple co-presence questionnaires [36,38]. It measured two dimensions: perception of the presence of others and their perceived influence (I was in the presence of others; I forgot the others, and I was focused on the task as if I were alone; I felt observed; My performance was influenced by the presence of others in the VE), and the negative or positive impact of this perceived influence (I was embarrassed by the presence of others in the VE; The presence of others in the VE helped me perform the task; I felt embarrassed by what others might think of me). The QPO uses a Likert scale (1 = not at all; 7 = extremely; 7 questions). In addition to the SSSQ, the Empatica E4[2] wristband was used to assess the cardiac activity of the user. This wristband is an unobtrusive wearable device that uses photoplethysmography signals to monitor the heart rate (HR).

3.2   Participants

The experiment was conducted with 57 unpaid users: 16 females and 41 males, aged from 19 to 59 years old ($M_{age} = 35$, $sd_{age} = 10$), and with various backgrounds

---

[1] http://root-motion.com.

[2] https://www.empatica.com/research/e4/.

(i.e., students, human resources staff, engineers, managers, and assistants). Users were split into three groups: 18 participants in the ALONE condition, 20 in the IN condition, and 19 in the OUT condition. Fifteen users had never experienced VR, while 21 users had used VR less than 5 times, 14 users less than 20 times, and 7 users more than 20 times. The demographic characteristics and expertise in VR of the participants were well distributed among the groups.

3.3 Experimental Design

The experiment involved two exercises: (1) a short tutorial and (2) the main task (see Fig. 4).

Tutorial. A description of the HTC controller was written on the blackboard: the touchpad was divided into two colored sides, left (orange) and right (blue). Then, users performed a short training task during which they were asked to click on the right or left side of the touchpad eight times (see Fig. 3, left).

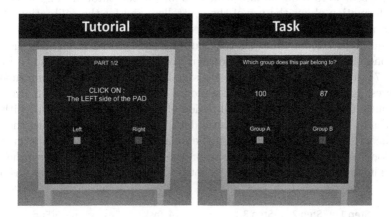

Fig. 3. Screenshots of instructions given in the tutorial and the task. (Color figure online)

Main Task. This task consisted of a categorization of numbers and was based on the work of Blascovich et al. [7] and Hoyt et al. [25]. There were two categories: numbers between 25 and 68 were included in category A, and numbers between 69 and 112 were included in category B. Participants executed several trials to discover the rules of categorization. Twenty-five trials formed a block and at least ten blocks formed the experiment. For each trial, the participant had 3 s to provide an answer. Specifically, in each trial, two numbers were displayed on a board in the VE, and the user was allowed 3 s to say whether the two numbers belonged together in category A or category B (see Fig. 3, right). The possible answers were correct, categorization found (OK); incorrect, mistake on the given categorization (NOK); or out of time, no answer given after 3 s

(OT). The participants received audio and visual feedback: a soft beep and a green check mark for OK answers or a buzzer and a red-cross for NOK and OT answers. Category A numbers followed one normal distribution ($\mu = 46.5$, $\sigma = 8$, lower limit $= 25$, upper limit $= 68$), and category B numbers followed another normal distribution ($\mu = 90.7$, $\sigma = 8$, lower limit $= 69$, upper limit $= 112$). The numbers were the same for each participant. After each block, the score (as a percentage) was displayed on the blackboard. To successfully complete the task, users needed to obtain 80% correct answers on two consecutive blocks. If the user did not find the categorization rule after ten blocks, the task was stopped.

3.4 Experimental Protocol

Step 1. All participants read and signed a consent form that briefly described the experiment and its purpose, the data recorded, the anonymity of the data, and the possibility to stop the experiment whenever the participant wished. Furthermore, each participant filled out a demographic questionnaire.

Step 2. Users were brought into a new room for the tutorial. The instructor gave information about the use of the controllers and for the calibration of the user's avatar. Then, the user was equipped with the HMD and the Empatica E4 wristband. The HR baseline was taken during the tutorial given that the user was alone, not facing others, and not performing the task. According to Fishel et al. [17], "the base-line period sets the standard against which the information of interest is compared. Setting the standard [...] referred to [...] comparing the mean output of a given standardized period of data (i.e., baseline data) with the new data of interest (e.g., experimental data)." After having equipped the user with the wristband, the instructor left the room and told the user to continue the task alone. All instructions were given on the blackboard and by a synthesized voice. The instructor then returned to notify the user that the tutorial was over.

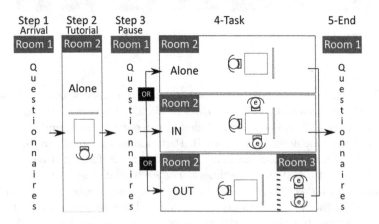

Fig. 4. Design and steps of the experiment

Step 3. Users were directed to another room to fill out three questionnaires to establish their initial perceived state: the SSSQ, the RTLX, and the SUS. Then participants were redirected to the experiment room.

Step 4. Depending on the condition, participants received different information before performing the main categorization of numbers task. The answering method was the same as in the tutorial. To elicit more social inhibition, the two examiners (i.e., one female and one male, who was also the experimenter) were introduced as an evaluative audience. During the task, examiners could only cough or move their arms, hands, and head. All noises were recorded and then played through headphones for the three conditions. Examiners were neither allowed to speak nor to answer the user. In the IN condition, participants saw and greeted the examiners before performing the task. In the OUT condition, participants never physically met the examiners. In this condition, the participants knew only that they shared the same VE as the examiners, and that the avatars embodied real people. Next, the examiners equipped themselves and invited the user to continue the experiment. Participants were also informed that their performance could not be observed by any distant person (except the audience) and that the instructor would leave the room in the OUT condition. In the IN condition, the instructor remained in the room because he was one of the two examiners. The instructions and mechanism of the task were displayed on the blackboard before beginning. The following quantitative performance data (the dependent variable) were recorded: type of answers, including number of correct (OK), incorrect (NOK), and out of time (OT) answers, and answering time (AT; between 0.00 s and 3.00 s).

Step 5. Participants completed three or four questionnaires (depending on the condition) to record their final perceived state: the SSSQ, the RTLX, the SUS, and the QPO.

3.5   Results

As all of the trials were performed by each participant (i.e., repeated measures), linear mixed models were used [19]. To evaluate the effect of one variable using linear mixed models, two nested models were compared based on their deviance (chi-square): one without this variable (i.e., the null model), and one with this variable. We compared the effects among the three conditions (i.e., ALONE, IN, and OUT) on levels of stress, cognitive workload, and presence using Kruskal-Wallis (not normally distributed data). Then, we performed an unpaired two-samples *t*-test (normally distributed data) to analyze differences in the levels of perceptions of others. Only the significant results of main or interaction effects ($p < .05$) are discussed below. The main results concern the following points: performance of participants, perceptions of others, stress, cognitive workload, and presence.

Objective Performance. To better evaluate variations, differences were measured between the first and the last block performed by users (1 block = 25 trials, and 1 trial = 3 s to categorize 2 displayed numbers). It was expected that this approach would allow us to better evaluate how the behavior of users varied according to the condition in which they performed the task. Table 1 presents the descriptive results of the participants' performance. To conduct these analyses, we used linear mixed-effects models and generalized linear mixed-effects models to model the participants' behaviors.

Table 1. Mean and Standard Deviation of performances.

Variable	ALONE		IN		OUT	
	Mean	SD	Mean	SD	Mean	SD
AT (s) $\epsilon[0.00; 3.00]$	1.29	.71	1.37	.71	1.54	.81
OK (%) $\epsilon[0.00; 1.00]$	.70	.46	.68	.47	.61	.49
NOK (%) $\epsilon[0.00; 1.00]$	.25	.43	.27	.44	.30	.46
OT(%) $\epsilon[0.00; 1.00]$	.05	.22	.05	.22	.08	.28

Answering Time. For the analysis, different models are compared (M0[3], M1[4], M2[5], M3[6], M4[7]; see Table 2 for model comparisons for the AT variable). The analysis showed an effect of the condition over the AT (M0 vs. M1; $\chi^2 = 7.88, p = .019$) and an additive effect of the condition and trial (M1 vs. M3; $\chi^2 = 1053.47, p < .001$). The answering time varied from one trial to an other (see Fig. 5). Comparisons between conditions (post-hoc tests) showed a significant difference between ALONE and OUT ($z = -2.76, p = .015$), partially supporting **H1**. There was no significant interaction effect (M3 vs. M4; $\chi^2 = 3.23, p = .198$). In other words, the AT was diminished when the audience was distant as opposed to when no audience was present. The comparisons between OUT and IN and between IN and ALONE were not significant; **H1** and **H4** are not supported. The AT was not significantly diminished when the audience was colocated as opposed to when no audience was present, and similar results were obtained for the distant audience compared to the colocated audience condition.

Type of Answers. We conducted the analyses on the number of OK, NOK, and OT answers given by participants between models. The values registered for each

---

[3] M0 is the null model only with the random effect of the participant:
$M0 = AT \sim (1|Participant)$.

[4] M1 is the model with the random effect of the participant and the effect of the condition: $M1 = AT \sim Condi + (1|Participant)$.

[5] M2 is the model with the random effect of the participant and the effect of the trial: $M2 = AT \sim Trial + (1|Participant)$.

[6] M3 is the model with the random effect of the participant plus the effect of the condition and the effect of the trial: $M3 = AT \sim Condi + Trial + (1|Participant)$.

[7] M4 is the model with the random effect of the participant plus the effect of the condition and the effect of the trial and their interaction:
$M4 = AT \sim Condi * Trial + (1|Participant)$.

Table 2. Comparisons of models - answering time.

Compared Models	DV	Evaluated Effect	χ^2	p-value
M0 vs. M1	AT	CONDI	7.88	.019
M1 vs. M3	AT	CONDI+TRIAL	1053.47	< .001
M3 vs. M4	AT	CONDI×TRIAL	3.23	.198

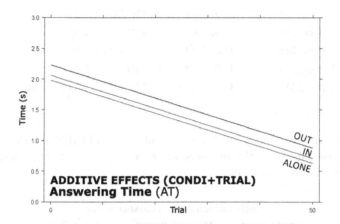

Fig. 5. Additive effects of Trial and Condition on answering time

answer were as follows: for OK, 0 (i.e., not correct) or 1 (i.e., correct); for NOK, 1 (i.e., incorrect) or 0 (i.e., not incorrect); and for OT, 1 (i.e., out of time) or 0 (i.e., in time). We used mixed-effects logistic regression with random effects. Table 3 presents the results of comparisons of models for the variables OK, NOK, and OT. The effect of the trial was significant over the number of OK, NOK, OT answers (M0 vs. M2 models; $\chi^2_{ok} = 351.45, p_{ok} < .001; \chi^2_{nok} = 146.81, p_{nok} < .001; \chi^2_{ot} = 183.49, p_{ot} < .001$). The interaction effects between the condition and the trial were also significant (M3 vs. M4 models; $\chi^2_{ok} = 15.25, p_{ok} < .001; \chi^2_{nok} = 11.09, p_{nok} = .004; \chi^2_{ot} = 18.33, p_{ot} < .001$).

The number of OK answers grew more quickly in the ALONE condition than in the IN and OUT conditions (see Fig. 6). The number of NOK and OT answers decreased more quickly in the ALONE condition than in the IN and OUT conditions. This interaction between the conditions and trials (CONDI*TRIAL) in these three variables supports **H1**, but not **H4**. In other words, the evolution of the type of answers over trials was significantly different in relation to the location of the audience. Specifically, the number of OK answers increased more slowly over the trials in the presence of the audience (i.e., IN or OUT) as opposed to without an audience present (i.e., ALONE), but the evolution occurred more quickly in the presence of the colocated audience compared to the distant audience condition. Furthermore, the number of NOK and OT answers decreased more slowly over trials in the presence of the audience (i.e., IN or OUT) as

Table 3. Comparisons of models - three types of answer.

Compared models	DV	Evaluated effect	χ^2	p-value
M0 vs. M2	OK	TRIAL	351.45	< .001
M2 vs. M3	OK	CONDI+TRIAL	2.46	.292
M3 vs. M4	OK	CONDI×TRIAL	15.25	< .001
M0 vs. M2	NOK	TRIAL	146.81	< .001
M2 vs. M3	NOK	CONDI+TRIAL	1.03	.596
M3 vs. M4	NOK	CONDI×TRIAL	11.09	.004
M0 vs. M2	OT	TRIAL	183.49	< .001
M2 vs. M3	OT	CONDI+TRIAL	7.50	.024
M3 vs. M4	OT	CONDI×TRIAL	18.33	< .001

opposed to trials without the audience present (i.e., ALONE), but the evolution occurred more quickly in the presence of the colocated audience compared to the distant audience condition.

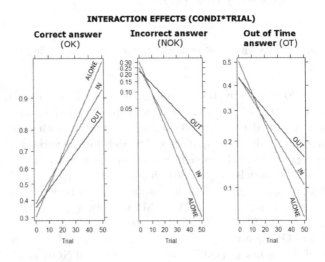

Fig. 6. Interaction effects of Trial and Condition on type of answers

Subjective Feelings and Perceptions. *Perception of others.* Using the QPO, the *t*-test showed a main effect on the Perception of Others and their Influence ($t(31.33) = 2.43, p = .021$) (see Fig. 7). Users perceived the examiners more significantly and felt more influenced by them when the examiners were physically colocated ($M_{in} = 4.99$, $sd_{in} = 0.83$) than when they were distant ($M_{out} = 4.09$, $sd_{out} = 1.40$). No other significant difference was found. **H3** is supported by these results.

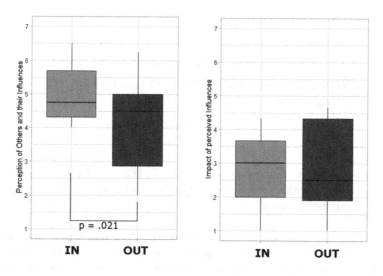

Fig. 7. Boxplots, per condition, of scores from the QPO

Stress. The Kruskal-Wallis tests did not show significant differences regarding all dimensions of the SSSQ: Engagement ($M_{alone} = 3.75$, $sd_{alone} = 1.13$; $M_{in} = 3.46$, $sd_{in} = 1.11$; $M_{out} = 3.54$, $sd_{out} = 1.30$), Worry ($M_{alone} = 1.78$, $sd_{alone} = 1.02$; $M_{in} = 1.99$, $sd_{in} = 1.17$; $M_{out} = 2.12$, $sd_{out} = 1.22$), and Distress ($M_{alone} = 1.83$, $sd_{alone} = 1.07$; $M_{in} = 1.69$, $sd_{in} = 1.03$; $M_{out} = 1.86$, $sd_{out} = 1.10$). **H2** and **H4** are not supported by these results. In other words, participants' stress levels were not significantly affected by audience location.

Additionally, we used HR measurements in beats per minute (bpm) to explore variability during the task performance. We extracted the mean of the HR from the baseline and we extracted the mean of the HR from each block. Due to the inter-individual variability, we subtracted the mean of the baseline from the mean of the blocks[8]. Table 4 reports the descriptive results (means, standard deviations, and boxplots) of these physiological measurements. No significant difference was found (Kruskal-Wallis tests) regarding DHRi between conditions. These results do not support **H2** and **H4**. In other words, participants' HR measurements were not significantly different in relation to the location of the audience.

Cognitive Workload. The RTLX questionnaire had six dimensions: Mental Demand, Physical Demand, Temporal Demand, Effort, Performance, and Frustration. Only the means of Physical Demand were low ($M_{ALONE} = 16.32$, $sd_{ALONE} = 15.80$, $M_{IN} = 15.28$, $sd_{IN} = 16.04$, and $M_{OUT} = 11.00$, $sd_{OUT} = 10.95$), while the means of the other dimensions varied around the middle score of 50.00 ($M \epsilon [42.00; 62.00]$). The Kruskal-Wallis tests did not find significant

---

[8] Equation to obtain the value used of the HR for analyses: $DHR_{block_i} = HR_{block_i} - HR_{baseline}$.

Table 4. Means and Standard Deviations for recorded data of HR.

Variable	Cos		Dist		Alone	
	Mean	SD	Mean	SD	Mean	SD
$HR_{baseline}$ (bpm)	81.3	16.13	76.15	11.29	73.01	8.71
DHR_{block_1} (bpm)	7.55	6.92	6.29	10.43	4.05	5.01
DHR_{block_2} (bpm)	3.98	5.78	3.93	9.01	2.47	4.85

differences regarding all dimensions of the RTLX. **H2** and **H4** are not supported by these results. In other words, participants' workload was not significantly affected by audience location.

Presence. The SUS questionnaire had two scores: Mean and Count (i.e., number of scores equal to or higher than 6). The one-way ANOVA test did not find significant differences regarding all scores of the SUS. Users felt a moderate presence ($M_{ALONE} = 3.5$, $sd_{ALONE} = 2.05$, $M_{IN} = 4.10$, $sd_{IN} = 1.88$, $M_{OUT} = 4.17$, $sd_{OUT} = 1.79$).

Gender Effect. The gender effect was evaluated for objective performance and for subjective feelings and perceptions. No significant effect was found outside on the Engagement (dimension of SSSQ). Indeed, women were significantly less engaged than men ($M_{women} = 3.27$, $sd_{women} = 0.75$; $M_{men} = 3.70$, $sd_{men} = 0.64$; $\chi^2(2) = 4.05, p < .044$).

4   Discussion

The results show that the presence of the examiners influenced the participant's natural performance improvement (i.e., answering time and type of answers) when performing a repeated task.

First, objective measures show a significant improvement of correct answers within the time frame as well as a reduction of false and out of time answers (i.e. "OK", "NOK", and "OT"). This can be explained by a natural improvement due to repetitions during the task. But the improvement is not the same between conditions. The interaction effects between the audience and the trials showed that the evolution within the time frame, whether positive or negative (depending on the objective measure), was slower when an audience was present compared to absent. The manifestation of social inhibition among users due to the presence of an audience seemed to result in a decrease of the natural performance evolution during this specific task. Our results are consistent with previous social inhibition studies [25]. Thus, **H1** is partially supported because answering time results show no clear distinction between the presence or absence of the audience. The only significant difference is between the distant and the colocated audiences.

Second, social inhibition is not perceptible in the participants' cognitive work-load and stress. The results of the questionnaires did not demonstrate any differences, despite the anxiety about an evaluative audience that could have been induced by the presence of the examiners. Thus, **H2** is not supported. This result could be due to the variability of mathematical skill among the participants [27]. Indeed, the perceptual abilities and resources used to perform the task may vary between different participants. Unfortunately, mathematical aptitude was not evaluated in the current study.

Third, results comparing participants' subjective perception of others between colocated (i.e., IN) and distant (i.e., OUT) audiences show significant differences. Participants seemed to perceive the examiners more significantly and appeared to feel more influenced by them when the examiners were physically colocated than when they were distant. Thus, **H3** is supported. However, participants did not find significant differences between conditions that resulted in a negative influence. Moreover, the overall score of the negative influence of the examiners was probably not high because the examiners were passive during the experiment and did not cause any additional stress.

Finally, users' performance refutes **H4**. The statistical analysis demonstrated significant differences between conditions (i.e., IN, and OUT). Indeed, previous interaction effects (i.e., audience over trial) also show that the positive or negative evolution of the performance occurred even more slowly when the users and the audience were distant. Therefore, a stronger social inhibition seems to occur in distant users compared to users who are next to one another. This finding is most likely the explanation for the slower natural performance improvement (i.e., type of answers) of the participants. The results seem to indicate that the reason users negatively experience their performance (when all participants and examiners are in the same real room) is not related to the extent to which they perceive or feel the presence of others. To sum up, the performance of the participants seems to be affected by both the presence of an audience and the type of the audience (i.e., IN, OUT). Furthermore, the significance of the participants' perceptions of others seems to also depend on the type of the audience.

5   Conclusion

Our goal was to investigate differences in social inhibition. An experimental study was conducted to induce this social effect in two different conditions. The user and the audience shared the same virtual environment, with the difference in the conditions consisting in the real audience's location, which was either a different or the same room as the user. Performance and subjective results were obtained during an unknown and challenging task. The results of the two conditions were compared with a control condition (i.e., the user alone). Two major outcomes have been found and no gender effect has been detected.

First, the presence of observers causes a difference in users' reactions compared to when users are alone in the VE. Indeed, the natural performance improvement occurred more slowly when the audience was colocated than when no audience was present, and even more slowly with a distant audience than with a colocated audience. A slower improvement with a distant audience could be due to a weaker perception of others compared to a colocated audience.

Second, and more generally, social inhibition seems to occur when the users in VR are in the presence of an audience. Moreover, in a remote room, the physically distant audience seems to affect the users' social inhibition even more strongly. A learning or training process using repetition could therefore be influenced by the presence of an audience. The designers of such applications should pay attention to this aspect of the setup before building the application.

As the user's personality could impact their perceptions, it could be interesting to explore the variation of social inhibition among different personality traits and through the same audience types. The type of the task could also be investigated by analyzing, for example, the variation of social inhibition in fire drills, training for maintenance, and evaluation of a service. The mere presence of an audience in reality, without its presence in VR, could also be investigated corresponding to a demonstration in an exhibition scenario.

Acknowledgement. This study was carried out within b<>com, an institute of research and technology dedicated to digital technologies. It received support from the Future Investments program of the French National Research Agency (grant no. ANR-07-A0-AIRT).

References

1. Argelaguet Sanz, F., Multon, F., Lécuyer, A.: A methodology for introducing competitive anxiety and pressure in VR sports training. Front. Robot. AI **2**, 10 (2015)
2. Aymerich-Franch, L., Bailenson, J.: The use of doppelgangers in virtual reality to treat public speaking anxiety: a gender comparison. In: Proceedings of the International Society for Presence Research Annual Conference, pp. 173–186. Citeseer (2014)
3. Bailenson, J.N., Beall, A.C., Blascovich, J.: Gaze and task performance in shared virtual environments. J. Visual. Comput. Anim. **13**(5), 313–320 (2002)
4. Bailenson, J.N., Segovia, K.Y.: Virtual Doppelgangers: Psychological Effects of Avatars Who Ignore Their Owners. In: Bainbridge, W. (ed.) Online Worlds: Convergence of the Real and the Virtual. Human-Computer Interaction Series, pp. 175–186. Springer, London (2010). https://doi.org/10.1007/978-1-84882-825-4_14
5. Bailenson, J.N., Yee, N., Blascovich, J., Beall, A.C., Lundblad, N., Jin, M.: The use of immersive virtual reality in the learning sciences: digital transformations of teachers, students, and social context. J. Learn. Sci. **17**(1), 102–141 (2008)
6. Blascovich, J., Loomis, J., Beall, A.C., Swinth, K.R., Hoyt, C.L., Bailenson, J.N.: Target article: immersive virtual environment technology as a methodological tool for social psychology. Psychol. Inq. **13**(2), 103–124 (2002)
7. Blascovich, J., Mendes, W.B., Hunter, S.B., Salomon, K.: Social "facilitation" as challenge and threat. J. Pers. Soc. Psychol. **77**(1), 68 (1999)
8. Bond, C.F., Titus, L.J.: Social facilitation: a meta-analysis of 241 studies. Psychol. Bull. **94**(2), 265 (1983)
9. Byers, J.C.: Traditional and raw task load index (TLX) correlations: Are paired comparisons necessary? Advances in Industrial Ergonomics and Safety 1: Taylor and Francis (1989)

10. Campos-Castillo, C.: Copresence in virtual environments. Sociol. Compass **6**(5), 425–433 (2012). https://doi.org/10.1111/j.1751-9020.2012.00467.x
11. Chartrand, T.L., Bargh, J.A.: The chameleon effect: the perception-behavior link and social interaction. J. Pers. Soc. Psychol. **76**(6), 893 (1999)
12. Claypoole, V.L., Dewar, A.R., Fraulini, N.W., Szalma, J.L.: Effects of social facilitation on perceived workload, subjective stress, and vigilance-related anxiety. In: Proceedings of the Human Factors and Ergonomics Society Annual Meeting, vol. 60, no. 1, pp. 1169–1173 (2016)
13. Cottrell, N.B., Wack, D.L., Sekerak, G.J., Rittle, R.H.: Social facilitation of dominant responses by the presence of an audience and the mere presence of others. J. Pers. Soc. Psychol. **9**(3), 245 (1968)
14. Dijksterhuis, A., Bargh, J.A.: The perception-behavior expressway: automatic effects of social perception on social behavior. In: Advances in Experimental Social Psychology, vol. 33, pp. 1–40. Academic Press (2001)
15. Durlach, N., Slater, M.: Presence in shared virtual environments and virtual togetherness. Presence: teleoperators and Virtual Environments **9**(2), 214–217 (2000)
16. Emmerich, K., Masuch, M.: Watch me play: Does social facilitation apply to digital games? In: Proceedings of the 2018 CHI Conference on Human Factors in Computing Systems, CHI 2018, pp. 100:1–100:12. (2018)
17. Fishel, S.R., Muth, E.R., Hoover, A.W.: Establishing appropriate physiological baseline procedures for real-time physiological measurement. J. Cogn. Eng. Decision Making **1**(3), 286–308 (2007). https://doi.org/10.1518/155534307X255636
18. Garau, M., Slater, M., Pertaub, D.P., Razzaque, S.: The responses of people to virtual humans in an immersive virtual environment. Presence Teleop. Virt. Environ. **14**, 104–116 (2005)
19. Gueorguieva, R., Krystal, J.H.: Move over anova: progress in analyzing repeated-measures data and its reflection in papers published in the archives of general psychiatry. Arch. Gen. Psychiatry **61**(3), 310–317 (2004)
20. Guerin, B., Innes, J.M.: Social facilitation and social monitoring: a new look at zajonc's mere presence hypothesis. Br. J. Soc. Psychol. **21**(1), 7–18 (1982)
21. Guerin, B.: Mere presence effects in humans: a review. J. Exp. Soc. Psychol. **22**(1), 38–77 (1986)
22. Hartanto, D., Kampmann, I.L., Morina, N., Emmelkamp, P.G.M., Neerincx, M.A., Brinkman, W.P.: Controlling social stress in virtual reality environments. PLOS ONE **9**(3), 1–17 (2014)
23. Helton, W.S., Näswall, K.: Short stress state questionnaire. Eur. J. Psychol. Assess. **31**(1), 20–30 (2015)
24. Henchy, T., Glass, D.C.: Evaluation apprehension and the social facilitation of dominant and subordinate responses. J. Pers. Soc. Psychol. **10**(4), 446 (1968)
25. Hoyt, C.L., Blascovich, J., Swinth, K.R.: Social inhibition in immersive virtual environments. Presence Teleop. Virt. Environ. **12**(2), 183–195 (2003)
26. Innes, J.M., Young, R.F.: The effect of presence of an audience, evaluation apprehension and objective self-awareness on learning. J. Exp. Soc. Psychol. (1975)
27. Jamieson, J.P., Peters, B.J., Greenwood, E.J., Altose, A.J.: Reappraising stress arousal improves performance and reduces evaluation anxiety in classroom exam situations. Soc. Psychol. Personal. Sci. **7**(6), 579–587 (2016)
28. Knowles, E.S.: Social physics and the effects of others: tests of the effects of audience size and distance on social judgments and behavior. J. Pers. Soc. Psychol. **45**(6), 1263 (1983)
29. Kushnir, T.: Stress and social facilitation: the effects of the presence of an instructor on student nurses' behaviour. J. Adv. Nurs. **11**(1), 13–19 (1986)

30. Lemoine, J.E., Roland-Lévy, C.: The effect of the presence of an audience on risk-taking while gambling: the social shield. Soc. Influence **12**(2–3), 101–114 (2017)
31. Sanchez-Vives, M.V., Slater, M.: From presence to consciousness through virtual reality. Nat. Rev. Neurosci. **6**(4), 332 (2005)
32. Schroeder, R.: Being there together and the future of connected presence. Presence Teleop. Virt. Environ. **15**(4), 438–454 (2006)
33. Shriram, K., Oh, S.Y., Bailenson, J.: 22 virtual reality and prosocial behavior. Social signal processing, p. 304 (2017)
34. Skarratt, P.A., Cole, G.G., Kingstone, A.: Social inhibition of return. Acta Psychol. **134**(1), 48–54 (2010)
35. Slater, M., et al.: A virtual reprise of the stanley milgram obedience experiments. PLOS ONE **1**(1), 1–10 (2006). https://doi.org/10.1371/journal.pone.0000039
36. Slater, M., Sadagic, A., Usoh, M., Schroeder, R.: Small-group behavior in a virtual and real environment: a comparative study. Presence Teleop. Virt. Environ. **9**(1), 37–51 (2000)
37. Smeesters, D., Wheeler, S.C., Kay, A.C.: Indirect prime-to-behavior effects: the role of perceptions of the self, others, and situations in connecting primed constructs to social behavior. In: Advances in Experimental Social Psychology, vol. 42, pp. 259–317. Academic Press (2010)
38. Steed, A., Slater, M., Sadagic, A., Bullock, A., Tromp, J.: Leadership and collaboration in shared virtual environments. In: Proceedings IEEE Virtual Reality (Cat. No. 99CB36316), pp. 112–115 (1999)
39. Stotland, E., Zander, A.: Effects of public and private failure on self-evaluation. J. Abnormal Soc. Psychol. **56**(2), 223–229 (1958)
40. Swinth, K.R., Blascovich, J.: Perceiving and responding to others: human-human and human-computer social interaction in collaborative virtual environments. In: Proceedings of the 5th Annual International Workshop on PRESENCE, vol. 392 (2002)
41. Terrier, R., Martin, N., Lacoche, J., Gouranton, V., Arnaldi, B.: Am I better in VR with a real audience? In: Gavrilova, M., Chang, J., Thalmann, N.M., Hitzer, E., Ishikawa, H. (eds.) CGI 2019. LNCS, vol. 11542, pp. 28–39. Springer, Cham (2019). https://doi.org/10.1007/978-3-030-22514-8_3
42. Usoh, M., Catena, E., Arman, S., Slater, M.: Using presence questionnaires in reality. Presence Teleoper. Virt. Environ. **9**(5), 497–503 (2000)
43. Velho, L., Lucio, D., Carvalho, L.: Situated participatory virtual reality. In: In Proceedings of XVI Simposio Brasileiro de Jogos e Entretenimento Digital (2017)
44. Wienrich, C., Gross, R., Kretschmer, F., Müller-Plath, G.: Developing and proving a framework for reaction time experiments in vr to objectively measure social interaction with virtual agents. In: 2018 IEEE Conference on Virtual Reality and 3D User Interfaces (VR). pp. 191–198 (March 2018)
45. Wolf, L.K., Bazargani, N., Kilford, E.J., Dumontheil, I., Blakemore, S.J.: The audience effect in adolescence depends on who's looking over your shoulder. J. Adolesc. **43**, 5–14 (2015)
46. Yu, R.F., Wu, X.: Working alone or in the presence of others: exploring social facilitation in baggage X-ray security screening tasks. Ergonomics **58**(6), 857–865 (2015)
47. Zajonc, R.B.: Social facilitation. Science **149**(3681), 269–274 (1965)

Physical Environment Reconstruction Beyond Light Polarization for Coherent Augmented Reality Scene on Mobile Devices

A'aeshah Alhakamy[1,2](✉) and Mihran Tuceryan[1](✉)

[1] Indiana University-Purdue University Indianapolis, Indianapolis, USA
{aalhakam,tuceryan}@iu.edu, aalhakam@iupui.edu, aalhakam@purdue.edu
[2] University of Tabuk, Tabuk, Saudi Arabia
aalhakami@ut.edu.sa

Abstract. The integration of virtual objects to appear as part of the real world is the base of photo-realistic augmented reality (AR) scene development. The physical illumination information, environment features, and virtual objects shading materials combined are considered to reach a perceptually coherent final scene. Other research investigated the problem while assuming availability of scene geometry beforehand, pre-computation of light location, or offline execution. In this paper, we incorporated our previous work of direct light detection with real scene understanding features to provide occlusion, plane detection, and scene reconstruction for improved photo-realism. The whole system tackles several problems at once which consists of: (1) physics-based light polarization, (2) location of incident lights detection, (3) reflected lights simulation, (4) shading materials definition, (5) real-world geometric understanding. A validation of the system is performed by evaluating the geometric reconstruction accuracy, direct illumination pose, performance cost, and human perception.

Keywords: Augmented and mixed environments · Interaction design · Scene perception · Texture perception

1 Introduction

The immersive experience in augmented and mixed reality can only be reached when the virtual objects are indistinguishable from the physical world. This level of realism requires both spatial coherence and visual coherence. While the correct tracking and registration of the virtual object in the physical space can provide the spatial coherence, an accurate rendering and light transport calculation could equip the system with visual coherence [20]. Realism is a computer graphics problem that has been developed for several years and is still under improvement by multiple researchers. In our previous work, we extracted the

© Springer-Verlag GmbH Germany, part of Springer Nature 2020
M. L. Gavrilova et al. (Eds.): Trans. on Comput. Sci. XXXVII, LNCS 12230, pp. 19–38, 2020.
https://doi.org/10.1007/978-3-662-61983-4_2

illumination information from the real physical environment in order to render the virtual object with light transport calculation in the final scene without real scene geometric understanding. An additional feature of that work required 3D real space reconstruction where tracking and registration are not limited to image-based markers but also provide motion tracking and understanding of the feature points in the whole environment. This paper is an extended version of a paper previous published at CGI 2019 [4], which is invited to submit to Transactions on Computer Science. We have extended our work to include a geometric understanding step which strengthens the application. The incorporation of old and new methods include: (1) physics-based light polarization, (2) location of detected incident light, (3) simulation of reflected lights from real objects, (4) definition of shading materials and properties for the virtual objects, and (5) understanding of the physical world through feature points analysis and reconstruction. The improved system uses mobile devices as the main camera, while the environment map is read using a live-feed from the 360° camera for a full peripheral vision at first glance.

The purpose behind each method in the system is to tackle some of the major problems in photo-realism which could help produce real-time coherent augmented reality environment. First method is **physics-based light polarization** which eliminates the false positives from reflections, white surfaces, or glares using filtering sheets. The second method **detects the incident lights locations** from the real light sources which is updated automatically in real-time to reflect the changes in lighting conditions. The third method **simulates the reflected lights** extracted from the real space as applied to the virtual objects, see Fig. 1.

The fourth method **defines the shading properties** of the virtual object where the material design and reflections of lights are capture instantly. the last method **reconstructs the real-world geometry** that detects features points of the physical environment then builds a mesh triangulation of the 3D surfaces based on these points. The integration of these methods in one system can achieve a high level of photo-realism. Some of these technique were introduced and explained in detail in our previous work [1–4] but it will be covered briefly here in order to provide context and investigate the additional technique of real-world reconstruction using feature points.

The system was tested using several types of experiments for performance and capabilities on different platforms such as PC alone, Mobile alone, and PC and Mobile mixture. Some constraints on resources must be simulated for the new build, while algorithms are refined to support some limitations. Some features and methods are substituted with compatible version to the platform build.

Furthermore, it is worth mentioning that the virtual objects will always appear synthetic, as long as the laws of physics are ignored. For instance, a flying object in the middle of the room that doesn't normally fly without context never seems to be real even if it has a realistic lighting and shading properties.

2   Related Work

2.1   Real-World Features

Electronic devices and developed AR tools have a motion tracking module estimating the pose of the device based on feature points that correspond to the visual appearance of the objects' spatial features in the environment [25]. A 3D visual representation of the physical scene is built through mapping module based on stored depth map, feature points, and estimated device poses [31]. A localization module receives the 3D visual representation from the mapping module to identify

Fig. 1. An example showing the difference between the direct incident light (direct illumination) and the indirect reflected light (indirect illumination).

similarities between stored and observed features points [36]. A loop closure correction is performed by the localization module to minimize the error between matching feature points to compute a localized pose [29].

Simultaneous localization and mapping (SLAM) technique that provides motion tracking based on the platform used are incorporated in current mobile devices [24]. SLAM features come in different forms such as concurrent odometry and mapping (COM), visual-inertial odometry (VIO), and six DOF camera pose tracking combined with/without inertial measurement unit (IMU) sensors to estimate the pose of the device relative to the world over time [10,24]. Device camera calibration with the virtual camera in the virtual scene [5] allows the developers to render the virtual objects into the real space from correct perspective including occlusion, light estimation, shading properties [6]. Every feature point that is captured provides spatial information that could be used for both spatial and visual coherence. A full 3D reconstruction of the real world can be achieved using a depth map for feature points and planes which contain location, color, and other data that could build some of the real environment in the virtual space [7,18,38,39,42].

2.2   Light Polarization in Computer Vision

Professional photographers are familiar with the polarization concept in order to eliminate some faulty features or add a certain tone to a photo-Figure 2. In (1975) Horn introduced the optical model of reflection and imaging which advanced the physics-based computer vision [7]. The human perception of light color and intensity can be modified significantly under polarization. Classification of Object materials were theoretically developed and practically built utilizing polarization phase-based method as stated by the intrinsic electrical conductivity [9]. A shape reconstruction technique also used polarization to recover the surface normals, the light directions, and the object refractive indexes [26]. An image dehazing and denoising scheme was developed by collecting polarizing images on several days to validate the noise reduction algorithm and details optimization [37].

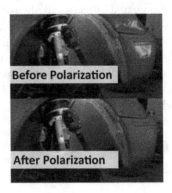

Fig. 2. Illustration how the Circular Polarizer/Linear (CPL) camera filter used to reduce reflections and glare.

2.3   Detection of Incident Light Location

The illumination information of the physical scene can be extracted from the environment map of the scene known as Image-Based Lighting (IBL) [11]. The evolution of IBL and radiance map techniques to detect the incident lights have expanded to work in real-time. The Spherical Harmonic (SH) projection coefficients are used in light factorization technique to compute the dominant light direction and color [27,30]. An Image based representation of the scene including geometry and radiance are used to capture the illumination then render in the final AR scene [23,34]. A variance minimized median cut algorithm is used to sample and extract multiple light sources from a hemispherical camera for each frame. Spherical coordinates (θ, ϕ) for light sources are calculated and placed on a sphere around the virtual object [14]. Several algorithms were enhanced to estimate the 3D position and intensity of light sources without a light probe or user interaction but could rely on RGB-Depth sensors [19]. Detection and estimation of light sources pose and color are the base for accurate virtual objects casting shadows with more realistic materials intensity.

2.4   Indirect and Global Illumination

The visual coherence can be increased significantly when inter-reflections between real and virtual objects are addressed in the final image. In 1997 Keller [22] introduced the concept of Instant Radiosity which replaced the Virtual Point Lights (VPLs) to approximate the indirect lights. A radiance map in form of texel in atlas used to store radiance value that is spatially varying world-space area based on indirect light source position and normal to accurately place and rotate the light [35]. Photon map used to simulate the reflected lights at the ray-tracing rendering by performing a density estimation on every hit diffuse surface [21]. The physical scene geometry was reconstructed to enable user interaction with indirect illumination utilizing RGB-Depth sensors which support fast updating [17].

2.5   360° Live-Feed Video

Virtual and mixed reality (VR/MR) applications have been streaming a 360° video to archive wholesome physical space understanding for years. In order to reduce the missing video ratio and increase quality in online video streaming a system is implemented using QUIC/UDP protocol instead of the HTTP/1.1 and HTTP/2 stacks with different network bandwidth, user behavior, and video characteristics [40]. A Low Dynamic Range (LDR) 360° video on Head-Mounted Displays (HMDs) to extract illumination information from the physical scene and render it to the final immersive scene [32]. A fixation prediction networks of Field-of-Views (FoVs) was developed which used sensor- and content-related features [13]. In this paper, streaming 360° Live-feed Video in augmented reality applications is considered to extract realistic lighting conditions from the real scene.

3   Method and Implementation

The methods and techniques used to investigate the extracting and integration of the physical illumination are described in this section. Although These methods are working simultaneously in real-time, The system is broken down to five subsections to explain the specifics of each method in detail. A visualized version of the overview is shown in Fig. 3.

Physics-Based Light Polarization. False positives from the light reflections, white surfaces, and glare are eliminated or reduced for more accurate and robust incident light detection [4].

Incident Light Detection. A polarized 360° environment map of the real scene is used to detect the light sources then calculate their pose relative to the device [1,2].

Reflected Light Simulation. A sample extracted from the physical environment surrounding the virtual objects is rendered into the image-based lighting mode of these objects to simulate the bouncing lights between the virtual and real objects [2,3].

Shading Materials Definition. Shading textures and normal map of the virtual object are predefined in specified shaders that interact with the light in real-time.

Real-Scene Geometry Reconstruction. A fast form of 3D reconstruction of the real world geometry surfaces and walls is achieved to provide realistic real to virtual objects interactions.

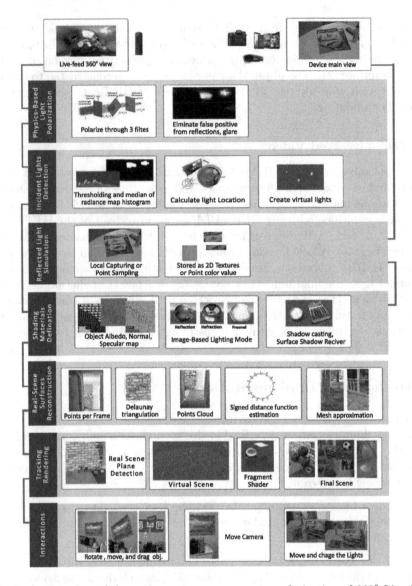

Fig. 3. An overview of the entire system components: polarization of 360° Live-feed, detection of incident light, simulation of reflected light, and creation shading property followed by rendering and interaction.

Rendering. Differential rendering allows the virtual object to be augmented into the real scene where light sources are part of the input. The final image in the 3D engine uses Deferred shading rendering path where the scene is rendered into a G-Buffer storing position, normal and material coefficients for each pixel. In this case, illumination is decoupled from the object geometry into direct (incident) and indirect (reflected) lights by performing lighting calculations in image space. The point geometries covering the light-influenced regions are rendered, while the radiance is computed in fragment/vertex programs and accumulated by additive blending to get the final illumination including shadows [33]. The support of modern GPUs' computing capabilities provides two passes; one for the main light and other for any additional lights. The augmented reality package enables the 3D engine's multi-platform API which implements several subsystems and functionality including depth, ray-cast and point cloud. Ray-cast provides methods and properties querying portions of the physical scene by casting a ray from a screen point against selected track-able planes and feature points.

Tracking. For Mobile implementation, motion tracking supported by ARCore is utilized to understand where the device is relative to the physical world surrounding it through concurrent odometry and mapping (COM) process. For PC implementation, The positional device tracker supported by Vuforia AR engine is used for a robust 6 degree-of-freedom (DOF) target tracking. Furthermore, several modifications are added through separate scripts to support the lighting conditions in dynamic environment.

Hardware Description. For Mobile implementation, Galaxy note 10 with Android system is used that accepts the minimum requirement of ARCore API level. For PC implementation, a machine that has Intel®Core^{TM} i7-3930k CPU @ 3.20 GHz 3201 MHz, six core(s), 64.0 GB RAM, and NVIDIA GeForce GTX 970 GPU is used. For data input devices, a DSLR Nikon D7200 is used as the main AR camera and alive-feed RICOH THETA S 360° is dedicated to read the radiance maps. For physics-based light polarization, three filters are utilized.

3.1   Real-Scene Geometry Reconstruction

For fully realistic interactions between the real and virtual objects, understanding the physical environment beyond image-based marker tracking can increase realism significantly and provides a sense of occlusion and inclusion of the real scene into the virtual scene, which is addressed in this section. The reconstruction of the real surfaces (vertically and horizontally) where the colors and dimensions of these surfaces are added to our system can provide a sense of the real scene. The purpose of this step is providing a sense on understanding to the real environment and not to build a perfect mesh reconstruction which reduce the real-time performance cost. The virtual object only need to feel the existence of the real objects with a sense of lighting color for reflected light estimation, see Fig. 4.

A physical model in the process of surface reconstruction goes through scanning device and registration to acquire cloud points in order to achieve geometric reconstructions. A set of sample points as input with/without normal vectors estimation is the most general approach [12]. A set of feature points obtained utilizing augmented reality tool $P = \{p_1, ..., p_n\}$ where $p_i \in \mathbb{R}^3$ is transformed into screen coordinates. The implicit geometry representations has zero set of 2D distance function $F(x, y) = \sqrt{(x^2 + y^2)} - r$ to define a 1D curve with which it is easy to handle different topologies. The goal is to find a manifold surface $S \subset \mathbb{R}^3$ that approximates P where $S = \{x|d(x) = 0\}$ with $d(x)$ a signed distance function (SDF).

Fig. 4. Physical environment understanding: (a) plane detection, (b) fast mesh reconstruction that merge the color of original plane for more realistic reflected light simulation.

It is important to note that the motion tracking provided by the AR tool is not always accurate which makes it impossible to create homogeneous point clouds, then reconstruct surfaces based on that, however, these points can be accurate per frame. Thus, a Delaunay triangulation is performed on the convex hull of the points from the actual frame in which every circumcircle of a triangle is an empty circle [28] to provide a regular distribution of points for estimating SDF.

The direct use of SDF without Delaunay triangulation enables scanning with uniform grid 15 cm which is too smooth for our purposes, i.e., the vertices in range ±15 cm are smoothed together. The reconstructed model would cover the area and it works great for a grid of 4 cm $d(i), i = [i, j, k] \in \mathbb{R}^3$. For reduced performance cost, working with grid of 2 cm was not considered.

In order to construct SDF from the points samples, the normal vectors are reconstructed. For each sample point p_i to estimate the normal n_i, we examine the local neighborhood using a set of k nearest neighbors KNN using Binary Space Partitioning (BSP) tree for closest point. Then, we compute the best approximating tangent plane using Principal Component Analysis (PCA) using co-variance analysis. The normal orientation is determined by applying the minimal spanning tree (MST) propagation. Finally, we extract zero isosurface by Marching Cubes to create the mesh by approximation of input points which results in a closed two-manifold surface.

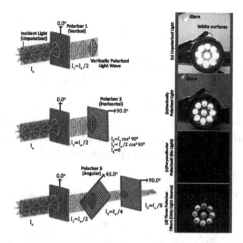

Fig. 5. Polarization of light waves through three filters: Vertical, Horizontal, and angular in order to capture the light source only.

3.2 Physics-Based Light Polarization

While working on the direct illumination detection algorithm in Sect. 3.3, false positive data are detected and need to be eliminated to get more accurate and robust results. As known, the light polarization depends on the quantum state of a photon described in [8,41]. Light waves are examined in this section to depict the original sources of lights. When three polarizing filters are aligned in certain way, the false positive lights from reflections, white surfaces, and glare are completely absorbed or significantly reduced making detecting the light sources more reliable. The light traveling from the first filter is vertically polarized, then transmitting through a perpendicular filter which blocks the light completely. But, introducing a third filter inserted between the previous filters at 45° angle allows the light sources to pass through without any additional false positive data, see Fig. 5.

The principle of the mathematical apparatus of the polarizing filters and the matrix representations to calculate the probability of lights passing through each filter are explained in detail in our previous work [4].

Briefly, the polarizing filters; $|\uparrow\rangle\langle\uparrow|$ vertical $\hat{V}'$, $|\rightarrow\rangle\langle\rightarrow|$ horizontal $\hat{H}'$, and $|\nearrow\rangle\langle\nearrow|$ angular $\hat{\Theta}'$ can represented with following matrices:

$$\hat{V}' = \begin{pmatrix} 1 & 0 \\ 0 & 0 \end{pmatrix}, \hat{H}' = \begin{pmatrix} 0 & 0 \\ 0 & 1 \end{pmatrix}, \tag{1}$$

$$\hat{\Theta}' = \begin{pmatrix} \cos^2(\theta) & \cos(\theta)\sin(\theta) \\ \sin(\theta)\cos(\theta) & \sin^2(\theta) \end{pmatrix} = \begin{pmatrix} 0.5 & 0.5 \\ 0.5 & 0.5 \end{pmatrix} \tag{2}$$

The final calculation shows that 12.5% of the un-polarized light is transmitted through this arrangement of polarizing filter.

$$\frac{1}{\pi} \int_0^\pi \left| (0\ 1) \begin{pmatrix} 0 & 0 \\ 0 & 1 \end{pmatrix} \begin{pmatrix} 0.5 & 0.5 \\ 0.5 & 0.5 \end{pmatrix} \begin{pmatrix} 1 & 0 \\ 0 & 0 \end{pmatrix} \begin{pmatrix} \cos(\theta) \\ \sin(\theta) \end{pmatrix} \right|^2 d\theta = 0.125 \qquad (3)$$

As shown in Fig. 5 the computed probability depicts only the light sources while the false positive from reflections, white surfaces, and glares are ignored or reduced in the radiance map. The concept of light polarization can support some methods, albeit it has some disadvantages in similar systems-see Table 1.

Table 1. The advantage and disadvantage of using polarization in AR.

Pros	Cons
Produce more true color of the real light source	Requires additional physical resources (Polarizing filters)
Fast and practical determination of the automatic statistical thresholds	Environment maps cannot be used for indirect illumination simulation

3.3 Incident Light Detection

A radiance map captured from a panoramic 360° camera to sample the light sources in real-time. The intensity of the pixel colors are sampled when it is above the threshold which was calculated automatically based on the overall environment illumination level. The resulting kernels are mostly sampled from a connective white color-space areas after image gray-scale converging. The threshold range value is determined based on: (1) the median of radiance map histogram where the temporal and spatial variations of the dynamic environment is updated constantly affecting the overall threshold value. (2) the radiance after polarization only capture the light sources where one static predefined range reduced the performance cost.

The color of the light source is calculated based on the mean color for each kernel that identified as direct illumination to provide more a realistic overall illumination of the final scene. The shadow strength of the virtual objects is also determined based on the intensity of light source. The location of direct light is computed based on the centroid of each light kernel which is transformed from the screen coordinates (x, y) to the spherical coordinates (θ, ϕ) using the inverse spherical projection after normalization as shown in Fig. 3 in the incident light detection. The spherical coordinates are represented as: $(\theta, \phi) = (\tan^{-1} \frac{y}{x}, \cos^{-1} \frac{z}{r})$. Where $r = \sqrt{x^2 + y^2}$ in the panoramic 360° view which influences the inverse spherical projection. Eventually, the pose of each light source (θ, ϕ) in the spherical coordinates is representing with a virtual light L for several number of lights $Lights$ as follows:

$$L = f(x, y, z) = \left(\frac{\sin\phi \cos\theta}{\pi \times dh}, \frac{\cos\phi}{\pi \times dw}, \frac{\sin\phi \cos\theta}{\pi \times 90} \right), \forall L \in Lights \qquad (4)$$

On the other hand, these coordinates have a negative direction in the reverse direction of the view as shown:

$$L = f(x, y, z) = (\frac{\sin \phi \cos \theta}{\pi \times (dh - 90)}, -\frac{\cos \phi}{\pi \times (dw - 180)}, \frac{\sin \phi \cos \theta}{\pi \times 90}), \forall L \in Lights$$

$$(5)$$

A normalization of the virtual lights are performed to be compatible for 3D engine quaternions representing the light rotation/angle.

3.4   Reflected Light Simulation

The intra-lights bouncing between the real and virtual objects are extracted and integrated onto the virtual object to simulate indirect illumination or reflected light from the environment surroundings. When a virtual object is placed in the physical scene, the area around the object is sampled and stored as 2D texture and then fed into the image-based lighting mode in the shading materials definition. The reconstructed mesh vertices use filters to keep updating the value at 100 fps rate. A mask is used to only sample the points around the object while ignoring the rest of the main view. The plane mesh dispatches every 10 fps to obtain the main texture assigned to the video texture.

The virtual object obtains the collective colors from the points cloud that reflect the surrounding area based on the mesh approximation. The device pose and point of view affects the reflected lights on the virtual object as seen in Figs. 6 and 7 where the objects falling under the shadows, the sun light or indoor lights are exposed to different indirect illumination.

3.5   Shading Materials Definition

Predefined shading programs are usually installed in 3D engines, but due to the online performance requirement creating specified shading programs is essential. The virtual objects are collective of vertices that are wrapped using UV mapping and more properties to produced realistic shading materials. Most shading programs have predefined features such as main texture, normal map, specular map while lighting mode is assigned in real-time. However, the pre-computed properties in our system are updated constantly at run-time to reflect the physical environment lighting. Thus, two types of shading programs are built to meet this requirement.

3.5.1   Lit Surface

When the surface of the virtual object exhibits variation in lighting and material features these properties are addressed using surface shading programs. Every frame runs passes as needed: (i) fast forward base for main direct light, (ii) forward add for additional lights, (iii) shadow caster.

The shading program allows vertex of fragment rendering options for the lighting mode. It provides local additional reflected lights and other properties as follows:

- *Object/World Transformation.* The main material of the virtual object is transformed from 2D space to 3D space using Tangent, Binormal, Normal matrix (TBN).
- *Lambert Diffuse.* The diffuse reflection is calculated using the famous Lambert model:

$$d = \sum_{i=0}^{n} c \times f \times a \times max(0, \overrightarrow{N} \cdot \overrightarrow{L}) \tag{6}$$

where c is the light color, f diffuse factor, a attenuation, $\overrightarrow{N}$ normal direction, and $\overrightarrow{L}$ light direction, $\cdot$ represents the dot product.
- *Blinn Phong Specular.* The popular specular model was computed on the shining surfaces as:

$$S = \sum_{i=0}^{n} S_c \times S_f \times a \times max(0, \overrightarrow{N} \cdot \overrightarrow{h})_p^S \tag{7}$$

Where $\overrightarrow{h}$ the halfway direction is a normalized $(\overrightarrow{L} + \overrightarrow{v})$ while $\overrightarrow{v}$ represent view direction. the S_c is the specular color, S_f specular factor, S_p refer to the specular power.
- *IBL Reflection.* The simulated reflected lights that was captured from the surrounding regions of the virtual objects can be assigned in part. The uploaded texture keeps updating in real-time to extract any instantaneous changes in the lighting conditions.
- *IBL Refraction.* the same texture is used here but it bends based on Snell's law of refraction which represents as:

$$e = \frac{n_i}{n_r}$$

$$R = e \times i + [(e \cos_i \theta) - \sqrt{1 - e^2(1 - \cos_r^2 \theta)}]\overrightarrow{N} \tag{8}$$

where n is refraction index, and i the velocity of the light in the vacuum, r the velocity of the light in the medium. This concepts is basis of the polarization described above.
- *IBL Fresnel.* The reflections falling on glass or water surfaces are different which can be addressed using Fresnel model where the main camera point of view influences the normals as:

$$Fresnel = f + (1 - f)(1 - \overrightarrow{v} \cdot \overrightarrow{h})^5 \tag{9}$$

3.5.2   Unlit Surface

The mesh that represent the real objects in the virtual scene only receive shadows falling from the virtual object without any other shading properties. An alpha test with cut off range are placed on the surfaces of the physical planes for transparent materials that receives shadows from the virtual objects. discarding this features reduce the virtual objects realism because without shadows objects seem floating into the real space.

Fig. 6. Output with different scenes (a) Plane detection without shading materials, (b) Plane detection, and shading properties, (c) Plane detection with sense of lights where objects in the shadow, (d) Light and shadow changing on the objects, (e) Vertical plane detection also with the ability to place objects on them. Virtual objects [cubes, teapot, picture frame]

4 Results and Evaluation

Indoor and outdoor environments with different lighting conditions are examined to evaluate the system from several perspectives. The general outputs seem promising for a real-time Augmented Reality applications-See Figs. 6 and 7. Although the virtual objects are not significant but the experiment include cube, picture frame, rock and tree, and our previous work include calculator, pen, statue, ball, and bottle.

4.1 Geometric Evaluation

A geometric comparison to the ground truth model is the approach used to evaluate the scene reconstruction. Although the final model is not built to create a well reconstructed mesh, an accuracy evaluation of the features points is conducted on a small-scale.

The ground truth model is denoted as T and the reconstructed result to be evaluated as R. The goal is to assess the accuracy of R which means how close R is to T. For the purposes of this evaluation, we assume that R is itself a triangle mesh. The reconstruction accuracy is measured by computing the distance between the points in R and the nearest points on T which can be on its boundary or on a distant part of the mesh. In theory, R is considered a surface that should have measures applied entailing integration over R, but in practice, the vertices of R are sampled for the evaluation.

When the nearest valid points on T are determined from R, the signed distances are computed whether the reconstruction is over- or under-estimated the true geometry. The sign of each distance is set to be equal to the sign of dot product between the normal facing outward at the nearest point on T and the vector from that point to the inquired point on R.

Fig. 7. Output with different scenes (A) A virtual rock that depict the sun light condition, (B) The virtual rock from different angle where the shading is changing based on the perspective, (C) Virtual tree branch that capture similar colorization to the real objects around it, (D) A whole virtual tree that show sense of occlusion behind the real trees.

Fig. 8. Camera frames from the datasets

The distribution of signed distances from the vertices of R to T can be visualized to compute statistics comparing the accuracy of the reconstruction process. The Root Mean Square Error (RMSE), mean, median and standard deviation are computed against the ground truth. The results are shown in Table 2.

Table 2. Evaluating the system using the datasets in Fig. 8

Statistic	Exploring points	
	Dataset1	Dataset2
RMSE	0.80901	2.7302
Mean	0.80250	2.3754
STDEV	0.09420	0.3425
Median	0.80510	2.5920

4.2 Direct Illumination Evaluation

The ground truth model represented in the real object in the physical environment casting shadow is an indication of the correct location of the light source. For more accurate result we repeated the calculation for six scenes with different lighting conditions. For instance, the first scene has one lamp and sunlight coming from a window, while the second scene represent the same scene from different camera angle. One big white lamp is available in scene three, other scenes have three yellow lamps and others were outdoor. The method used to calculate the light direction from the shadow in real environment to evaluate the angle of incident lights computed in the system. Lets denote the shadow length of the real object as s and the object's height as h to calculate the ground truth angle θ of light source location as $\theta = \tan^{-1}\frac{h}{s}$. Then, this angle is compared with the detected angle ϕ that was computed in Sect. 3.3.

Table 3. The measured angle θ compared with detected angle ϕ in degrees and the corresponding errors.

Scene No.	Shadow length (s)	Measured ($\theta°$)	Detected ($\phi°$)	Error
1	8	32.00	33.05	−1.05
2	24	−168.69	−166.01	2.68
3	35	8.13	10.22	−2.09
4	1	78.69	77.60	1.69
5	17	16.38	15.40	0.98
6	10	−153.43	−154.62	−1.19

Table 3 indicate the small margin of error between the measured angle θ and the angle detected by the system ϕ. The root-mean-square-error (RMSE) is applied to measure of the differences between values detected by the model and the values observed in the ground truth as:

$$RMSE = \sqrt{\frac{\sum_{i=1}^{6} Error_i^2}{6}} = 1.72 \tag{10}$$

4.3   Performance Evaluation

The global illumination in a dynamic scene at real-time impacts the performance cost of the entire system. The previous versions of the system are investigated to evaluate the total cost of each version. Some features of the system were removed or replaced with other methods that provide the same feature to reduce the performance cost. The system versions include cube map (CM) [2], 2D Textures Sub-Sampling (2D) [1], physics-based polarization (PZ) [4], and geometric reconstruction of the physical scene(GS) which are also compared with the models presented in other related work: GR12 [16], GR14 [15], GR15 [17]. Figure 9 provides some of the previous work results in order to see the different in features and perspectives.

Table 4 presents the criteria used to evaluated the system performance such as **(FPS)** which refer to the number of frame per second where the real-time range of (30fps/60fps) is achieved in the latest versions of the system, **(Update)** reflects the time spent for the entire pipeline process in [ms], **(Input)** is the data captured from the main AR view and the 360° view. While **(Tracking)** is the time took for the geometry reconstruction or 6-DOF camera tracking, the **(Surfaces)** is the renderer time to extract including occlusion computation. Lastly,**(Rendering)** is for objects rasterization, rendering procedure and composition of the final scenes.

Table 4. Performance evaluation comparing the previous versions of the system: cube map (CM) [2], 2D Textures Sub-Sampling (2D) [1], physics-based polarization (PZ) [4], and geometric reconstruction of the physical scene (GS), which also compared against methods from other research (GR12 [16], GR14 [15], GR15 [17]).

Operation	Related work			Ours			
	GR12	GR14	GR15	CM	2D	PZ	GS
FPS[1/s]	5.8	12.29	22.46	6	45	50	55
Update[ms]	172.4	81.36	44.53	173.4	35.9	32.4	30.0
Input[ms]	7.3	7.44	7.02	0.04	0.05	0.06	0.07
Tracking[ms]	11.1	10.24	10.64	2.31	1.9	1.10	1.00
Surfaces[ms]	6.69	6.69	12.6	4.21	4.42	4.56	5.55
Rendering[ms]	0.92	0.98	0.87	0.51	0.43	0.32	0.31

Fig. 9. A previous results of the physics-based polarization system with different lighting conditions and locations where each case has: (1) Original 360° view "the red circles indicate the locations of unwanted reflections and glares mistaken with light sources", (2) the view after polarization, (3) Threshold with minimal requirements, (4) the final image of the scene [4]. (Color figure online)

5   Conclusion and Future Work

The extraction and integration of illumination model for realistic final scene can increase the visual coherence but is lacking the spatial coherence. Environment understanding and acquiring the depth data of the real scene is addressed for complete immersive experience in augmented reality. In this work, we include the real-scene geometric reconstruction in order to obtain and integrate the depth data and improve real-to-virtual interactions in our system. Although the features installed in the previous versions of the system provide a perfect sense of light source especially after removing false positive light sources through physics-based polarization [4], the virtual objects were only tracked by image-based marker. The ability to integrate the virtual object where the physical surfaces are detected and then this information is added to the final scene, thus increasing the realism in the system. We noticed the impact of shading materials in Sect. 3.5 and how the virtual object can easily looks synthetic without suitable shading materials. Future work will include further investigations into more realistic shading properties that work uniquely with each object's normals and depicts the illumination model with the depth data to improve photo-realism and perception in the final image. There is always room to reduce the cost of the system performance to be more robust in dynamic environment at the real-time be improving the system algorithms.

Acknowledgement. The first author is very grateful for the PhD committee support and encouragement: Dr. Mihran Tuceryan, my committee chair; Dr. Shiaofen Fang; Dr. Jiang Yu Zheng; Dr. Snehasis Mukhopadhyay. The completion of this research could not have been accomplished without the sponsor of the Saudi Arabian Cultural Mission (SACM). Also, the authors would like to thank CGI 2019 committee for their invitation to submit an extended version of the paper [4] on Transactions on Computer Science.

References

1. Alhakamy, A., Tuceryan, M.: AR360: dynamic illumination for augmented reality with real-time interaction. In: Proceedings of The 2019 IEEE 2nd International Conference on Information and Computer Technologies (ICICT), pp. 170–175. IEEE Press (2019). https://doi.org/10.1109/INFOCT.2019.87109822

2. Alhakamy, A., Tuceryan, M.: CubeMap360: interactive global illumination for augmented reality in dynamic environment. In: 2019 Southeast Conference IEEE Press, pp. 1–8. https://doi.org/10.1109/SoutheastCon42311.2019.9020588

3. Alhakamy, A., Tuceryan, M.: An empirical evaluation of the performance of real-time illumination approaches: realistic scenes in augmented reality. In: De Paolis, L.T., Bourdot, P. (eds.) AVR 2019. LNCS, vol. 11614, pp. 179–195. Springer, Cham (2019). https://doi.org/10.1007/978-3-030-25999-0_16

4. Alhakamy, A., Tuceryan, M.: Polarization-based illumination detection for coherent augmented reality scene rendering in dynamic environments. In: Gavrilova, M., Chang, J., Thalmann, N.M., Hitzer, E., Ishikawa, H. (eds.) CGI 2019. LNCS, vol. 11542, pp. 3–14. Springer, Cham (2019). https://doi.org/10.1007/978-3-030-22514-8_1

5. Tuceryan, M., et al.: Calibration requirements and procedures for a monitor-based augmented reality system. IEEE Trans. Visual Comput. Graphics **1**(3), 255–273 (1995)

6. Breen, D.E., Whitaker, R.T., Rose, E., Tuceryan, M.: Interactive occlusion and automatic object placement for augmented reality. In: Computer Graphics Forum, vol. 15, pp. 11–22. Wiley Online Library (1996)

7. Winston, P.H., Horn, B.: The psychology of computer vision, Chap. Obtaining shape from shading information. McGraw-Hill Companies, New York (1975)

8. Brom, J.M., Rioux, F.: Polarized light and quantum mechanics: an optical analog of the stern-gerlach experiment. Chem. Educ. **7**(4), 200–204 (2002)

9. Chen, H., Wolff, L.B.: Polarization phase-based method for material classification in computer vision. Int. J. Comput. Vision **28**(1), 73–83 (1998)

10. Dai, Y., Hou, W.: Research on configuration arrangement of spatial interface in mobile phone augmented reality environment. In: Tang, Y., Zu, Q., Rodríguez García, J.G. (eds.) HCC 2018. LNCS, vol. 11354, pp. 48–59. Springer, Cham (2019). https://doi.org/10.1007/978-3-030-15127-0_5

11. Debevec, P.: Rendering synthetic objects into real scenes: bridging traditional and image-based graphics with global illumination and high dynamic range photography. In: Proceedings of ACM SIGGRAPH 1998 the 25th Annual Conference on Computer Graphics and Interactive Techniques, vol. 10, pp. 189–198. ACM (1998). https://doi.org/0-89791-999-8

12. Dey, T.K.: Curve and Surface Reconstruction: Algorithms with Mathematical Analysis, vol. 23. Cambridge University Press, Cambridge (2006)

13. Fan, C.L., Lee, J., Lo, W.C., Huang, C.Y., Chen, K.T., Hsu, C.H.: Fixation pre-diction for 360 video streaming in head-mounted virtual reality. In: Proceedings of the 27th Workshop on Network and Operating Systems Support for Digital Audio and Video, pp. 67–72. ACM (2017)
14. Franke, T.A.: Delta light propagation volumes for mixed reality. In: 2013 IEEE International Symposium on Mixed and Augmented Reality (ISMAR), pp. 125–132 (Oct 2013). https://doi.org/10.1109/ISMAR.2013.6671772
15. Gruber, L., Langlotz, T., Sen, P., Hoherer, T., Schmalstieg, D.: Efficient and robustradiance transfer for probeless photorealistic augmented reality. In: 2014 IEEE Virtual Reality (VR), pp. 15–20. IEEE (2014)
16. Gruber, L., Richter-Trummer, T., Schmalstieg, D.: Real-time photometric registration from arbitrary geometry. In: 2012 IEEE International Symposium on Mixed and Augmented Reality (ISMAR), pp. 119–128. IEEE (2012)
17. Gruber, L., Ventura, J., Schmalstieg, D.: Image-space illumination for augmented reality in dynamic environments. In: 2015 IEEE Virtual Reality (VR), pp. 127–134. IEEE (2015)
18. Handa, A., Whelan, T., McDonald, J., Davison, A.J.: A benchmark for RGB-D visual odometry, 3D reconstruction and slam. In: 2014 IEEE international conference on Robotics and automation (ICRA), pp. 1524–1531. IEEE (2014)
19. Jiddi, S., Robert, P., Marchand, E.: Estimation of position and intensity of dynamic light sources using cast shadows on textured real surfaces. In: 2018 25th IEEE International Conference on Image Processing (ICIP), pp. 1063–1067, October 2018. https://doi.org/10.1109/ICIP.2018.8451078
20. Kán, P.: High-quality real-time global illumination in augmented reality. Ph.D. thesis (2014)
21. Kán, P., Kaufmann, H.: High-quality reflections, refractions, and caustics in augmented reality and their contribution to visual coherence. In: 2012 IEEE International Symposium on Mixed and Augmented Reality (ISMAR), pp. 99–108. IEEE (2012)
22. Keller, A.: Instant Radiosity. In: Proceedings of the 24th annual conference on Computer graphics and interactive techniques, pp. 49–56. ACM Press/Addison-Wesley Publishing Co. (1997)
23. Meilland, M., Barat, C., Comport, A.: 3D high dynamic range dense visual slam and its application to real-time object re-lighting. In: 2013 IEEE International Symposium on Mixed and Augmented Reality (ISMAR), pp. 143–152, October 2013.https://doi.org/10.1109/ISMAR.2013.6671774
24. Mladenov, B., Damiani, L., Giribone, P., Revetria, R.: A short review of the SDKs and wearable devices to be used for ar application for industrial working environment. Proc. World Congress Eng. Comput. Sci. 1, 23–25 (2018)
25. Nerurkar, E., Lynen, S., Zhao, S.: System and method for concurrent odometry and mapping, 23 November 2017, uS Patent App. 15/595,617
26. Ngo Thanh, T., Nagahara, H., Taniguchi, R.i.: Shape and light directions from shading and polarization. In: Proceedings of the IEEE Conference on Computer Vision and Pattern Recognition, pp. 2310–2318 (2015)
27. Nowrouzezahrai, D., Geiger, S., Mitchell, K., Sumner, R., Jarosz, W., Gross, M.: Light factorization for mixed-frequency shadows in augmented reality. In: 201110th IEEE International Symposium on Mixed and Augmented Reality, pp. 173–179, October 2011. https://doi.org/10.1109/ISMAR.2011.6092384
28. Okabe, A., Boots, B., Sugihara, K., Chiu, S.N.: Spatial Tessellations: Concepts and Applications of Voronoi Diagrams, vol. 501. Wiley, Hoboken (2009)

29. Parisotto, E., Chaplot, D.S., Zhang, J., Salakhutdinov, R.: Global pose estimation with an attention-based recurrent network. In: 2018 IEEE/CVF Conference on Computer Vision and Pattern Recognition Workshops (CVPRW), pp. 350–35009, June 2018. https://doi.org/10.1109/CVPRW.2018.00061

30. Ramamoorthi, R., Hanrahan, P.: An efficient representation for irradiance environment maps. In: Proceedings of the 28th Annual Conference on Computer Graphics and Interactive Techniques, pp. 497–500. ACM (2001)

31. Rettenmund, D., Fehr, M., Cavegn, S., Nebiker, S.: Accurate visual localization in outdoor and indoor environments exploiting 3d image spaces as spatial reference. Int. Arch. Photogramm. Remote Sens. Spatial Inf. Sci. **XLII-1**, 355–362 (2018). https://doi.org/10.5194/isprs-archives-XLII-1-355-2018

32. Rhee, T., Petikam, L., Allen, B., Chalmers, A.: Mr360: mixed reality rendering for360 panoramic videos. IEEE Trans. Visual. Comput. Graphics **23**(4), 1379–1388 (2017)

33. Rohmer, K., Grosch, T.: Tiled frustum culling for differential rendering on mobile devices. In: 2015 IEEE International Symposium on Mixed and Augmented Reality, pp. 37–42, September 2015. https://doi.org/10.1109/ISMAR.2015.13

34. Rohmer, K., Jendersie, J., Grosch, T.: Natural environment illumination: coherent interactive augmented reality for mobile and non-mobile devices. IEEE Trans. Visual Comput. Graphics **23**(11), 2474–2484 (2017). https://doi.org/10.1109/TVCG.2017.2734426

35. Rohmer, K., Büschell, W., Dachselt, R., Grosch, T.: Interactive near-field illumination for photorealistic augmented reality on mobile devices. In: 2014 IEEE International Symposium on Mixed and Augmented Reality (ISMAR), pp. 29–38. IEEE (2014)

36. Schneider, T., Li, M., Burri, M., Nieto, J., Siegwart, R., Gilitschenski, I.: Visual-inertial self-calibration on informative motion segments. In: 2017 IEEE International Conference on Robotics and Automation (ICRA), pp. 6487–6494. IEEE(2017)

37. Shen, L., Zhao, Y., Peng, Q., Chan, J.C.W., Kong, S.G.: An iterative image dehazing method with polarization. IEEE Trans. Multimed. **21**(5), 1093–1107 (2018)

38. Wang, J., Liu, H., Cong, L., Xiahou, Z., Wang, L.: CNN-monofusion: online monocular dense reconstruction using learned depth from single view. In: 2018 IEEE International Symposium on Mixed and Augmented Reality Adjunct (ISMAR-Adjunct), pp. 57–62, October 2018. https://doi.org/10.1109/ISMAR-Adjunct.2018.00034

39. Weingarten, J., Siegwart, R.: EKF-based 3D slam for structured environment reconstruction. In: 2005 IEEE/RSJ International Conference on Intelligent Robots and Systems, pp. 3834–3839. IEEE (2005)

40. Yen, S.C., Fan, C.L., Hsu, C.H.: Streaming 360°; videos to head-mounted virtual reality using dash over quic transport protocol. In: Proceedings of the 24th ACM Workshop on Packet Video, PV 2019, pp. 7–12. ACM, New York (2019). https://doi.org/10.1145/3304114.3325616, http://doi.acm.org/10.1145/3304114.3325616

41. Zerner, M.C.: Semiempirical molecular orbital methods. Rev. Comput. Chem. **2**, 313–365 (1991)

42. Zhang, C.: Cufusion2: accurate and denoised volumetric 3d object re-construction using depth cameras. IEEE Access **7**, 49882–49893 (2019). https://doi.org/10.1109/ACCESS.2019.2911119

Integrated Analysis and Hypothesis Testing for Complex Spatio-Temporal Data

Krešimir Matković[1]([✉])(iD), Denis Gračanin[2](iD), Michael Beham[1](iD),
Rainer Splechtna[1], Miriah Meyer[3], and Elena Ginina[1](iD)

[1] VRVis Research Center, Vienna, Austria
`{Matkovic,Beham,Splechtna,elena.ginina}@VRVis.at`
[2] Virginia Tech, Blacksburg, VA, USA
`gracanin@vt.edu`
[3] University of Utah, Salt Lake City, UT, USA
`miriah@cs.utah.edu`

Abstract. Analysis of unstructured, complex data is a challenging task that requires a combination of various data analysis techniques, including, among others, deep learning, statistical analysis, and interactive methods. A simple use of individual data analysis techniques addresses only a part of the overall data exploration and analysis challenge. The visual exploration process also requires exploration of what-if scenarios, a continuous and iterative process of generating and testing hypotheses. We describe a comprehensive approach to exploration of complex data that combines automatic and interactive data analysis and hypotheses testing techniques. The proposed approach is illustrated on a publicly available spatio-temporal data set, a collection of bird songs recorded over an extended period of time. Convolutional Neural Network is used to identify and classify bird species from the bird songs data. In addition, two new interactive views, integrated within a coordinated multiple views setup, are introduced: the what-if view and the spectrogram view. The proposed approach is used to develop a unified tool for exploration of bird songs data, called Bird Song Explorer.

Keywords: Visual analysis · Complex spatio-temporal data · Hypothesis testing

1 Introduction

Recent advances in data analysis techniques (e.g., deep learning and advanced statistical analysis) have enhanced exploration of complex spatio-temporal data. However, suitable algorithms and techniques for all tasks included in the analysis of such data are not always readily available. Due to ill defined problems, or simply too complex problem statements, there is a strong need for interactive visual exploration methods to analyze complex spatio-temporal data.

© Springer-Verlag GmbH Germany, part of Springer Nature 2020
M. L. Gavrilova et al. (Eds.): Trans. on Comput. Sci. XXXVII, LNCS 12230, pp. 39–56, 2020.
https://doi.org/10.1007/978-3-662-61983-4_3

The visual exploration process can be viewed as an exploration of a sequence of what-if scenarios. That exploration is a continuous and iterative process of generating and testing hypotheses. A hypothesis can be generated by a human (a visual analyst) or based on machine learning results. Furthermore, more than one hypothesis can be tested at the same time. Interactive techniques help to speed up complex analysis and provide better insight.

Hypothesis testing can be used on any type of data. However, we discuss spatio-temporal data as an important category of complex data An example of spatio-temporal data is the IEEE VAST Challenge 2018—Mini-Challenge 1 data set that includes a collection of bird songs recorded over several decades [13]. This data set includes individual labeled bird songs (in a form of audio recordings) of 19 different bird species. The recordings were taken at specific place and time and labeled with supplementary metadata. In addition, there are 15 recordings which, according to a questionable source, all belong to a single bird species. The main task is to identify patterns of bird movements and to classify bird song recordings.

We describe a comprehensive approach to exploration of complex spatio-temporal data sets that combines automatic and interactive techniques. In order to meet the analyst's needs, we combine an interactive, human in the loop solution with automatic classification of bird songs based on a deep learning technique. By doing so, we exploit the best of the two worlds, superior sound classification done by computers and exploratory capabilities of a human analysts, supported by interactive visualization.

It is easy to imagine other examples, such as human voice recordings in public spaces such as airports. Moreover, since we use deep convolutional neural network (CNN) for the classification step, the initial data could also be images of people or animals or any other kind of complex object data enhanced with timestamp and location information. Finally, pure numeric data can also be used.

We describe the entire process, from raw data processing to the final analysis. We deploy a well established coordinated multiple views technology and introduce the what-if view used to specify the hypotheses tested and to display the corresponding statistics. We also introduce the spectrogram view, designed to view the audio data that is part of the example data set. The results of the automatic analysis are available in the interactive visualization tool, so the system represents a unified exploration tool that includes multiple hypotheses testing.

A preliminary version of this work has been reported at the Computer Graphics International 2019 (CGI'19) conference [18]. The CGI'19 paper describes the interactive part only, based on two novel views, the centroid scatter plot view and the distance plot view. This paper includes three additional contributions. First, we propose and discuss an analysis approach and the decisions made during the design process. The approach includes automatic and interactive techniques. Second, we propose two new views—the what-if view and the spectrogram view. These views are integrated into ComVis coordinated multiple views system [17] that also provides many additional views. All views are linked and composite brushing is supported. Third, we describe a unified tool, Bird Song Explorer, which combines automatic and interactive approach to the exploratory analysis of complex spatio-temporal data.

2   Related Work

2.1   Automatic Data Analysis

Data analysis help us detect outliers, clusters, to classify data or to model data. For big data the analysis is performed automatically, using various techniques. In particular, deep learning techniques are very popular. They are applied to a wide range of problems, including computer vision, speech recognition, sound classification and natural language processing. Several recent papers provide an overview of deep learning techniques, both supervised and unsupervised [1, 11, 12, 22, 24].

Sprengel et al. [26] describe a new audio classification method for bird species identification that is based on speech recognition and deep learning techniques. They use CNN with five convolutional and one dense layer. We rely on their approach and develop our convolutional neural network in order to classify data. Similarly, Takahashi et al. [27] demonstrate the use of CNN with data augmentation method. Experimental results show that their approach significantly outperforms the state of the art methods. Martinsson [16] conducted a study showing that deep residual neural networks can be used to classify bird species based on bird songs.

2.2   Visual Data Analysis

It is often difficult to interpret deep learning results so it is important to make deep learning interpretable and controllable by analysts [5]. That requires a combination of visual analytics, information visualization, and machine learning perspectives into a single framework [7]. For example, TensorFlow Graph Visualizer [29] visualizes the underlying dataflow graphs of the TensorFlow machine learning architecture to help analysts to understand, debug, and share models.

Using deep learning techniques and making them understandable to analysts is just one side of the story. We need to include the findings produced by these techniques within the overall spatio-temporal context of the data set and related visualization techniques. A more recent information visualization survey by Liu et al. [15] provides insights into current advances and challenges in interactive visualization.

Technologies like Global Positioning System (GPS), Radio-frequency identification tags (RFID), and mobile phones make it feasible to provide the spatio-temporal context for a data set and collect large amounts of location and mobility data. A comprehensive coverage of the visual analysis of movement data is provided in [2].

Some examples of mobility and trajectory visualization approaches include an approach for human mobility discovery through the analysis of GPS data with

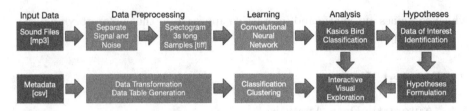

Fig. 1. We combine automatic and interactive techniques to analyze complex data. Neither technique alone would have been sufficient for the analysis. Hypothesis testing provides for better insight. The IEEE VAST Challenge 2018—Mini-Challenge 1 data set is used to illustrate the process [13].

M-Atlas [10]; a survey of traffic visualization system to analyze large amounts of spatio-temporal multi-dimensional traffic trajectory data [3]; an integrated solution for interactive visual analysis and exploration of events along trajectories data [6,19]; and automatic analysis of the movement patterns of people in outdoor recreational areas [20].

Some examples of related application domains include BirdVis, an interactive visualization system that supports the analysis of spatio-temporal bird distribution models [8] and a visual query model for taxi traffic that allows analysts to quickly select data slices and explore large amounts of spatio-temporal data [9]. We build on the state of the art and introduce new views which support hierarchical data exploration, and combine them with results of automatic classification.

2.3   Interactive Hypothesis Testing

In statistics, testing a hypothesis is a well-known technique. Typically, an analyst makes an assumption regarding a population parameter and tests the validity. First, the null hypothesis is defined, and an alternative, opposite hypothesis. The test tells if the null hypotheses or the alternative hypothesis is true. The methodology, used by the analysts, depends on the data and hypothesis. Multiple hypotheses testing is a subset of multiple or simultaneous inference. That can significantly increase the likelihood of Type I errors. There are many methods that deal with this problem that address specific situations [25].

Our technique enables interactive visual hypothesis tests. We compare the data, which is a challenging problem in visualization. Data can be compared by showing visualizations one after another. Another technique is to visualize the differences by overlay the chart with some visual annotations or another chart. A common example are small arrows, which visualize changes in a scatter plot. We use the principle of small multiples [28]. Each item is shown using a basic chart (e.g, bar and box plot) side-by-side. Each of the chart uses the same scales, resulting in effective visualizations.

While hypothesis testing can be done automatically, interactive testing of hypothesis allows focus on the data exploration. The analyst gets more insights into the data and can interpret/reason the data in an interactive process.

3 Data and Tasks

The IEEE VAST Challenge 2018—Mini-Challenge 1 data set describes possible endangerment of the Rose Crested Blue Pipit bird species in the Mistford Natural Preserve [13]. The likely reduction of the birds' nesting pairs is tied to the local manufacturing company Kasios. However, the company denied these charges and provided their data set—a collection of bird calls/songs recordings, consisting of 15 anonymous audio files, alleged to be recent recordings of healthy Rose Crested Blue Pipits in the Preserve. The nearby Mistford College has a large, validated collection of bird calls/songs from all over the Preserve. The question is if the two collections are consistent and support the Kasios's position. How can we validate Kasios's data?

The collection provided by Mistford College describes the 19 known bird species living in the Wildlife Preserve, and consists of audio files in the mp3 format. The recordings were made between 1986 and 2018. A large csv file includes the relevant metadata such as information about the type of the recording (call or song), position, date, time, and quality of the recordings.

The high-level analysis tasks include:

- characterizing movements of items of interest (persons, animals, objects, . . .) in space and time;
- classifying unknown recordings based on available data;
- identifying (interactively or automatically) data points or a combination of attributes' values that are of interest;
- formulating a hypothesis or multiple hypotheses based on identified data points of interest; and
- comparing and analyzing selected cases.

The first step is data structuring. We structure the data so that each audio recording is represented as a record that contains the audio recording, all relevant metadata and the derived data necessary for the analysis.

The data processing part (Fig. 1) has two major components: audio files (recordings) processing and data table generation. The audio files are processed so that they can be analyzed using deep learning techniques. The original mp3 audio files are converted into spectral files of equal length (three seconds) separated into signal and noise. Once this is done, the classifier can be constructed.

In the second step, the metadata is cleaned and various additional attributes are derived, such as the angle of sunlight (differentiating daylight and night), or centroids of birds positions per year.

The structured data and the developed Bird Song Explorer tool make it possible to solve the identified tasks. We describe the deep learning technique in more details in Sect. 4 and the new views, along with the design requirements and justifications, in Sect. 5.

4 Deep Learning for Bird Song Classification

A classification of unknown items based on known data is a typical task for machine learning. Current solutions provide high accuracy for many data types.

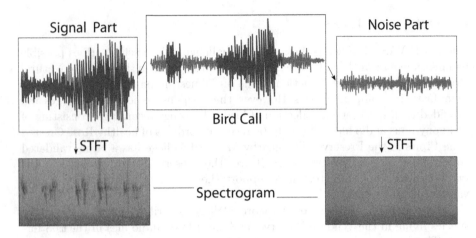

Fig. 2. Pre-processing of the audio files (recordings) to create spectrograms for the classification. Each recording is split into a signal (blue) and a noise (orange) part based on the amplitude. Both parts are then transformed to the frequency domain using a short-time Fourier transformation (STFT). (Color figure online)

However, it is a challenge to get high accuracy when analyzing complex data sets, such as the spatio-temporal data described in Sect. 3.

In this study we want to have an automatic classification of audio recordings (bird songs) and support the analyst in evaluating the classification results. In order to distinguish between patterns in the calls/songs of the different bird species we "project" them onto pictures. We further use deep learning technique to identify these patterns and a custom designed CNN to classify them accordingly. That requires significant data pre-processing.

Firstly, the original mp3 audio files that are of different length and noise level, are converted into 32 bits per pixel (tiff) spectral files, each three seconds long. This choice of the sample's lenght has been found optimal for analysis of bird song data in [16]. The obtained spectrograms are further separated into signal (shown in blue in Fig. 2) and noise (shown in orange in Fig. 2) by filtering the frequency ranges. For these steps, we follow the approach of Sprengel et al. [26], adopting their publicly available code. Furthermore, the spectrograms are converted into 16 bits per pixel png files, and such, used as input data for the CNN classifier.

To differentiate the calls and songs of all the different bird species we train a multi-class classifier using the Python library Keras [4]. Our classifier has a simple architecture (Fig. 3) and consists of two convolutional layers with 32 and 64 (3×3) kernels, both followed by MaxPooling layers with filter size of (2×2), a flattening layer, one fully connected layer of 128 units and an output layer of 39 units for all 19 bird species's calls and songs and the noise files as additional class. The optimization is done with the *Adam* method [14]. We use categorical crossentropy for the loss function and accuracy criteria for the metrics. The original size of the images is reduced to 64×64 pixels to achieve faster computation.

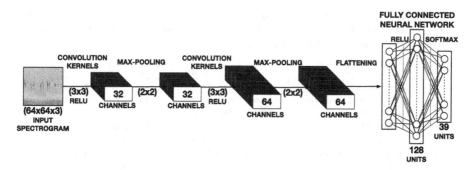

Fig. 3. The CNN architecture consists of two convolutional layers with 32 and 64 (3×3) kernels, both followed by MaxPooling layers with filter size of (2×2), a flattening layer, one fully connected layer of 128 units and an output layer of 39 units for all 19 bird species's calls and songs and the noise files as additional class.

The classifier is trained on ~26,000 (three seconds) sample files, including data augmentation with zoom and shear, and tested on only about 10% of those: ~2,800 files. The model converges well within ten epochs, with batch size of 32 samples. We use the Keras' default learning rate of 0.01. The training time per epoch on CPU is about 12 h and on GPU is, of course, significantly faster. Despite some measures taken to reduce overfitting, such as dropout technique, the difference between the model's training and validation accuracy stays large: 91% versus 68%, respectively. One reason for low classification accuracy might be the initially very unbalanced data set. Some of the bird species have an order of magnitude more data files than other bird species. Moreover, bird song/call patterns in the training data are rare in comparison with silence pauses and/or background noise. While deep learning analyses show excellent results on "rich" (on patterns) data sets, they can easily overfit on "poor" ones.

After performing the same data prepossessing steps on the test audio files provided by Kasios, we predict the bird species for each of the 15 test audio files. The results are shown in Table 1, with the ground truth results in a separate column for reference purposes.

In particular, the results are obtained by first predicting the bird species of each of the three seconds samples in the test audio files. This classification is not unique, as different "mini" predictions originating from the same recording may differed from each other. Therefore, we identify the *primary* bird species prediction of a sample in an audio file with the one predicted by the greatest number of "mini" samples corresponding to that file. The audio file with the second greatest number of "mini" predictions is our *secondary* bird species prediction. For example, in Table 1 the row for File ID 2 has the equal number of "mini" predictions for Blue Collared Zipper and Bombadil so they are both considered to be primary predictions.

Table 1 shows that eight bird species are correctly classified with primary prediction and four bird species with secondary prediction. The correct classifi-

Table 1. Classification of the test audio files provided by Kasios. Eight bird species are correctly classified with the primary prediction and four bird species with the secondary prediction. The correct classifications are shown in bold.

File ID	Primary prediction	Secondary prediction	Ground truth
1	**Bent Beak Riffraff**	Orange Pine Plover	Bent Beak Riffraff
2	Blue Collared Zipper/Bombadil	**Rose Crested Blue Pipit**	Rose Crested Blue Pipit
3	**Bombadil**	Blue Collared Zipper	Bombadil
4	**Bombadil**		Bombadil
5	Scrawny Jay	Orange Pine Plover	*Undefined*
6	**Bent Beak Riffraff**	Broad Winged Jojo	Bent Beak Riffraff
7	Qax		*Undefined*
8	Canadian Cootamum	**Lesser Birchbeere**	Lesser Birchbeere
9	Bombadil	**Rose Crested Blue Pipit**	Rose Crested Blue Pipit
10	**Orange Pine Plover**		Orange Pine Plover
11	Rose Crested Blue Pipit	**Bent Beak Riffraff**	Bent Beak Riffraff
12	**Orange Pine Plover**		Orange Pine Plover
13	**Rose Crested Blue Pipit**	Bombadil	Rose Crested Blue Pipit
14	Canadian Cootamum		*Undefined*
15	**Bent Beak Riffraff**		Bent Beak Riffraff

cations are shown in bold. That is about consistent with the classifier accuracy. The three wrong predictions are of bird species not included in the training. Since the classifier wasn't initially designed to classify unknown bird species as such, it was technically not possible to predict them.

When the classifier recognizes patterns related to more than one bird species in the spectrogram samples, we conclude that there must be more than one bird species in the recordings. Another possibility is that some of the recordings could be of bird species not known by the classifier. We also notice more bird calls compared to songs. According to our deep learning analysis, the possibility that the Kasios' recordings are of Rose Crested Blue Pipit is small, which is consistent with the ground truth. The interactive component of the Bird Song Explorer tool helps in evaluating classification results, and makes the analysis more integrated with the classification. It also helps in identifying possible causes of uncertain classifications (two birds, low quality of recording, etc.).

We illustrated the benefits and outlined the possible issues, thus demonstrating the potential of using deep learning techniques for automatic classification of complex data, and, in particular, of bird songs/calls. Further improvement of the classifier itself is, however, a subject of another study.

5   Visualization Design

The design process was guided by our main requirement, supporting evaluation of the classification results. The automatic classification is based on spectrogram data, and there are many potential sources of uncertainty in the pipeline, so we can not take the results for granted. Furthermore, Kasios company claims that all

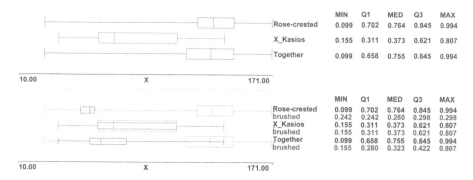

	MIN	Q1	MED	Q3	MAX
Rose-crested	0.099	0.702	0.764	0.845	0.994
X_Kasios	0.155	0.311	0.373	0.621	0.807
Together	0.099	0.658	0.755	0.845	0.994

10.00   X   171.00

	MIN	Q1	MED	Q3	MAX
Rose-crested	0.099	0.702	0.764	0.845	0.994
brushed	0.242	0.242	0.280	0.298	0.298
X_Kasios	0.155	0.311	0.373	0.621	0.807
brushed	0.155	0.311	0.373	0.621	0.807
Together	0.099	0.658	0.755	0.845	0.994
brushed	0.155	0.280	0.323	0.422	0.807

10.00   X   171.00

Fig. 4. Top: Box plots of X attribute values for the Rose Crested Blue Pipit data from the original data, Kasios data, and the combined data. The table on the right shows the corresponding minimum, median, maximum, first quartile and third quartile values. Bottom: Brushed data (year 2018). Kasios data has a wider distribution of X values. The table shows the corresponding values for the original data (blue) and the brushed data (red). (Color figure online)

their recordings belong to the Rose Crested Blue Pipit. As Kasios is considered to be an unreliable source, we have to evaluate this claim as well.

As existing views do not support the tasks directly, we propose two new views to support efficient data analysis. The new views, alongside with the automatic analysis complement the previously introduced centroids scatter plot view and the distance plot view [18]. We first describe the new views design and then provide a use case scenario in Sect. 6.

5.1 What-If View

The main idea of the new what-if view is to use basic descriptive statistics in order to show what would be if the data is classified right. In the case of Kasios claim, we can check what would happen to the Rose Crested Blue Pipit data if the data provided by Kasios would really belong to Rose Crested Blue Pipits. We compute classical box-plots for the Rose Crested Blue Pipit metadata for certain cases, for Kasios cases only, and for merged data. Figure 4 shows such an example for the X coordinate of the recordings. The top box-plot shows the data characteristics for the known recordings. The bottom box-plot shows the data for Kasios recordings. We see that Kasios recordings are grouped within a smaller range, and have much lover median, the first quartile, and the third quartile values. This is already suspicious. As we know that the Kasios data is from 2018 only, we brush the year 2018 (brushing is done in another view not shown in Fig. 4). The brushed data statistics (Fig. 4 bottom) shows that Kasios data has been recorded within a much larger area in X direction.

The tables (Fig. 4 right) enhance qualitative visualization by showing the exact values for the main properties for all data and for the brushed data. The values can be displayed using normalized (0 to 1) or absolute values.

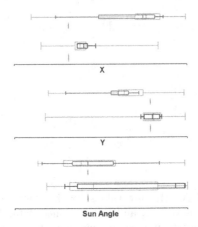

Fig. 5. The what-if view for the three additional data available, X (top) and Y (middle) coordinates, and the *SunAngle* (bottom) when the recording was taken. The Rose Crested Blue Pipit box-plots are shown in rose, and the Bombadil box-plots in brown. The Kasios File ID 9 is shown in cyan. Since there is only one recording, the box-plot becomes a single line. Only 2017 and 2018 data are brushed.

Let us illustrate how the what-if view can help to resolve uncertain decision. If we use the File ID 9 record (Table 1), the automatic classification results in Bombadil as the first choice, and the Rose Crested Blue Pipit as the second choice. Figure 5 shows the what-if view for the three properties available, X and Y coordinates, and the *SunAngle* when the recording was taken. The Rose Crested Blue Pipit box-plots are shown in rose, and the Bombadil box-plots in brown. The Kasios File ID 9 record is shown in cyan. Since there is only one recording, the box-plot becomes a single line. Only 2017 and 2018 are brushed. We can see that X coordinate is far out of range of Bombadils, the Y coordinate is out of range for Rose Crested Blue Pipit, and the Sun Angle is much better match for Rose Crested Blue Pipit. So, the parameters inspection gives a slight advantage to the Rose Crested Blue Pipit. Note that we do need automatic classification as entry points in the analysis. Testing all possible combinations would be a very tedious task. An experienced analyst can start from the deep learning results and further inspect them in order to determine the correct answer.

5.2   Spectrogram View

Since we use spectrograms for the automatic classification we want to show the spectrograms to an analyst. The analyst can then see the basis for the classification and compare spectrograms. In addition, the spectrogram view makes it possible to play the original audio files. The analyst can hear the bird songs/calls and decide which classification is correct.

Figure 6 shows the spectrogram view for Purple Tooting Tout and Queenscoat. The analyst can visually inspect the spectrograms, and a simple click on the spectrogram will play the three seconds audio recording which is used in the

Fig. 6. The spectrogram view shows the spectrograms for two bird species at the time. The analyst can visually inspect the spectrograms. By clicking on an icon, the corresponding audio recording is played. The view is normally used as a floating view shown on the second display. It is linked with all other views, so in case of an active brush only brushed data are shown.

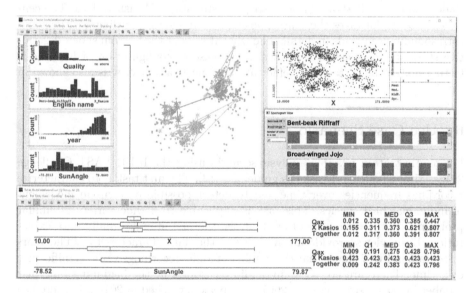

Fig. 7. A screenshot from an analysis session. A combination of histogram, centroid scatter plot, spectrogram, and what-if views.

analysis. The spectrograms are shown as 64×64 pixels icons. Since the spectrograms are scaled-down versions of the larger files, we used an extrema preserving approach, as suggested by Piringer et al. [21]. The algorithm preserves minimum and maximum values, so the patterns are being better preserved in the reduced size image. In our implementation we use logarithmic scale because of the data characteristics.

The spectrogram view is especially useful for checking the classification of unknown files, or for checking the audio recordings with uncertain classification. When in doubt or when the automatic classification results in several possible matches, the analyst can quickly check visually and audibly which one is correct. It perfectly complements the what-if view that is based on descriptive statistics. A more qualitative nature of the spectrogram view takes advantage of humans intuition and abilities.

5.3   Overall System

The above proposed approach is integrated into ComVis coordinated multiple views system [17] that supports composite brushing and numerous standard views. During our analysis sessions we used the what-if view and the spectrogram view, complemented by histograms and scatter plots, including the centroids scatter plot view. This resulted in a suggested views configuration shown in Fig. 7. The metadata is shown on the left using histograms, and on the right using scatter plots. We also use statistics enhanced scatter plot as suggested by Radoš et al. [23]. It shows basic descriptive statistics of brushed data. The centroids scatter plot takes the central position, as it shows recording positions and corresponding centroids in detail. The what-if view at the bottom shows descriptive statistics for selected hypothesis. The ease of configuration of hypothesis testing makes the system very efficient. The spectrogram view is also shown in Fig. 7.

6   Use Case Scenario

Let us illustrate a possible analysis scenario using the IEEE VAST Challenge 2018—Mini-Challenge 1 tasks as guidelines [13]. The first task is to characterize recordings frequencies over time and to detect possible patterns in movement of individual bird species. This task is applicable to a wide variety of similar problems. At the beginning of an analysis, the first step is usually data exploration. Basic views provide an overview of the data characteristics. The years histogram in Fig. 7 shows that the number of audio recordings varies significantly over time. There are not so many audio recordings at the beginning but their number increases starting with 2007. The peak is reached in 2016 and there is a drop in 2018. Data is available only for the first three months of the 2018 which explains the drastic drop in the year histogram.

We are interested in birds moving patterns. These pattern can be easily identified using linking and brushing. We select the bird species which move the most and the least (a simple brush is sufficient). Figure 8 shows the corresponding centroid scatter plot views. As expected, the centroids are either clustered or spread around.

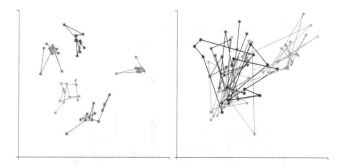

Fig. 8. The centroids trails of bird species. Left: the smallest changes in location. Right: the biggest changes in location.

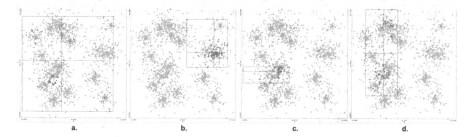

Fig. 9. Recording locations, their bounding boxes, and the one standard deviation from the average cross hair are shown for four different bird species. (a) Green Tipped Scarlet Pipit moves all around. (b) Ordinary Snape does not move much. (c) Qax does not move much. (d) Scrawny Jay is present at two locations. It might be that there are two colonies present in the preserve.

A detailed examination using linking and brushing shows various patterns. For example, Green Tipped Scarlet Pipit has been recorded all over the preserve. Figure 9a shows the positions, the bounding box, and the central cross-hair. The cross-hair is positioned at the average location and shows one standard deviation in X- and Y-directions. Figure 9 shows the patterns for other birds using the same technique. Ordinary Snape and Qax are the bird species that do not move much. All audio recordings are limited to a relatively small area (Figs. 9b and 9c). Scrawny Jay bird species is present at two locations (Fig. 9d). We could not find a temporal pattern which would correspond to those two locations, so we reason that there are two colonies of the Scrawny Jay in the preserve.

Figure 10 shows that some bird species do not appear between October and January (cold weather). We can brush these months and observe the bird species presence. In the distribution histogram the winter recordings are depicted in orange and all recordings in gray. A tall orange bin indicates many winter recordings. There are two exceptions with more winter than summer recordings, Qax and Carries Champagne Pipit. It is reasonable to assume that this seasonal variations are due to the bird species that leave the preserve in summer or winter.

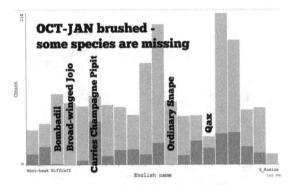

Fig. 10. By brushing the cold weather months (October–January) in a histogram (not shown) we can see that some bird species are not present in the preserve during these months. At the same time there are some bird species that were recorded more often during the cold weather months than during the rest of the year (the height of the orange part of the bin is more than a half of the overall bin height).

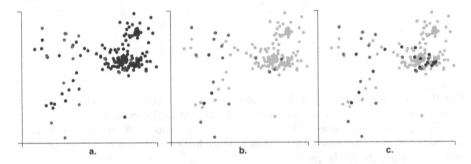

Fig. 11. Positions of all audio recordings of Rose Crested Blue Pipit (rose) and Kasios provided audio recordings (cyan) which are claimed to be the same bird species. (a) All available recordings show that cyan points are located unusually south and north west. (b) Rose points are shown for 2018 only (all cyan points are from 2018). The claim that cyan points represent Rose Crested Blue Pipits seems completely wrong now. (c) The year 2017 is added to the rose points. Again, the Kasios claim does not seem plausible. It certainly deserves further examination. (Color figure online)

Let us focus on Kasios audio recordings that are supposed to be of Rose Crested Blue Pipits. We are not considering the classification data yet, we are just checking the positions. Figure 11a shows all positions of Rose Crested Blue Pipit (rose) and Kasios recordings (cyan).

At the first sight it might look plausible that Kasios recordings are indeed Rose Crested Blue Pipits. A careful observation shows that some of the cyan points are more south than any rose point, and also more north west than any rose point. This observation justifies further exploration. As all Kasios audio recordings are from the year 2018, we only show 2018 points in Fig. 11b. The claim does not seem that plausible now. The cyan points are present in a much larger area. If we add the year 2017 (Fig. 11c), the situation looks better, but it is still suspicious. The cyan points are simply way too south and too west, compared to the rose points.

The what-if view (Fig. 4) makes it possible to compare descriptive statistics for the Kasios and the Rose Crested Blue Pipit data. Again, a clear mismatch is obvious. It is time to check the results of the automatic analysis. First we use the spectrogram view to visually compare the spectrograms of the Kasios audio recordings with the actual Rose Crested Blue Pipit audio recordings.

An audio inspection reveals a clear mismatch between the audio recordings. The Kasios audio recordings are classified by means of deep learning (Sect. 4). Based on the classification data there are only three confirmed audio recordings of Rose Crested Blue Pipit, but there are 12 more Kasios audio recordings. We compare the assumed bird species by means of visualization and by audio inspection, as well. When the automatic classification offers several possibilities, we can easily check which one is the most probable by using the what-if view and other views. The human analyst can gain confidence in the results and does not need to rely solely on the automatic results. Based on our analysis, it seems plausible to suspect Kasios claims. The visual and audio comparisons clearly show that most of the recordings do not belong to Rose Crested Blue Pipits. The ground truth data confirms this hypothesis.

7   Discussion

The initial approach to learn the bird songs patterns from pictures presented the challenge of non-trivial data pre-processing. The key point was to shape the data in a proper format for the classifier (spectrogram pictures). Knowing that CNN has good performance for "normal pictures" did not guarantee good results for the spectrograms, but it was worth a try. Eventually, the results were surprisingly good and through this process we learned a lot about the particularities of deep-analyzing such kind of data.

Section 4 briefly discusses the prospects of using deep learning for automatic classification of complex data. The analyzed bird songs data certainly belongs to complex, non-trivial class of data. Facing the challenges also provoked our curiosity about possible improvements and generalizations of this technique for other applications.

An interactive approach provides many advantages for understanding complex data sets. Development of the new views to support the interactive analysis was an iterative process. Although we could spot patterns in conventional views, we realized very soon that a more quantitative evaluation would improve the analysis. The what-if view can be used whenever a hypothesis has to be tested. Still, we do not provide a solution for the analyst, we present the data and the analyst decides what is plausible and what is not. However, such a quantitative view can certainly help in decision making as well as in justification and communication of the analysis results.

The spectrogram view with the audio reproduction adds additional dimension to the analysis, and lets the analyst hear the bird songs. Instead of relying on metadata or complexly derived spectrograms, the analyst can listen to the audio recording to check the data. It is usually better to deal with the original than with the derived data if possible.

After analyzing the data set we realized that none of the techniques is sufficient alone. Automatic classification is simply unmatched by any interactive approach. At the same time, having the results presented visually, seeing the data and their descriptive statistics, as well as seeing the spectrograms and hearing the bird songs, tremendously simplifies the evaluation of the classification. Spotting the outliers, seeing differences in the movement patterns between species and over the years is trivial by means of interactive visualization. That would be a serious challenge for automatic approaches.

Finally, the tool can be applied to other domains, beyond the motivating data set [13]. The core idea—enabling exploration of classified entities as they move through space and time—applies in domains such as tracking people through urban environments for security concerns, or tracking vehicles to understand and address traffic congestion. The combined techniques of automatic classification of entities and interactive capabilities to discover important space-time patterns could broadly support analysts in these, and other similar areas.

8   Conclusions

We described an analysis approach that combines deep learning techniques and visualization techniques with a special focus on interactive hypothesis testing to evaluate different what-if scenarios. We used this approach to analyze the VAST Challenge 2018 Mini-Challenge 1 data set [13]. However, this approach can be applied to any other data sets with similar structure. Two new views were designed and implemented to support the analysis, the what-if view and the spectrogram view.

The visualization alone could not solve the problem sufficiently. At the same time, deep learning classification alone would not provide any means of exploring its findings. Only a combination of both techniques, interactive and automatic, makes it possible to efficiently explore the data and helps analysts to create a mental model of various data patterns. In case of uncertain classification, the newly proposed views, combined with previously introduced views [18] in the Bird Song Explorer tool, make it possible to solve uncertain classification, and to make decisions faster and with more confidence.

Acknowledgements. VRVis is funded by BMK, BMDW, Styria, SFG and Vienna Business Agency in the scope of COMET - Competence Centers for Excellent Technologies (854174) which is managed by FFG. This work also was supported, in part, by a grant from the Virginia Tech Institute for Creativity, Arts, and Technology.

References

1. Abdel-Hamid, O., Mohamed, A.R., Jiang, H., Deng, L., Penn, G., Yu, D.: Convolutional neural networks for speech recognition. IEEE/ACM Trans. Audio Speech Lang. Process. **22**(10), 1533–1545 (2014)

2. Andrienko, G., Andrienko, N., Bak, P., Keim, D., Wrobel, S.: Visual Analytics of Movement. Springer, Berlin (2013). https://doi.org/10.1007/978-3-642-37583-5
3. Chen, W., Guo, F., Wang, F.Y.: A survey of traffic data visualization. IEEE Trans. Intell. Transp. Syst. **16**(6), 2970–2984 (2015)
4. Chollet, F., et al.: Keras (2015). https://keras.io
5. Choo, J., Liu, S.: Visual analytics for explainable deep learning. IEEE Comput. Graphics Appl. **38**(4), 84–92 (2018)
6. Cibulski, L., Gračanin, D., Diehl, A., Splechtna, R., Elshehaly, M., Delrieux, C., Matković, K.: ITEA–interactive trajectories and events analysis: exploring sequences of spatio-temporal events in movement data. Vis. Comput. **32**(6), 847–857 (2016)
7. Endert, A., et al.: The state of the art in integrating machine learning into visual analytics. Comput. Graph. Forum **36**(8), 458–486 (2017)
8. Ferreira, N., et al.: Birdvis: visualizing and understanding bird populations. IEEE Trans. Visual Comput. Graphics **17**(12), 2374–2383 (2011)
9. Ferreira, N., Poco, J., Vo, H.T., Freire, J., Silva, C.T.: Visual exploration of big spatio-temporal urban data: a study of New York city taxi trips. IEEE Trans. Visual Comput. Graphics **19**(12), 2149–2158 (2013)
10. Giannotti, F., et al.: Unveiling the complexity of human mobility by querying and mining massive trajectory data. VLDB J. **20**(5), 695 (2011)
11. Goodfellow, I., Bengio, Y., Courville, A.: Deep Learning. MIT Press, Cambridge (2016)
12. Hatcher, W.G., Yu, W.: A survey of deep learning: platforms, applications and emerging research trends. IEEE Access **6**, 24411–24432 (2018)
13. IEEE VIS 2018 Conference: VAST challenge 2018: Mini-challenge 1 (2018), note. http://www.vacommunity.org/VAST+Challenge+2018+MC1
14. Kingma, D.P., Ba, J.: Adam: a method for stochastic optimization. arxiv:1412.6980v9 [cs.LG], arXiv.org, 30 January 2017
15. Liu, S., Cui, W., Wu, Y., Liu, M.: A survey on information visualization: recent advances and challenges. Vis. Comput. **30**(12), 1373–1393 (2014). https://doi.org/10.1007/s00371-013-0892-3
16. Martinsson, J.: Bird species identification using convolutional neural networks. Master's thesis in computer science – algorithms, languages and logic, Department of Computer Science and Engineering, Chalmers University of Technology and University of Gothenburg, Gothenburg, Sweden, April 2017
17. Matković, K., Freiler, W., Gračanin, D., Hauser, H.: ComVis: a coordinated multiple views system for prototyping new visualization technology. In: Proceedings of the 12th International Conference on Information Visualisation (IV 2008), pp. 215–220, 9–11 July 2008
18. Matković, K., Gračanin, D., Beham, M., Splechtna, R., Meyer, M., Ginina, E.: Visual analysis of bird moving patterns. In: Gavrilova, M., Chang, J., Thalmann, N.M., Hitzer, E., Ishikawa, H. (eds.) CGI 2019. LNCS, vol. 11542, pp. 388–394. Springer, Cham (2019). https://doi.org/10.1007/978-3-030-22514-8_35
19. Matković, K., Gračanin, D., Splechtna, R., Diehl, A., Elshehaly, M., Delrieux, C.: Exploring trajectory data using ComVis CMV tool VAST 2015 mini-challenge 1. In: Proceedings of the IEEE Conference on Visual Analytics Science and Technology (VAST 2015), pp. 167–168, 25–30 October 2015
20. Orellana, D., Bregt, A.K., Ligtenberg, A., Wachowicz, M.: Exploring visitor movement patterns in natural recreational areas. Tour. Manag. **33**(3), 672–682 (2012)
21. Piringer, H., Pajer, S., Berger, W., Teichmann, H.: Comparative visual analysis of 2D function ensembles. Comput. Graph. Forum **31**(3pt3), 1195–1204 (2012)

22. Pouyanfar, S., et al.: A survey on deep learning: algorithms, techniques, and applications. ACM Comput. Surv. **51**(5), 92:1–92:36 (2018)
23. Radoš, S., Splechtna, R., Matković, K., Đuras, M., Gröller, E., Hauser, H.: Towards quantitative visual analytics with structured brushing and linked statistics. Comput. Graph. Forum **35**(3), 251–260 (2016)
24. Schlüter, J., Grill, T.: Exploring data augmentation for improved singing voice detection with neural networks. In: Proceedings of the 16th International Society for Music Information Retrieval Conference (ISMIR 2015), pp. 121–126 (2015)
25. Shaffer, J.P.: Multile hypothesis testing. Annu. Rev. Psychol. **46**, 561–584 (1995)
26. Sprengel, E., Jaggi, M., Kilcher, Y., Hofmann, T.: Audio based bird species identification using deep learning techniques. In: Proceedings of the Conference and Labs of the Evaluation Forum (CLEF) 2016, pp. 547–559, 5–8 September 2016
27. Takahashi, N., Gygli, M., Pfister, B., Van Gool, L.: Deep convolutional neural networks and data augmentation for acoustic event detection. arxiv:1604.07160v2 [cs.SD], arXiv.org, 8 December 2016
28. Tufte, E.R.: Envisioning Information. Graphics Press, Cheshire (1990)
29. Wongsuphasawat, K., et al.: Visualizing dataflow graphs of deep learning models in TensorFlow. IEEE Trans. Visual Comput. Graphics **24**(1), 1–12 (2018)

Action Sequencing in VR, a No-Code Approach

Flavien Lécuyer[1]([✉]), Valérie Gouranton[1], Adrien Reuzeau[1], Ronan Gaugne[2], and Bruno Arnaldi[1]

[1] Univ Rennes, INSA Rennes, Inria, CNRS, IRISA, Rennes, France
flavien.lecuyer@irisa.fr
[2] Univ Rennes, Inria, CNRS, IRISA, Rennes, France

Abstract. In many domains, it is common to have procedures, with a given sequence of actions to follow. To perform such procedures, virtual reality is a helpful tool as it allows to safely place a user in a given situation as many times as needed, without risk. Indeed, learning in a real situation implies risks for both the studied object – or the patient – (e.g. badly treated injury) and the trainee (e.g. lack of danger awareness). To do this, it is necessary to integrate the procedure in the virtual environment, under the form of a scenario. Creating such a scenario is a difficult task for a domain expert, as the coding skill level needed for that is too high. Often, a developer is needed to manage the creation of the virtual content, with the drawbacks that are implied (e.g. time loss and misunderstandings).

We propose a complete workflow to let the domain expert create their own scenarized content for virtual reality, without any need for coding. This workflow is divided in two steps: first, a new approach is provided to generate a scenario without any code, through the principle of *creating by doing*. Then, efficient methods are provided to reuse the scenario in an application in different ways, for either a human user guided by the scenario, or a virtual actor controlled by it.

1 Introduction

In our daily lives, many procedures imply to follow a specific sequence of actions, in order to reach a good result. Some of those procedures force the user to respect it to the letter, such as for a surgical operation where even the slightest mistake generates critical problems. On the contrary, some of them serve more as indications to guide a user, like a signposted route in a museum. When those situations are recreated in virtual reality, this action sequencing must be made explicit, through the use of a scenario.

Usually, the scenario is designed by a domain expert (i.e. the expert, working in the application domain, such as a teacher, a medical doctor, an archaeologist, etc.). However, due to the need for coding skills to integrate the scenario in virtual

This work is part of the ANR-16-FRQC-0004 INTROSPECT project, and the SUNSET project funded by the ANR-10-LABX-07-01 "Investing for the Future" program.

M. L. Gavrilova et al. (Eds.): Trans. on Comput. Sci. XXXVII, LNCS 12230, pp. 57–76, 2020.
https://doi.org/10.1007/978-3-662-61983-4_4

reality, the help of a developer is almost always needed. Since the developer needs to understand correctly the needs of the domain expert before being able to translate the scenario into machine code, this step is usually time consuming, and error prone. The strong presence of implicit constraints in most domains is also an important source of difficulties in that process. Even when the scenario is obtained, the domain expert needs a way to reuse it. According to the needs of the application (*learn by doing*, *monitor by seeing*, *collaborate by doing* or *learn by seeing*), the integration of the scenario is done quite differently.

A common way of guiding someone through a procedure is to demonstrate it. This way, every action composing the sequence is made explicit, since it is directly shown to the observer. Based on this metaphor, we propose a new workflow to create scenarios translating the procedures through a demonstration in a virtual environment. A preliminary version of this work has been reported in [19]. In this paper, we add an efficient way of reusing the generated scenario in the virtual reality application, adapted to different needs. After the analysis of related works in Sect. 2, we present how a scenario can be easily generated and reused by a domain expert, through the use of efficient metaphors and tools, with five points: the *create by doing* approach for the creation of scenarios, in Sect. 3; the presentation of a scenario authoring tool based on this approach, in Sect. 4; the reuse of the scenario with both real users and virtual actors, in Sect. 5; the description of two use cases demonstrating the creation and reuse of the scenarios, in Sect. 6; and a short user study in Sect. 7. We finish with a discussion on future works in Sect. 8. This is an extended version of the paper presented at CGI 2019 [19].

2   Related Work

For the management of scenarios in virtual reality application, some works proposed a way to model scenarios. Out of those scenario models, the majority is provided without any graphical representation. This limitation, forcing the scenario author to write code, makes it difficult to create new scenarios for a non-computer scientist. On the contrary, graphical representations provide a better abstraction. However, it is to note that this abstraction must be done with caution, so as to not lose expressiveness [13]. Some works propose a graphical

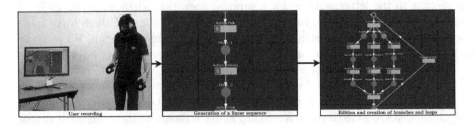

Fig. 1. The proposed workflow starts from the action recording to generate a straight scenario, which can then be edited to obtain a more complex sequence

representation for the scenarios. Thanks to this, the scenario becomes understandable for the domain experts, who are generally unfamiliar with computer science, but are the ones who know best what is expected of the scenario. The graphical representation associated with those scenario models highly depends on the kind of representation formalism it is based on. For instance, HAVE [8] uses UML representation, as it is based on activity diagrams. The use of such a representation eases the learning for a developer, and can be understood by an expert with some learning, although it is difficult for someone other than the developer to create the content. Similarly, a Grafcet-like representation is used for LORA++, since it uses similar concepts [12]. This has the main advantage of presenting an easily understandable representation for a domain expert but this requires more effort for the fine tuning of the actions, since the graphical representation is not completely adapted for this. In order to integrate this directly in the model, some made a lower level model, which is close to the scripts used by the application. This is the case for HPTS++ [18], in which the designer needs to write scripts based on finite state machines, as described in the presentation of HCSM [10]. On the other hand, Story Nets proposes to make finite state machines which are very close to the code [5]. The major problem that is encountered is that a regular representation is often not enough to fully represent the concepts we need. This can be seen with IVE [5], in which the concept of place from the Petri nets is derived into two separate concepts (actor and preconditions) to make the representation expressive enough to define a scenario. Instead, it is possible to specialize and extend an existing concept, as ABL does for finite state machines [23], as well as #SEVEN for Petri nets [9]. While #SEVEN focuses more on the interactions in the environment, ABL is designed to define the behaviour of virtual agents. Even though the domain experts can understand such a scenario, the authoring can still be difficult to apprehend. For instance, the logic of how to build a working scenario may still be difficult to apprehend, as it requires a link to the code to be functioning. To help with the authoring, the concept of *"creating by doing"* aims to create the scenarios through the recording of the actions. As an example, the work presented by Angros et al. [2] starts from a recording of the user to generate a first version of a scenario, which is then generalized. To do this, the application creator informs the scenario manager what are the objectives of the scenario to be used. This method is interesting to create short scenarios, with atomic sequences, but the recording of a long scenario is done step by step, require more time.

Another efficient way to define a scenario is to define hierarchical goals. An example of this approach is given in [22], in which the expert can define the main elements of the scenario, before giving more details to integrate it with the virtual environment. This kind of top-down approach is efficient for the creation of such scenarios since it allows the expert to intervene at a higher level of abstraction. However, it is less suited for precise procedures, since the expert may forget to mention some of the actions to perform. Indeed, it is not unusual for the expert to explain the procedure at a high level, with too few details for the implementation. Although it can be fixed by iterating between the expert and the developer, the time required for this could be saved.

In parallel, Some works proposed to provide a replay function in virtual environments, which can be seen as a way to record the user actions to generate a scenario, or at least a trace of what the user has been doing. For instance, MoCap can be seen as a way to record the user's actions, such as in Chan et al.'s work [7], or Bailenson et al.'s work [3]. Another interesting work is the one done by the MIT Education Arcade with *Mystery at the Museum* (*M@M*) [16] and *Environmental Detectives* [17], in which replaying the previous actions is possible, and provided as a means to remind the players of what already happened. Unfortunately, their approach is not really detailed, and the replay function seems to rely more on a log of the events than on a reusable scenario. A scenario that is generated through the execution can also be reused to generate a final product, as done in [25], where the user can influence the evolution of the story. Those choices are recorded in order to produce a movie taking into account every choice made by the user. This means that the scenario can be reused only in a passive way. A better possibility would be to create a mixed reality application through an immersive environment, as proposed in [20]. However, the creation of a scenario for a virtual reality application is a tedious task for a domain expert.

To conclude to this section, we can observe that the question of simplifying the creation of scenarios for virtual reality has been asked multiple times. To ease the creation of scenarios, several models have been proposed, with visual representations of the scenarios to make them more easily understandable. However either coding skills or a learning phase is needed to be able to use them. On the contrary, hierarchical scenarios are easily understandable, but make the definition of the precise actions more difficult. Other works focused on the principle of creating scenarios through the actions of a user, to reuse the scenario afterwards, with reuses varying from a logging of the past actions to a movie generated from the scenario. Still, none of them reuses the scenario directly in the virtual environment.

3   Scenario Creation

The authoring of scenarios for virtual reality applications is a tedious task for both the domain expert and the developer, since both of them hold a part of the necessary knowledge to create it, and the communication between them can be difficult. In this section, we first define some important notions for our approach in Sect. 3.1, to detail the creation of the scenario in Sect. 3.2.

3.1   Definitions

Before we present in more details our approach, it is important to define what we call a "scenario" in this paper. In our context, a scenario is a sequence of actions linked in a specific way. The links between the actions define a temporal order, to prevent an action from being executed if other ones are not done before.

This kind of scenario is particularly useful if the internal states of the objects are not enough to ensure the coherency of the environment. Of course, the scenario can be enriched with loops, to define that a part of the sequence must be repeated a given number of times. It can also contain branches, to let the user choose between several ways of continuing the scenario, or represent two sequences that may be done in parallel.

To make the *create by doing* possible, we focus on atomic actions, so that they can be considered executed instantly, instead of considering continuous actions such as walk. Indeed, to define the order of actions, the fact that an action is executed bears consequences that can impact the state of the virtual environment. The way the action is performed, however, does not impact the feasibility of other actions, which is why we do not take it into account when describing the scenario. An illustration of this separation into atomic actions is presented in Fig. 2. In the example provided, the user grasps an object, resulting in the action Take being triggered. Then the user moves the object however they want to, which does not impact the state of the environment, as the object is still taken, and the hand of the user is still full. The user finishes by placing the object somewhere, resulting in the Place action, meaning that the place is now occupied, the hand is free and the object can be taken. Even though we are not interested in the precise path of the object, checkpoints can be defined to trigger an action. In this case, the action Move to is triggered when the object is placed at a given spot, but is still in the hand of the user. This kind of action can be used to force the user to place an object under a stream to wash it, or under a light to observe it thoroughly, for instance.

This definition of the actions is derived from the object-relation concept, presented in *Cause and Effects* [21], and based on two main concepts: the typed objects and the relations. The typed objects are the objects present in the environment, which are enriched with properties, or types, to make them interactible. In the object-relation paradigm, any element of the environment can be considered an object. Because of this, not only the visible inanimate objects are included: the user's avatar and more conceptual elements, such as spatial zones of the environment, can be defined as objects. The second concept is the relation, which define the actions. Instead of using the objects directly, the relations use the types placed on them. Thanks to this, a relation needs to be defined only once to be reused as many times as needed, with as many objects as possible, as long as the objects bear the necessary types.

3.2   Recording of the Expert

We propose to use the *create by doing* approach to create scenarios through a recording of a user. Thanks to this approach, the authoring of a scenario becomes as natural as possible, since only a demonstration by the expert (e.g. the teacher in a nurses school) of the said procedure is needed to obtain the corresponding action sequence, in a format legible for the application. The main steps of this approach, summarized in Fig. 1, are:

- **Defining the interactions in the virtual environment.** Before being able to create the scenario, the types and relations must be defined, so that the environment can be really interactive. Although this part is often the role of the developer, a possible way to do it is presented in [19].
- **Run the application in a free mode.** The expert is free to perform any action in the environment, with the actions being logged into a scenario. At the end of this step, the expert obtains a scenario composed of a linear sequence, listing the actions performed in order.
- **Edit the scenario.** If the expert needs a more complex scenario, with branches and loops, the edition can be done using the sequences as a base. It is also possible to create several sequences to combine them as a scenario.

The main improvement provided by the *create by doing* approach is the translation of sequenced actions into a digital data. The data obtained is a scenario, in which the states correspond to the moments between the steps of the sequence recorded by the scenario generator. The transitions bear the information as to which action should be performed to make the scenario change state. In doing so, the resulting scenario is the scenario that can only be completed if a final user performed the exact same actions as the expert did during the record. Since the actions are only the important events triggered by the final user, however, the latter could be free to walk or to move an object around between each transition.

By letting the domain expert evolve freely in the environment, no constraints other than the need to be immersed in the virtual environment, is needed to create the scenario. This helps the domain expert to get a digital representation of the sequence, without having to seek help from a developer to translate the sequence. The result from this step can also be manipulated directly by the developer to add fine-grain modifications. For instance, the developer can add transitions between the scenario states, that are not triggered by an action, but rather by an event in the virtual environment. A common case is to let the scenario wait for a few seconds.

Since a scenario is composed of actions, with temporal constraints between them, it can easily be represented by an oriented graph, such as the one shown in Fig. 2. Thanks to this, it is easy for the domain expert to modify the sequencing with graphical tools, with a WYSIWYG metaphor.

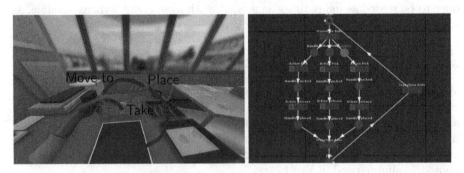

Fig. 2. The actions recorder for a pick and place task, and the corresponding scenario

To let an expert create a scenario through the *create by doing* principle, we designed a set of tools, helping both in the authoring and the reuse of the scenario. In Sect. 4, we present a tool to create scenarios through the actions of the expert. In Sect. 5, we focus on the tools provided to reuse the scenario in a virtual reality application.

4   Scenario Authoring Tool

To enable the creation of scenarios for virtual reality applications, a domain expert needs tools that can be easily used. Based on the *create by doing* approach, we propose a tool, completely integrated in Unity, to let the domain expert create their own scenario with as few manipulations as possible.

To implement the *create by doing* approach, we needed to integrate both a model for the interactions, and a model for the scenarios. The approach in itself is not dependent from any given model, as it only defines a metaphor for the creation of the scenario. However, to implement it in our tool, we choose to base the interactions on #FIVE [4], and the scenarios on #SEVEN [9]. The main advantage of both models is that they are designed to be as versatile as possible, which allows us to create a tool usable for a large range of domains. They are also already integrated to work together in Unity, which makes the integration of the actions in the scenario easier.

In #SEVEN, the sequencing is represented by a Petri net, where the places indicate the state the scenario is in, and the transitions are triggered by changes in the environment. The main interest of this kind of representation is that the Petri net formalism is interesting for the creation of scenarios with collaboration between multiple agents. Indeed, there can be different branches of the scenario functioning in parallel, allowing several agents to share the tasks. To make the link with the virtual environment, the transitions are enriched with sensors and effectors, which respectively listen to the environment and act on it. Neither the sensor nor the effector are mandatory for the transitions: a transition without a sensor will be triggered automatically, when the state of the scenario allows it. Similarly, a transition without any effector change the state of the scenario, without any impact for the virtual environment.

#FIVE is an object-relation model based on four main concepts: the objects, the types, the relations, and the object patterns. The objects, types and relations correspond to the ones defined by the object-relation paradigm. The objects are enriched with types to make them interactible, and the relations use those types to perform the interaction. Objects pattern can be used to define more complex conditions for the objects to be used in the relations. Their main use is to define that a relation needs, for some objects, multiple types at once. When a relation is possible in #FIVE, it is instantiated in the form of a *realization*. The realization is directly linked to the objects manipulated, as opposed to the relation.

During the recording of the expert, all the relations in the environment are allowed. Thanks to this, the expert can manipulate the objects as much as they want. Each time the expert performs an action, the corresponding relation is recorded in the scenario under the form of a new transition, creating a scenario as illustrated in Fig. 3. This phase generates a sequence, with each transition corresponding to a relation. The created transition contains two pieces of information: the relation executed by the expert, and the objects involved in it.

The recording is done thanks to a specific scenario, which simply waits for a relation to be executed. Once it is done, the effector on the transition writes a new part for the scenario under construction. Then, the scenario just loops to the original place to be ready to listen to a new relation.

It is to note that the actions done by the user during the recording impact the state of the environment. Because of this, the environment is reset when the expert ends the recording. Before that, the recorded scenario cannot be re-injected in the application, to preserve the coherency of the virtual environment.

To help the expert visualize the scenario, a graphical editor is provided in Unity. This editor shows the scenario as illustrated in Fig. 3, with tools to modify it. During the creation of the scenario, the editor can display the scenario in real-time, as the transitions and places are added according to the actions done by the expert. The graphical editor can be used to modify the sequencing of the actions, by deleting and adding links between the places and the transitions. Of course, the expert is also free to modify the sensors and effectors on the transitions, although it is more pertinent for a developer to do those finer modifications. With the graphical editor, the domain expert can also easily combine multiple scenarios into a single, more complex one, by adding the sequences as branches in the final scenario.

5 Scenario Reuse

Once the scenario has been created, the goal of the domain expert is of course to use it in an application. Similarly to the creation of the scenario, its reuse in the environment is difficult without the necessary knowledge in coding. To allow the expert to reuse the scenario obtained through the *create by doing* approach, we propose some tools to ease the workflow of re-integrating the scenario in the virtual environment. In Sect. 5.1, we first present how the expert can reuse the scenario for a simulation with a human user. In Sect. 5.2, we describe how a

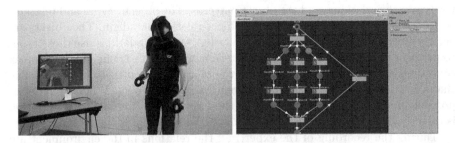

Fig. 3. On the left, an expert creates a scenario. On the right, the scenario editing tool

virtual agent can be connected to the scenario in an application. We can list four different reuses available for the scenario: the *learn by doing*, the *monitor by seeing*, the *collaborate by doing* and the *learn by seeing*.

For more customization when reusing the scenario, the developer can also directly access the resulting scenario, which is in the #SEVEN format. With it, the developer can either use the graphical editor, along with the Unity scene, or even modify the file directly. An example of customization is the creation of variations for the scenario to use it under different pedagogy conditions.

5.1   Reuse with a Human User

The main objective of the scenario is often to be reused by a human user, to have a set of tasks to complete in the virtual environment. The scenario created by the *create by doing* approach is, by nature, usable by the scenario engine, since it is the scenario engine itself that generates it. Thanks to this, the scenario can be easily re-injected in the application. However, to make a good use of this scenario, we propose two complementary uses, involving a human user: the *learn by doing*, and the *monitor by seeing*.

Learn by Doing. The most obvious reuse for a scenario is to re-inject it in the virtual environment, to guide the actions of a user. Indeed, scenarios in virtual reality are common for applications such as serious games [3]. In those applications, the interactivity is important, as the user feels more immersed, and hence more involved in the learning [11]. This guidance offered by the scenario is particularly useful for the training to procedures, we call this reuse the "learn by doing".

To make the *learn by doing* possible, the domain expert needs only to define the scenario they generated as the scenario used for the simulation. For this, the graphical editor we provide proposes a feature to automatically set the displayed scenario as the simulation's scenario. Thanks to this, the scenario will automatically be used when the application is launched again.

During the training to a procedure, different levels of guiding can be provided. In order to simulate this guidance, we provide highlights in the environment, with predefined settings depending on the kind of guidance wanted by the expert (more can be defined by tuning the behaviours of the guiding elements):

– **No guidance.** In some cases, for instance when the application is used to test the knowledge of a student, no guidance should be offered by the environment. In this case, all the highlights are disabled. However, the scenario is still present in the application, and can be used to notify the student about the success or failure of the procedure. Indeed, when the scenario arrives in a final state, this state can be used to define whether or not the student managed to perform the procedure successfully.

- **Step-by-step guidance.** For a first explanation of the procedure, it can be useful to show to the user what they should do to continue the scenario. For this, a setting is proposed to highlight the actions that would trigger the available transitions in the scenario, (i.e. the transitions for which the upstream places all have a token to use). For each pertinent action to highlight, the objects to manipulate are highlighted as shown in Fig. 4. Since the highlight alone is not enough to explain which action should be done with the object, the expert may associate each relation of the environment with a color, and with a different kind of highlight (contouring, flare, ...). This way, the objects will be highlighted differently depending on the actions to perform. To avoid giving too much information, only one highlight is displayed per object, depending on its priority (set for each action). Depending on the expert's choice, the actions doable by the user can either be limited to the ones proposed by the scenario or not.
- **Limited guidance.** For specific conditions, such as a rehearsal of the procedure, a lighter guidance is needed. To provide this kind of guidance, we propose to highlight all the interactible objects in the environment, regardless of the specific interactions indicated by the scenario. This indicates what objects can be manipulated, but nothing more.

Monitor by Seeing. When executing the scenario, a trainer can have difficulties to see what the user is doing. It is especially difficult when the user goes fast or when there are many objects in the environment.

To help the trainer determine what the user is doing, and to check if the user is correctly following the procedure, we propose a means to monitor the execution of the scenario. To do this, we propose to display the scenario, in the graphical editor integrated in Unity, during the runtime of an application.

When the application is playing, the scenario is displayed differently in the editor, to show its current state. More precisely, the tokens of the Petri net are moved according to the transitions that are triggered by the user. When a transition is available in the scenario, it is also highlighted in the editor. That way, it is easy for the observer to see how the scenario is being executed.

Fig. 4. On the left, a scalpel being highlighted to show that the user can take it. On the right, a trainee learning the scenario by interacting with the environment

This feedback of the running scenario can be combined with the visual feedback showing what the user sees. That way, a more complete information can be given to the observer.

5.2   Reuse with a Virtual Actor

To help with the use of the scenario, the application may need one or several virtual agents to perform some tasks. To help the domain expert use a virtual agent connected to the scenario in their virtual reality application, we propose a complete package to connect a humanoid to the scenario.

We designed this package so that it automatizes most of the behaviour of a virtual agent when it is linked to a scenario. Thanks to it, a virtual actor is able to move to a given location, grasp an object using inverse kinematics (with FinalIK[1]), and execute actions from the scenario.

With our package, the virtual agent executes the scenario as follows:

- The virtual agent lists the available actions given by the current state of the scenario. By default, the virtual agent can execute any available action. However, it is possible to limit its capacities, by adding roles to the actors (through their GameObject), and putting the same roles on the transitions: a transition with roles can only be triggered by an actor with the same roles. All of it can be done directly in Unity, through the scenario editor.
- For each one of those available actions, the virtual agent checks if the action can be done considering the state of the objects involved in the action. For instance, if the action proposed by the scenario is to take an object, and the agent already has its hands full, the action should not be taken into account. Thanks to the first two steps, a list of the actions that can be considered both useful and feasible is obtained.
- If there are more than one actions available for the virtual agent, one of them is chosen and executed. The choice of the action amongst the available ones is done according to a heuristic set by the expert. By default, the choice is done randomly, but the use of more detailed heuristics (e.g. computing the shortest path regarding the number of actions or choosing the closest items) allows to modify the behaviour of the virtual agent. For instance, it can try to minimize the number of actions needed to complete the task.

To make the virtual agent look more credible, all of its actions are animated. The tools provided can work with any humanoid, as long as it is compatible with Unity's humanoid system. To do this, we add some information to the objects and relations, to tune the avatar's behaviour accordingly. There are two kinds of features that can be used: additional methods in the relations, and descriptors for the objects.

Each relation defines the animation for its execution. When executing the relation, the virtual agent reads the necessary information in the relation, and performs the corresponding animation. To modify the animation for a given

---

[1] https://assetstore.unity.com/packages/tools/animation/final-ik-14290.

relation, a developer can decide how the avatar is supposed to behave, and modify the code of the relation accordingly.

To define more precisely how the object should be grasped by the avatar, we add descriptors on the objects. Those descriptors, which can be used for the virtual agent as well as for the user's avatar, define the pose of the hand when the object is grasped. It describes which hand can be used to take the object (either the left one, the right one, any hand or both hands simultaneously). For each hand, the pose is defined by describing the positions of the joints for each finger. For an easier setting of this descriptor, the rig can be displayed in Unity, to see how the hand is supposed to go around the object, like in Fig. 5.

The object descriptors also define how the hand transitions between poses when it does the animation. Indeed, we can distinguish two states for the hand: with a pose or loose. Depending on the object and the action, the hand either take a pose only when it is close to the object (for instance, to push a button), take a pose and keep it (to grasp an object), release the pose (to release an object) or stay as it is during the whole animation.

Thanks to the descriptors, and to the scenario system for the virtual agent, it is easy for the domain expert to get a virtual agent to execute some tasks in a scenario. We can distinguish two main uses for a virtual agent, controlled by a scenario, in virtual reality: the *collaborate by doing*, and the *learn by seeing*.

Collaborate by Doing. The first, called the *collaborate by doing*, is the most common one. It consists in using one or several virtual agents to collaborate with the user, in order to help/disturb them during the procedure.

Since the same scenario is used by both the human user and the virtual agent, the collaboration is implicitly defined in the scenario itself, with as many agents as wanted. If needed, the domain expert can tune this collaboration, by appointing roles to each actor. Those roles must also be placed on the transitions in the editor: only an actor with the needed roles can trigger the transition. This does not prevent the actors from executing the actions that would trigger the transition. However, the virtual agents only list the actions for which they have the necessary roles. Because of this, they are "blind" to the rest of the scenario, and will not execute actions that do not correspond to their part.

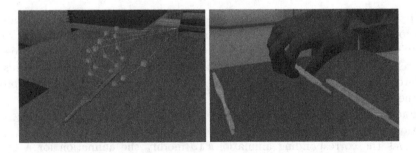

Fig. 5. The descriptors for a hand pose, and the resulting hand grasping the scalpel

Learn by Seeing. The virtual agent can also be useful on its own, without any human user in the virtual environment. Since it may not be always easy for a trainer to get the material needed for a demonstration, we propose to use the replay of the scenario by a virtual agent as a demonstration. The scenario defines a complete set of tasks, in order, which can be replayed by a virtual agent in the scenario, the same way as if the agent was collaborating with a user (Fig. 6).

Once the scenario is set in the virtual reality application, the domain expert only needs to launch the application, without any human user, to let the virtual agent perform the actions. A trainee can then observe the virtual agent perform the scenario to learn the procedure. Since the virtual agent is performing in real-time, in Unity, the trainee can easily change the viewpoint or be immersed in the scene to get the opportunity to observe from the most pertinent viewpoint at any moment. In the latter case, the trainee will just see the virtual agent perform the actions, and will be free to move around, with the possible help of a teacher to indicate what is interesting to look at. The demonstration performed by the virtual agent can also be easily recorded into a video, by recording the feedback given by the cameras in the Unity scene. This can be done with pre-integrated plug-ins in Unity, or by capturing the feedback given on screen. The recording can include a camera placed on the virtual agent's head, to give a first person view of the demonstration.

6 Use Cases

To demonstrate our approach and tools, we designed two use cases: a medical use case in Sect. 6.1, and a archaeology one in Sect. 6.2. Since the tool is designed to be independent of the application, it has been used as is for both use cases.

6.1 Surgical Procedure Training

In the medical domain, the knowledge of procedures is a crucial part of the success for a surgical intervention. Indeed, in order not to cause problems or slow down the whole group, each member of the team must know their tasks. When learning procedures, virtual reality can be a powerful tool to learn how to

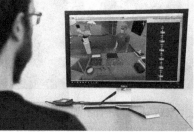

Fig. 6. A user is collaborating with a virtual nurse

work in a team [24]. To help the students learn the procedures for the preparation of a room before the surgical intervention, we designed, in collaboration with a medical team, an application for scrub nurses. It was also experimented in a nurses school, to evaluate its potential for training. In this application, the scrub nurse in training must prepare an operating table before the intervention.

In this use case, the trainee has to take some instruments, and place them on specific spots on the table, so that they can be rapidly found during the intervention. Some of the instruments must also be prepared during this preparation phase, such as scalpels that must be assembled. The preparation of the table differs for each intervention, which is why it is important to be able to create new scenarios easily. In one of the scenarios we tested, a part of the procedure makes the trainee assemble three scalpels (composed of a handle and a blade), by first putting the handle on the table, taking the blades, and placing back the assembled scalpels. For this task, the trainee must collaborate with a virtual agent, who brings the blades, which must be assembled with the handles, and placed on the table. The setup for this application is illustrated in Fig. 7.

In this application, we already integrated all the possible interactions in the virtual environment beforehand, with #FIVE. Thanks to this, only the creation of the scenario for each procedure remains to be done by the domain expert. To do this, the domain expert can simply perform the whole preparation, which results in the complete scenario.

In this scenario, some of the actions can be done in any order. For instance, there is no particular constraint for the assembling of the scalpels: the nurse can assemble them in any order. Because of this, the graphical editor was used to modify the sequencing of the actions. Instead of having a linear sequence, some of the actions were put in parallel branches, so that each scalpel assembly corresponds to a separate branch.

The help of a virtual agent was also needed. Because of this, we defined that the virtual agent could only bring the plate containing the scalpel blades to the user, once the handles are put on the table. This was defined using the roles of the scenario: the virtual agent cannot do the first part of the scenario, and is

Fig. 7. On the left, the preparation table in the virtual operating room. In the middle, the first person view of the environment. On the right, a real expert scrub nurse interacting with the application.

hence waiting for the user to do it. This way, the virtual agent has a specific role in the scenario, which does not collide with the trainee's actions.

Finally, we used the different levels of guidance in the scenario to help trainees to learn the table preparation procedure. The first version presented to them used a strong guidance, to highlight the following actions that were useful for the preparation of the table. Then, another version was presented to them, with only a limited guidance: all the possible actions were highlighted. During the execution of the procedure, a trainer can see the vision of the trainee, as well as the scenario being updated according to the trainee's actions.

While the first application allowed us to reuse the scenario for the *collaborate by doing* and the *monitor by seeing* cases, we were also able to use the scenario in the *learn by seeing* case. This second use of the scenario was done to demonstrate the assembly of the scalpels through a replay of the procedure by a virtual actor. To do this, we replaced the human user by a virtual agent, and recorded it assembling of the scalpels. The resulting replay shows the complete assembly, and can easily be presented to a group of students to explain the procedure, without having to be in the operating room, or to recreate it in a classroom.

6.2 Archaeological Virtual Tour

To test the genericity of our approach, we decided to use it with a second domain, namely archaeology. Once an archaeological excavation has been done, it is often difficult for the archaeologists to diffuse the newfound knowledge to the general public. To help in doing so, the archaeologists may organise guided tours on the excavation site at the end of the excavation, to explain what has been found, with the visual supported provided by the site itself. To be able to visit it after the site is closed, we designed a virtual tour application. This use case provides another *learn by doing* situation, with different stakes.

In this particular use case, we propose to visit the site of Beg-Er-Vil, in the west of France. The scenario for the virtual tour was designed with the collaboration of an archaeologist who worked on the excavation. This virtual tour allows a tourist to be immersed in the site as it was during the excavation, and to explain the discoveries, as well as the work of the archaeologists. To ensure a better understanding of the information presented in the virtual site, a precise path is defined, which brings the visitor to pertinent points of interest, with explanations at each point.

In order to keep the application simple for the visitors of the virtual site, we decided to limit the possible interactions. First, the user can move around the site through teleportation. On the external part of the site, specific teleportation targets are already placed, to provide the means to easily access each part of the environment. In the central part of the site, where the density of POIs is higher, the teleportation can be done to any location of the zone. They can also display and hide textual information for each point of interest in the virtual environment, in the form of a panel; and modify some parameters of the simulation.

When the visitors starts the application, they view something akin to what is presented in Fig. 8. For the creation of the scenario, the archaeologist is immersed in the virtual site. For the navigation in the site, teleportation targets are automatically placed so as to cover the maximum space in the environment. In the core of the site, however, the user is free to teleport anywhere in the zone, as the interesting spots are more condensed in that zone.

In the virtual environment, the archaeologist can place points of interest in the environment during the creation of the scenario. The creation of the POIs is done by adding a new point in the environment, and telling the content of the panel, which is automatically converted to text. Since the creation of the POIs should not be integrated in the final scenario, the relations associated to that interaction are specifically declared as ignored by the scenario recorded, in order to keep only the pertinent interactions.

At any moment, the archaeologist can also modify some parameters of the simulation. For instance, since this site is on the coast, the sea level can be modified, to show how it was at different times during the occupation of the site. Those modifications of parameters can be really helpful to make the visitors aware of the changes that occurred since the site was left by its occupants, and to understand their living conditions at the time.

Once the archaeologist recorded the scenario, the reuse is simply done by the re-injection of the scenario in the application. Thanks to it, a visitor can then use the application to virtually visit the archaeological site. For this reuse, we decided to use a *learn by doing* approach. To help the visitors follow the path designed by the archaeologist, a step-by-step guidance is used, with highlights showing where the user should go next, and with which POIs they should interact. However, their actions are not limited to the ones provided to the scenario, to let a user go back and visit freely other locations is they want to.

Fig. 8. User's view at the start of the virtual tour (with the teleportation points)

7   User Feedback

In order to evaluate our approach, we asked 5 experts (1 from the medical domain and 4 archaeologists). The participants were presented to the environment with a first, simple example (changing the wheel of a car). Once they were accustomed to it, they moved to the use case corresponding to their domain of expertise: the medical staff was presented with the operating room, and the archaeologists were immersed in an office (Fig. 9). The goal was to present an environment in which the user could be at ease, with exactly the same interactions between the two examples.

In both cases, the desk was filled with different tools, and the participant was asked to create the scenario corresponding to the following procedure; place some of those tools at a given place, in a certain order. At the end of the session, we showed them the resulting scenario in the editor, and let them modify it as they wanted, until they felt accustomed to the editor. Finally, we asked them to fill the UTAUT2 questionnaire [27], along with the NASA-TLX [14], the SUS questionnaire [26], a Simulator Sickness questionnaire [15], and a Personal Innovativeness questionnaire [1] (the final questionnaire is provided with this paper).

Overall, the experts feedback was strongly positive. They considered that the tool was useful (*"I think that this tool is useful to create scenarios"* $\rightarrow$ m $= 7$, $\sigma = 0.447$, 7 being the best score), simple (*"Few efforts are needed to be at ease with the tool"* $\rightarrow$ m $= 6$, $\sigma = 0.5477$) and fun to use (m $= 7$, $\sigma = 0.447$). All of them managed to obtain the expected scenario, without much effort. However, there were also some negative comments, mostly directed at the possibility to use virtual reality in their work (cost, accessibility). The participants who felt this way were also the same that scored the worst score for the personal innovativeness questionnaire. Also, one of them noted that he thought that the tool could be difficult to use for more complex scenarios in the open comments section. Still, all the participants found the tool interesting and really easy to use, and were satisfied to have been able to create a scenario without direct help.

Fig. 9. The environment for the experiment

8   Conclusion and Future Works

In this paper, we presented a new workflow for the creation of scenario-driven applications in virtual reality. Thanks to a *create by doing* approach, an expert with no particular coding skills is able to generate a complete scenario, and to reuse it in an application. This reuse can be done with a single user, or with virtual agents controlled by the scenario, to obtain different ways of presenting the scenario to a user. Thanks to this, a same scenario can be easily created and reused for either a *learn by doing*, a *learn by seeing*, a *collaborate by doing*, or a *monitor by seeing* application.

For the complete creation and reuse of the scenario, we provide three important tools for the domain expert. The first tool, also briefly presented in [19], allows the domain expert to create a scenario based on a demonstration of it done directly in the virtual environment. The second one is a tool to use the scenario to guide a user in the virtual environment, with different levels of guidance according to the kind of application wanted. Finally, the proposed methodology is supported by a tool to connect a virtual agent to a scenario. This tool allows the expert to define how a virtual agent should behave, to either perform a part of the scenario or demonstrate it completely.

We will enhance this approach in several ways in future works. First, the definition of scenarios with variations (e.g. different orders) could be simplified. For now, only the objects used during the recording are integrated, without any possibility of variation. To add this variation, we propose to record the expert multiple times, and to synthesize the result given by the set of observations to get the final scenario. Mathematical models such as test and flip synthesis [6] could also be used to detect patterns in the scenarios, allowing automatic creation of variations.

A second improvement could be the integration of pedagogy into the reuse of the scenario. While, in this paper, we focused on bringing tools for the experts, leaving the pedagogical aspect to the teachers and pedagogy experts, it could be interesting to bring more efficient tools to tune the experience of the learners, by taking into account known counterexamples for instance.

A final improvement could be to give tools to edit efficiently other kinds of sensors and effectors in the scenarios, so as to give the expert more ways to handle the creation of the application. Examples of such sensors and effectors are timers, or effectors that could change roles dynamically: while those are integrated in the editor, it is still difficult for the expert to understand them.

References

1. Agarwal, R., Karahanna, E.: Time flies when you're having fun: cognitive absorption and beliefs about information technology usage. MIS Q. 665–694 (2000). https://www.jstor.org/stable/3250951?seq=1
2. Angros, Jr., R., Johnson, W.L., Rickel, J., Scholer, A.: Learning domain knowledge for teaching procedural skills. In: Proceedings of the First International Joint Conference on Autonomous Agents and Multiagent Systems: Part 3, AAMAS 2002, pp. 1372–1378. ACM, New York (2002). https://doi.org/10.1145/545056.545134

3. Bailenson, J.N., Yee, N., Blascovich, J., Beall, A.C., Lundblad, N., Jin, M.: The use of immersive virtual reality in the learning sciences: digital transformations of teachers, students, and social context. J. Learn. Sci. **17**(1), 102–141 (2008). https://doi.org/10.1080/10508400701793141

4. Bouville, R., Gouranton, V., Boggini, T., Nouviale, F., Arnaldi, B.: #FIVE: high-level components for developing collaborative and interactive virtual environments. In: Proceedings of Eighth Workshop on Software Engineering and Architectures for Realtime Interactive Systems (SEARIS 2015), conjunction with IEEE Virtual Reality (VR), Arles, France, March 2015. https://hal.inria.fr/hal-01147734

5. Brom, C., Šisler, V., Holan, T.: Story manager in 'Europe 2045' uses petri nets. In: Cavazza, M., Donikian, S. (eds.) ICVS 2007. LNCS, vol. 4871, pp. 38–50. Springer, Heidelberg (2007). https://doi.org/10.1007/978-3-540-77039-8_4

6. Caillaud, B.: Surgical process mining with test and flip net synthesis. In: Bergenthum, R., Carmona, J. (eds.) Application of Region Theory (ART), Barcelona, Spain, pp. 43–54, July 2013. https://hal.inria.fr/hal-00872284

7. Chan, J.C.P., Leung, H., Tang, J.K.T., Komura, T.: A virtual reality dance training system using motion capture technology. IEEE Trans. Learn. Technol. **4**(2), 187–195 (2011). https://doi.org/10.1109/TLT.2010.27

8. Chevaillier, P., et al.: Semantic modeling of virtual environments using MASCARET. In: 2012 5th Workshop on Software Engineering and Architectures for Realtime Interactive Systems (SEARIS), pp. 1–8, March 2012. https://doi.org/10.1109/SEARIS.2012.6231174

9. Claude, G., Gouranton, V., Bouville Berthelot, R., Arnaldi, B.: Short paper: #SEVEN, a sensor effector based scenarios model for driving collaborative virtual environment. In: Nojima, T., Reiners, D., Staadt, O. (eds.) ICAT-EGVE, International Conference on Artificial Reality and Telexistence, Eurographics Symposium on Virtual Environments, Bremen, Germany, pp. 1–4, December 2014. https://hal.archives-ouvertes.fr/hal-01086237

10. Cremer, J., Kearney, J., Papelis, Y.: HCSM: a framework for behavior and scenario control in virtual environments. ACM Trans. Model. Comput. Simul. (TOMACS) **5**(3), 242–267 (1995). https://doi.org/10.1145/217853.217857

11. Fletcher, J.D.: Does this stuff work? A review of technology used to teach. Tech-Knowlogia **Jan-Mar**, 10–14 (2003)

12. Gerbaud, S., Mollet, N., Arnaldi, B.: Virtual environments for training: from individual learning to collaboration with humanoids. In: Hui, K., et al. (eds.) Edutainment 2007. LNCS, vol. 4469, pp. 116–127. Springer, Heidelberg (2007). https://doi.org/10.1007/978-3-540-73011-8_14

13. Green, T.R.G., Petre, M.: Usability analysis of visual programming environments: a 'cognitive dimensions' framework. J. Vis. Lang. Comput. **7**(2), 131–174 (1996). http://www.sciencedirect.com/science/article/pii/S1045926X96900099

14. Hart, S.G., Staveland, L.E.: Development of NASA-TLX (task load index): results of empirical and theoretical research. In: Advances in Psychology, vol. 52, pp. 139–183. Elsevier (1988). https://www.sciencedirect.com/science/article/pii/S0166411508623869

15. Kennedy, R.S., Lane, N.E., Berbaum, K.S., Lilienthal, M.G.: Simulator sickness questionnaire: an enhanced method for quantifying simulator sickness. Int. J. Aviat. Psychol. **3**(3), 203–220 (1993). https://doi.org/10.1207/s15327108ijap0303_3

16. Klopfer, E., Perry, J., Squire, K., Jan, M.F., Steinkuehler, C.: Mystery at the museum: a collaborative game for museum education. In: Proceedings of the 2005 Conference on Computer Support for Collaborative Learning, pp. 316–320. International Society of the Learning Sciences (2005). http://dl.acm.org/citation.cfm?id=1149293.1149334

17. Klopfer, E., Squire, K.: Environmental detectives-the development of an augmented reality platform for environmental simulations. Educ. Technol. Res. Dev. **56**, 203–228 (2007)

18. Lamarche, F., Donikian, S.: Automatic orchestration of behaviours through the management of resources and priority levels. In: Proceedings of the First International Joint Conference on Autonomous Agents and Multiagent Systems: Part 3, pp. 1309–1316. ACM (2002). https://doi.org/10.1145/545056.545124

19. Lécuyer, F., Gouranton, V., Reuzeau, A., Gaugne, R., Arnaldi, B.: Create by doing – action sequencing in VR. In: Gavrilova, M., Chang, J., Thalmann, N.M., Hitzer, E., Ishikawa, H. (eds.) CGI 2019. LNCS, vol. 11542, pp. 329–335. Springer, Cham (2019). https://doi.org/10.1007/978-3-030-22514-8_27

20. Lee, G.A., Nelles, C., Billinghurst, M., Kim, G.J.: Immersive authoring of tangible augmented reality applications. In: Proceedings of the 3rd IEEE/ACM International Symposium on Mixed and Augmented Reality, ISMAR 2004, pp. 172–181. IEEE Computer Society, Washington, DC (2004). https://doi.org/10.1109/ISMAR.2004.34

21. Lugrin, J.L., Cavazza, M.: Making sense of virtual environments: action representation, grounding and common sense. In: Proceedings of the 12th International Conference on Intelligent User Interfaces, pp. 225–234. ACM (2007). https://doi.org/10.1145/1216295.1216336

22. Marfisi-Schottman, I., George, S., Tarpin-Bernard, F.: Tools and methods for efficiently designing serious games. In: European Conference on Games Based Learning, ECGBL, Copenhagen, Denmark, pp. 226–234 (2010). https://hal.archives-ouvertes.fr/hal-00953318

23. Mateas, M., Stern, A.: A behavior language for story-based believable agents. IEEE Intell. Syst. **17**(4), 39–47 (2002). https://doi.org/10.1109/MIS.2002.1024751

24. Mitchell, L., Flin, R., Yule, S., Mitchell, J., Coutts, K., Youngson, G.: Evaluation of the scrub practitioners' list of intraoperative non-technical skills (splints) system. Int. J. Nurs. Stud. **49**(2), 201–211 (2012). http://www.sciencedirect.com/science/article/pii/S002074891100335X

25. Paiva, A., Machado, I., Prada, R.: Heroes, villians, magicians, & dramatis personae in a virtual story creation environment. In: Proceedings of the 6th International Conference on Intelligent User Interfaces, IUI 2001, pp. 129–136. ACM, New York (2001). https://doi.org/10.1145/359784.360314

26. Slater, M., Usoh, M., Steed, A.: Depth of presence in virtual environments. Presence: Teleoperators Virtual Environ. **3**(2), 130–144 (1994). https://doi.org/10.1162/pres.1994.3.2.130

27. Venkatesh, V., Thong, J.Y., Xu, X.: Consumer acceptance and use of information technology: extending the unified theory of acceptance and use of technology. MIS Q. **36**(1), 157–178 (2012). http://www.academia.edu/download/36422124/Venkateshutaut2.pdf

Single Color Sketch-Based Image Retrieval in HSV Color Space

Yu Xia$^{(\boxtimes)}$, Shuangbu Wang, Yanran Li, Lihua You, Xiaosong Yang, and Jian Jun Zhang

National Centre for Computer Animation, Bournemouth University, Poole, UK
`yxia@bournemouth.ac.uk`

Abstract. Sketch-based image retrieval is a fundamental computer vision problem. Instead of using hand-designed features to represent sketches and images, recent researches apply deep learning approaches combined with fine-grained matching to retrieve images with fine-grained details. Although these researches allow user to use hand-free sketches drawn for retrieving similar objects, the color matching is ignored which induces a low retrieval precision. To address this problem, we propose a single color sketch-based image retrieval (SCSBIR) approach using HSV color feature considering both shape matching and color matching in this paper. The SCSBIR problem is investigated using deep learning networks, in which deep features are used to represent color sketches and images. A novel ranking method considering both shape matching and color matching is also proposed. In addition, we build a SCSBIR dataset with color sketches and images, and train and test our method by using this dataset. The test results show that our method has a better retrieval performance. The research in this paper can not only promote its application in the commercial field, but also provide reference for the future research in this field.

Keywords: Single color sketch · Image retrieval · HSV color space · Deep learning · Triplet network

1 Introduction

Sketch-based retrieval techniques are getting increasing attention as new computer vision problems because the existing retrieval methods based on text and photos can no longer meet the growing needs of people. Currently, many researchers have studied several retrieval problems based on sketches, mainly including sketch-based image retrieval [1–3,11] and sketch-based 3D model retrieval [7–10]. In the field of sketch-based image retrieval, fine-grained matching between sketches and retrieved images attracts an increase attention. However, almost all of the current studies only focus on the shape detail matching between the black-and-white sketch and the retrieved image, ignoring color matching. Inspired by the work of Bui and Collomosse [11] and based on previous research [28], this paper aims to solve the problem of fine-grained image

© Springer-Verlag GmbH Germany, part of Springer Nature 2020
M. L. Gavrilova et al. (Eds.): Trans. on Comput. Sci. XXXVII, LNCS 12230, pp. 77–90, 2020.
https://doi.org/10.1007/978-3-662-61983-4_5

retrieval based on single color sketch, and make the retrieval results consider both shape detail matching and accurate color matching. Solving this problem is particularly important in commercial applications such as searching a specific item on an online shopping platform by color finger-sketching using a touchscreen device. For example, when a user draws a sketch of female wedding shoe with white color, he will obtain an image of white female wedding shoe rather than other color shoes even the shapes of these shoes are closer to the sketch.

In this paper, we propose a novel SCSBIR method based on the multibranch deep convolutional neural network. The network consists of three identical branches, one of which takes color sketches as input and the other two take images as input during training. With the network, we can not only obtain the objects with fine-grained similarity to the sketch, but also take into account the similarity of color. For achieving the optimal performance of the neural networks, a lot of training data are needed. Since the deep FG-SBIR model [6] provided a suitable CNN foundation for black-and-white sketch-based image retrieval, we build our pre-training model based on the deep FG-SBIR model and create a dataset of single color sketch-image pairs for SCSBIR based on the Shoe and Chair Datasets from [3] and the Handbag Dataset from [6].

The current research is an extended version of the conference paper presented at CGI 2019 [28]. Unlike the previous work, we make the following new contributions: 1) A single color sketch-image dataset is created which contains three categories, 419 shoe, 297 chair and 568 handbag single color sketch-image pairs, respectively; 2) We use a deep learning approach to achieve image retrieval based on single color sketch, and verify the generalization of this approach in different categories; 3) A new color similarity comparison method in HSV color space with Bhattacharyya distance is proposed to rank retrieval images after shape matching process.

2   Related Works

Our proposed method is related to category-level sketch-based image retrieval, fine-grained sketch-based image retrieval, color sketch-based image retrieval and sketch-based 3D model retrieval. In this section, we briefly review the most related work in these fields.

2.1   Category-Level Sketch-Based Image Retrieval

Many existing SBIR researches focused on category-level sketch-based image retrieval and employed hand-designed features to represent sketches and images. So far, numerous hand-designed feature representations have been proposed. An interactive system was presented in [23] for sketch-based image retrieval, and 43 sketch-image pairs were created to evaluate and compare the retrieval performance of 27 descriptor variants. Eitz et al. [1] developed the bag-of-features descriptors (BOF) and created a new dataset for category-level sketch-based image retrieval including 31 sketches with 31 × 40 images. Based on BOF code-book, Hu et al. [2, 24, 25] introduced Gradient Field HoG (GF-HOG) as a depiction invariant image descriptor to improve retrieval accuracy. Novel processing schemes for large-scale databases were proposed in [26, 27] to calculate the similarity between a query sketch and images. The limitation of hand-designed features is that the subtle detail information cannot be noticed and the retrieval result belongs to the category-level. Therefore, to meet the requirements for instance-level sketch-based image retrieval, a deep learning algorithm is used in this paper to obtain features containing more detailed information.

2.2 Fine-Grained Sketch-Based Image Retrieval

The concept of fine-grained retrieval was first proposed in 2014 [5], while previous SBIR methods mainly focused on category-level retrieval. After that, some scholars employed deep learning models to address the fine-grained SBIR problems. Yu et al. [3] created a dataset including two categories of shoes and chairs and used a triplet ranking homogeneous network with triplet ranking loss to train model parameters respectively for shoes and chairs, which is mainly used for face recognition. Subsequently, Song et al. [6] improved the method in [3] by introducing the shortcut connection architecture of ResNet and attention modeling which is mainly applied in NLP field, added a new handbag category, and proposed a novel loss function named HOLEF which was an improved version based on the classic triplet ranking loss. Sangkloy et al. [4] did a similar study on fine-grained sketch-based image retrieval. Their main contribution is the creation of the Sketchy database with 125 categories, and using a triplet ranking heterogeneous network with classical triplet ranking loss to train model parameters which can be applied for fine-grained image retrieval of multi-categories. Although some previous studies have been done on fine-grained retrieval, they all only focus on image retrieval based on black and white sketches, and there is no precedent for fine-grained image retrieval based on color sketches.

2.3 Color Sketch-Based Image Retrieval

Recent existing color sketch-based image retrieval methods mainly focus on the extraction and comparison of hand-designed features of color sketches and images based on gradients [1, 2]. These methods have some limitations and cannot preserve the subtle details of sketches and images well. As a result, the retrieval results cannot meet the requirements of fine-grained retrieval, such as good matching in the posture, direction and details of objects. Reddy et al. [13] used HSV color space to extract color features and gray-level co-occurrence matrix to extract texture features of free-hand color sketches or images separately. Then, the Euclidean distances of color features and texture features of query sketches and target images were calculated and added to obtain the similarities. This article mainly focuses on the category-level search, but ignores the subtle details and directions of the retrieved instances. Moreover, the query sketch is not the abstract hand-drawn color line sketch, but the photo edge extraction sketch with color blocks. The edge sketch provides more information than hand-drawn sketch and greatly reduces the difficulty of retrieval. Bui et al. [11] first used line-art query sketches and presented a gradient field HoG based on mathematical formulas for color sketch-based image retrieval. They converted the color sketch and image into GF-HoG descriptors separately and then made subsequent comparisons. Up to now, the deep learning method was rarely applied in color sketch-based image retrieval. Cheng et al. [12] used a convolutional neural network to address the pedestrian color naming problem. Their work is to obtain accurate color description of real world pedestrian images without paying attention to the extraction of subtle detailed features of sketches or images, which is quite different from what we are solving. Xia et al. [28] studied color sketch-based image retrieval in RGB color space with 11 specified colors. The limitation is that RGB color is not intuitive for human interpretation and the luminance and chrominance properties are not separated which cause errors in the color matching process.

2.4   Sketch-Based 3D Model Retrieval

Most of the previous sketch-based 3D shape retrieval methods work by comparing hand-crafted features [9,10] extracted from sketches and 2D contours projected from 3D models. With the development of deep learning in computer vision, the deep learning method is widely used in sketch-based 3D model retrieval to capture features. Wang et al. [7] adopted two Siamese convolutional neural networks to learn similarities between two domains. One of the two branches was used to extract deep features of sketches, and the other one was used to extract deep features of 2D projections of the 3D models. Qi et al. [8] proposed a new triplet heterogeneous model and introduced a joint semantic embedding space.

3   Fine-Grained Instance-Level SCSBIR Dataset

At present, almost all production retrieval applications of online shopping platforms are based on semantic retrieval. Since semantics cannot accurately describe the detailed shape and color of a product, users may not easily obtain desired retrieval results by using semantic retrieval. In this paper, we aim to solve this problem and propose a retrieval method based on color sketches. The color sketch has enough appearance information of the retrieval target which can be used to retrieve products and obtain optimal retrieval results. Since deep CNN is used to extract features of color sketches and images in this paper, a large number of color sketch-image datasets are needed to train network parameters for better feature representation. We create a SCSBIR dataset specifically to meet the requirements of our proposed method.

We created the SCSBIR dataset based on the Shoe Dataset [3], Chair Dataset [3] and Handbag Dataset [6]. It contains 419, 297 and 568 single color

Fig. 1. Examples of the SCSBIR dataset

sketch-image pairs of shoes, chairs and handbags. We use the edge maps extraction method [15] to extract the corresponding single color edge maps from images using the dominant color in the images and take them as the input of the image branches during model training.

Similarly, the creation of the color sketch corresponding to each image is obtained by using the dominant color of the image to color the original black-and-white sketch. Figure 1 shows some examples of single color sketch-image pairs in the SCSBIR dataset. Although our SCSBIR dataset is not very large, it can fully meet the needs of fine-tuning and testing of our model (see Sect. 5).

4 Methodology

The deep convolutional neural network used in this paper is a Triplet network which is an improved version of Siamese network. The three branches in the network are identical which are homogeneous. A soft attention model and two shortcut connection architectures are adopted to improve the retrieval precision of the network.

4.1 Siamese Network and Siamese Loss

Siamese network [16] has a pair of convolutional neural networks and each branch has a different input, i.e., a color sketch or corresponding image. After encoding the input in each branch, the distance between the two encodings is compared to see how similar or different the two inputs are, and it is represented by the norm of the difference between the encodings of the two inputs:

$$d(X^{(1)}, X^{(2)}) = \left\| f_{\theta_1}(X^{(1)}) - f_{\theta_2}(X^{(2)}) \right\|_2^2 \tag{1}$$

where $X^{(1)}$ and $X^{(2)}$ represent two different inputs, $d(\cdot)$ is Euclidean distance, θ_1 and θ_2 represent the respective parameters of the two branches, and $f_{\theta_1}(\cdot)$ and $f_{\theta_2}(\cdot)$ are the feature mappings of the two branches which map the two inputs to a common feature embedding space, respectively.

The two similar inputs need to have a smaller value of $d(\cdot)$ than dissimilar inputs. To this end, Siamese loss is used in the Siamese network to do back propagation and vary all parameters. It is defined as:

$$L = l * d(A, P) + (1 - l) * max(0, \alpha - d(A, N)) \tag{2}$$

where A is a query sketch, P is an image similar to A, N is an image dissimilar to A, $l = 0$ for negative pairs and $l = 1$ for positive pairs, and α is a margin which means the distance between $d(A, P)$ and $d(A, N)$.

4.2 Triplet Network and Triplet Loss

Different from Siamese network, Triplet network [17] has three convolutional neural networks. Three branches of Triplet network have three different inputs. Note that the second and the third branches share the same parameters. Given a triplet of a query sketch A, a similar image P and a dissimilar image N, the Triplet network needs to satisfy:

$$d(A, P) - d(A, N) + \alpha \leq 0 \tag{3}$$

To achieve this goal, Triplet Loss is defined as:

$$L(A, P, N) = max(d(A, P) - d(A, N) + \alpha, 0) \tag{4}$$

Considering all triplets in the dataset, the ultimate optimization goal is:

$$\min_{\theta_1, \theta_2} \sum_{i=1}^{m} L(A^{(i)}, P^{(i)}, N^{(i)}) \tag{5}$$

where m is the total number of triplets.

By minimizing Eq. 5, the distance between A and P will be narrowed while the distance between A and N will be widened. Triplet network can acquire the representations of inputs with detailed information if there are sufficient triplet annotations. We apply Triplet network with Triplet Loss to carry out shape matching and achieve single color sketch-based image retrieval.

4.3   Homogeneous vs. Heterogeneous

Triplet network is composed of three branches, and it needs a triplet for each training process. Since the inputs of the second and third branches belong to the same domain, these two branches share a set of parameters. If the first branch shares the same set of parameters with the second and third branches, the network is a triplet homogeneous network. If the parameters of the first branch are different from those of the second and third branches and have an independent set of weights, the network is a triplet heterogeneous network.

Since our training dataset is not enough for training needs, in order to avoid the overfit problem and alleviate the domain discrepancy, we select homogeneous network and process our dataset by extracting color edge maps which are used as inputs of the second and third branches instead of images.

4.4   Soft Attention Model and Shortcut Connection Architecture

Inspired by the work of Song et al. [6], we implement a soft attention model to improve the retrieval accuracy of SCSBIR. The vector distribution of the soft attention output is a kind of soft distribution, which means that an attention distribution probability of any region in the input image is given. Bahdanau et al. [18] first proposed the soft attention model and applied it to the field of machine translation. In this paper, the soft attention model is adopted in each branch of the triplet homogeneous network. In addition, the shortcut connection architectures [19] are employed to solve the problem of gradient disappearance in deep networks. The final retrieval results are obtained by calculating the color similarity values between the input color sketch and the top ten retrieval results of shape matching.

4.5   Shape Matching and Color Matching

To achieve SCSBIR, we need to solve two matching problems, i.e., the shape matching and the color matching. Since a single color sketch and edge map of an image are represented by the feature vectors which are outputted from the networks, we apply Eq. 1 to estimate the shape similarity of the single color sketch and image. In the color matching process, we choose the HSV color space for describing the color feature of single color sketchs and edge maps because RGB color space cannot exactly reflect the color information of objects and separate the luminance and chrominance properties. Compared with RGB color space, the HSV color space has decorrelated and uniform coordinates matching the human perception of color and its histogram is easy to extract [14]. Since the V coordinate in the HSV color space is easily affected by the lighting condition, we only use the $H - S$ coordinates to form a 2D histogram of the single color sketch and image respectively, and then apply Bhattacharyya distance to calculate the color similarity between the 2D histograms of the single color sketch and image, which can be expressed as:

$$dist(S, I) = (1 - \frac{1}{\sqrt{\bar{S}\bar{I}n^2}} \sum_{i=1}^{n} \sqrt{S_i I_i})^{\frac{1}{2}} \tag{6}$$

$$\bar{S} = \frac{1}{n} \sum_{i=1}^{n} S_i, \bar{I} = \frac{1}{n} \sum_{i=1}^{n} I_i \tag{7}$$

where S and I are the 2D histograms of the single color sketch and the image, and S_i and I_i are the ith bin in S and I, respectively.

4.6   Matching Color Sketches and Images Using Triplet Homogeneous Network

After obtaining the SCSBIR model trained by the training set of SCSBIR dataset, we apply it to the testing set to verify the retrieval accuracy of our method (see Sect. 5). Taking shoes as an example, the pipeline of our proposed SCSBIR is illustrated in Fig. 2.

In the pipeline of the SCSBIR method, all shoe images in the testing set have obtained their feature vector representations through pre-processing to improve the speed of real-time retrieval. The SCSBIR method includes three steps. First, the user inputs a color sketch of a shoe as probe into the SCSBIR model and gets its feature vector representation in real time. Second, the shape matching is applied to estimate shape similarity between the sketch feature vector and all the image feature vectors and find the top ten retrieval results which are most similar to the shoe sketch in the dataset. Third, we use color matching to estimate the color similarity between the color sketch and the top ten results of shape matching, and reorder the ten results according to the color similarity. As shown in the Fig. 2, the first retrieval result in final ten results is the most similar shoe to the input color sketch in the shape and color.

5   Experiments

5.1   Experiment Settings

The SCSBIR model employs the Sketch-a-Net [20] as the basic model and is pre-trained in three steps [3]. First, the basic network is trained to recognize 1,000 categories of the ImageNet dataset [22] with the edge maps extracted from images. Then, the model is fine-tuned to recognize the 250 categories of TU-Berlin 20,000 sketch dataset [21]. At last, fine-grained retrieval ability of the model is obtained by retraining the model in the dataset consisting of 187 sketch-image categories selected from the TU-Berlin dataset and the ImageNet dataset separately.

After pre-training, we fine-tune the pre-trained model using our SCSBIR dataset. The SCSBIR dataset contains three categories: shoe, chair, and handbag. Each category is split into two parts. Following the same splits as in [3]

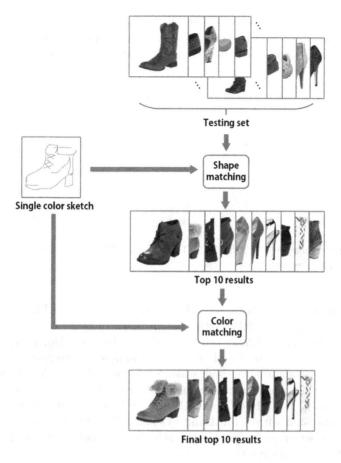

Fig. 2. Pipeline of the SCSBIR method

and [6], 304 pairs, 200 pairs and 400 pairs are used for fine-tuning training respectively, and 115 pairs, 97 pairs and 168 pairs are used for testing respectively. We use the training set of each category to fine-tune the model specifically for the target category. In fine-tuning process, we set the initial learning rate to be 0.001 and the mini-batch size to be 128. The attention module consists of 2 convolutional layers with kernel size 1×1.

5.2 Results

We compare our method with other two fine-grained sketch-based image retrieval methods, i.e., DTRM [3] and FG-SBIR [6], which apply DCNN for feature extraction. The DTRM was the first to use DCNN for fine-grained SBIR. To improve the retrieval accuracy, the FG-SBIR applied a soft attention model and shortcut connection architectures based on DTRM. We test our method, DTRM and FG-SBIR on our SCSBIR testing set and calculate the retrieval accuracies within top K $(K = 1, 2, \ldots, 10)$ retrieval results. We use accuracy @ K to describe the retrieval accuracy which is the percentage of the amount of times when the true-match image of a color sketch is ranked in the top K retrieval results.

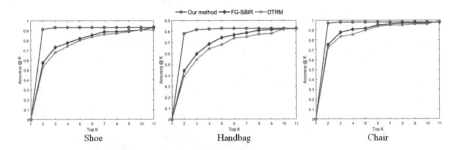

Fig. 3. Retrieval accuracy @ K for $K = 1$ to 10 of DTRM, FG-SBIR and our method in the shoe, handbag and chair dataset

The results of the comparison for $K = 1$ to 10 are shown in Fig. 3. Compared with the DTRM and FG-SBIR methods, our method has the best retrieval accuracy within top K $(K = 1, 2, \ldots, 10)$ on all three categories. Moreover, we choose three cases: $K = 1$, $K = 3$ and $K = 5$ to compare the retrieval accuracy of DTRM, FG-SBIR and our method, which is shown in Table 1. The results show that the retrieval accuracies of our method averagely increase around 33.90% and 29.83% at $K = 1$, 16.45% and 12.19% at $K = 3$, and 7.54% and 5.62% at $K = 5$ compared with DTRM and FG-SBIR. The results indicate that our method has a better performance than other two models in fine-grained single color sketch-based image retrieval.

5.3   Visualizing Retrieval Results

We visualize part of the retrieval results to show the better retrieval accuracy of our method compared with the DTRM and FG-SBIR. In Fig. 4, the first row is the retrieval results of our method with query color sketch, the second row is the retrieval results of DTRM with black-and-white sketch which has the same contour lines with the color sketch, and the third row is the retrieval results of FG-SBIR using the same black-and-white sketch as input.

By comparing the visual retrieval results, our method performs better in appearance matching including detailed shape matching and color matching. Unlike DTRM and FG-SBIR, our model can move the image with similar color up to the top of the retrieval results. For example, on the top shoe example in the right column, since the input color sketch is a brown boot sketch, the brown boots are moved up to the top while the boots of other colors are moved behind.

Table 1. Comparison of retrieval accuracy at $K = 1$, $K = 3$ and $K = 5$

Dataset-Shoe	$K = 1$	$K = 3$	$K = 5$
DTRM	53.04%	73.91%	83.48%
FG-SBIR	57.39%	77.39%	85.22%
Our method	91.30%	93.04%	93.04%
Dataset-Chair	$K = 1$	$K = 3$	$K = 5$
DTRM	72.16%	85.57%	93.81%
FG-SBIR	75.26%	90.72%	94.85%
Our method	96.91%	97.94%	97.94%
Dataset-Handbag	$K = 1$	$K = 3$	$K = 5$
DTRM	39.29%	64.29%	73.81%
FG-SBIR	44.05%	68.45%	76.79%
Our method	77.98%	82.14%	82.74%

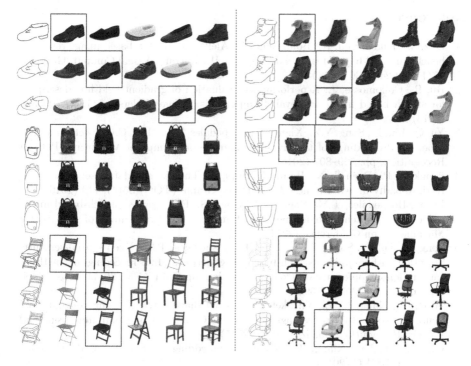

Fig. 4. The top five retrieval results by our method, FG-SBIR and DTRM. The true matches are highlighted in red. (Color figure online)

6   Conclusion

In this paper, we have proposed a fine-grained single color sketch-based image retrieval method based on multi-branch deep convolutional neural networks, and used a triplet homogeneous network to solve the fine-grained SCSBIR problem on three categories. In addition, we have created a SCSBIR dataset of color sketch-image pairs and proposed a new ranking method combined with the shape similarity matching and color similarity matching in HSV color space which makes the retrieval results get the best matching in appearance. Extensive experiments have been implemented to demonstrate the effectiveness and verify better retrieval performance of our proposed approach.

Acknowledgements. This research is supported by the PDE-GIR project which has received funding from the European Union's Horizon 2020 research and innovation programme under the Marie Skłodowska-Curie grant agreement No 778035. Yanran Li has received research grands from the South West Creative Technology Network.

References

1. Eitz, M., Hildebrand, K., Boubekeur, T., Alexa, M.: Sketch-based image retrieval: benchmark and bag-of-features descriptors. IEEE Trans. Visual Comput. Graphics **17**(11), 1624–1636 (2011)
2. Hu, R., Collomosse, J.: A performance evaluation of gradient field hog descriptor for sketch based image retrieval. Comput. Vis. Image Underst. **117**(7), 790–806 (2013)
3. Yu, Q., Liu, F., Song, Y.Z., Xiang, T., Hospedales, T.M., Loy, C.C.: Sketch me that shoe. In: Proceedings of the IEEE Conference on Computer Vision and Pattern Recognition, pp. 799–807 (2016)
4. Sangkloy, P., Burnell, N., Ham, C., Hays, J.: The sketchy database: learning to retrieve badly drawn bunnies. ACM Trans. Graph. (TOG) **35**(4), 119 (2016)
5. Li, Y., Hospedales, T.M., Song, Y.Z., Gong, S.: Fine-grained sketch-based image retrieval by matching deformable part models. In: Proceedings of the British Machine Vision Conference (2014)
6. Song, J., Yu, Q., Song, Y.Z., Xiang, T., Hospedales, T.M.: Deep spatial-semantic attention for fine-grained sketch-based image retrieval. In: Proceedings of the IEEE International Conference on Computer Vision, pp. 5551–5560 (2017). https://doi.org/10.1109/ICCV.2017.592
7. Wang, F., Kang, L., Li, Y.: Sketch-based 3D shape retrieval using convolutional neural networks. In: Proceedings of the IEEE Conference on Computer Vision and Pattern Recognition, pp. 1875–1883 (2015)
8. Qi, A., Song, Y., Xiang, T.: Semantic Embedding for Sketch-Based 3D Shape Retrieval. BMVC (2018)
9. Daras, P., Axenopoulos, A.: A 3D shape retrieval framework supporting multimodal queries. Int. J. Comput. Vision **89**(2–3), 229–247 (2010)
10. Eitz, M., Richter, R., Boubekeur, T., Hildebrand, K., Alexa, M.: Sketch-based shape retrieval. ACM Trans. Graph. **31**(4), 31–1 (2012)
11. Bui, T., Collomosse, J.: Scalable sketch-based image retrieval using color gradient features. In: Proceedings of the IEEE International Conference on Computer Vision Workshops, pp. 1012–1019 (2015). https://doi.org/10.1109/ICCVW.2015.133

12. Cheng, Z., Li, X., Loy, C.C.: Pedestrian color naming via convolutional neural network. In: Lai, S.-H., Lepetit, V., Nishino, K., Sato, Y. (eds.) ACCV 2016. LNCS, vol. 10112, pp. 35–51. Springer, Cham (2017). https://doi.org/10.1007/978-3-319-54184-6_3

13. Reddy, N., Reddy, G., Narayana, M.: Color sketch based image retrieval. Int. J. Adv. Res. Electrical Electron. Instrum. Eng. **03**, 12179–12185 (2014). https://doi.org/10.15662/ijareeie.2014.0309054

14. Ortega, M., Rui, Y., Chakrabarti, K., Porkaew, K., Mehrotra, S., Huang, T.S.: Supporting ranked boolean similarity queries in MARS. IEEE Trans. Knowl. Data Eng. **10**(6), 905–925 (1998)

15. Zitnick, C.L., Dollár, P.: Edge boxes: locating object proposals from edges. In: Fleet, D., Pajdla, T., Schiele, B., Tuytelaars, T. (eds.) ECCV 2014. LNCS, vol. 8693, pp. 391–405. Springer, Cham (2014). https://doi.org/10.1007/978-3-319-10602-1_26

16. Taigman, Y., Yang, M., Ranzato, M.A., Wolf, L.: Deepface: closing the gap to human-level performance in face verification. In: Proceedings of the IEEE Conference on Computer Vision and Pattern Recognition, Columbus, OH, USA, pp. 1701–1708. IEEE (2014). https://doi.org/10.1109/CVPR.2014.220

17. Schroff, F., Kalenichenko, D., Philbin, J.: Facenet: a unified embedding for face recognition and clustering. In: Proceedings of the IEEE Conference on Computer Vision and Pattern Recognition, Boston, MA, USA, pp. 815–823. IEEE (2015). https://doi.org/10.1109/CVPR.2015.7298682

18. Bahdanau, D., Cho, K., Bengio, Y.: Neural machine translation by jointly learning to align and translate. arXiv preprint arXiv:1409.0473 (2014)

19. He, K., Zhang, X., Ren, S., Sun, J.: Deep residual learning for image recognition. In: Proceedings of the IEEE Conference on Computer Vision and Pattern Recognition, Las Vegas, NV, USA, pp. 770–778. IEEE (2016). https://doi.org/10.1109/CVPR.2016.90

20. Yu, Q., Yang, Y., Song, Y.Z., Xiang, T., Hospedales, T.: Sketch-a-net that beats humans. arXiv preprint arXiv:1501.07873 (2015)

21. Eitz, M., Hays, J., Alexa, M.: How do humans sketch objects? ACM Trans. Graph. **31**(4), 44–1 (2012)

22. Deng, J., Dong, W., Socher, R., Li, L.J., Li, K., Fei-Fei, L.: Imagenet: a large-scale hierarchical image database. In: Proceedings of the IEEE Conference on Computer Vision and Pattern Recognition, Miami, FL, USA, pp. 248–255. IEEE (2009). https://doi.org/10.1109/CVPR.2009.5206848

23. Eitz, M., Hildebrand, K., Boubekeur, T., Alexa, M.: An evaluation of descriptors for large-scale image retrieval from sketched feature lines. Comput. Graph. **34**(5), 482–498 (2010)

24. Hu, R., Barnard, M., Collomosse, J.: Gradient field descriptor for sketch based retrieval and localization. In: Proceedings of 2010 IEEE International Conference on Image Processing, Hong Kong, China, pp. 1025–1028. IEEE (2010). https://doi.org/10.1109/ICIP.2010.5649331

25. Hu, R., Wang, T., Collomosse, J.: A bag-of-regions approach to sketch-based image retrieval. In: Proceedings of 2011 18th IEEE International Conference on Image Processing, Brussels, Belgium, pp. 3661–3664. IEEE (2011). https://doi.org/10.1109/ICIP.2011.6116513

26. Cao, Y., Wang, C., Zhang, L., Zhang, L.: Edgel index for large-scale sketch-based image search. In: CVPR 2011 Proceedings of the 2011 IEEE Conference on Computer Vision and Pattern Recognition, Colorado Springs, CO, USA, pp. 761–768. IEEE (2011). https://doi.org/10.1109/CVPR.2011.5995460

27. Cao, Y., Wang, H., Wang, C., Li, Z., Zhang, L., Zhang, L.: Mindfinder: interactive sketch-based image search on millions of images. In: ACM Multimedia, pp. 1605–1608. ACM, New York (2010)

28. Xia, Y., Wang, S., Li, Y., You, L., Yang, X., Zhang, J.J.: Fine-grained color sketch-based image retrieval. In: Gavrilova, M., Chang, J., Thalmann, N.M., Hitzer, E., Ishikawa, H. (eds.) CGI 2019. LNCS, vol. 11542, pp. 424–430. Springer, Cham (2019). https://doi.org/10.1007/978-3-030-22514-8_40

Integral-Based Material Point Method and Peridynamics Model for Animating Elastoplastic Material

Yao Lyu[1]([✉]), Jinglu Zhang[1], Ari Sarafopoulos[1], Jian Chang[1]([✉]), Shihui Guo[2], and Jian Jun Zhang[1]

[1] National Centre for Computer Animation, Bournemouth University, Dorset, UK
{ylyu,zhangj,asarafop,jchang,jzhang}@bournemouth.ac.uk
[2] School of Software, Xiamen University, Xiamen, China
guoshihui@xmu.edu.cn

Abstract. This paper exploits the use of Material Point Method (MPM) for graphical animation of elastoplastic materials and fracture. Previous partial derivative based MPM studies face challenges of underlying instability issues of particle distribution and the complexity of modeling discontinuities. This paper incorporates the state-based peridynamics structure with the MPM to alleviate these problems, which outweighs differential-based methods in both accuracy and stability. The deviatoric flow theory and a simple yield function are incorporated to animate plasticity. To model viscoelastic material, the constitutive model is developed with the linearized peridynamics theory which regards the current configuration as equilibrated and is only influenced by current incremental deformation. The peridynamics theory doesn't involve the deformation gradient, thus it is straightforward to handle the problem of cracking in our hybrid framework. To ease the implementation of the fracture divergence under MPM, two time integration methods are adopted to update the crack interface and continuous parts separately. Our work can create a wide range of material phenomenon including elasticity, plasticity, viscoelasticity and fracture. Our framework provides an attractive method for producing a variety of elastoplastic materials and fracture with visual realism and high stability.

Keywords: Material Point Method · Peridynamics · Elastoplastic modeling · Computer animation

1 Introduction

Physically-based modeling of elastoplastic material has been an active research topic for many years in computer graphics, particularly for its appealing

This work is supported by National Natural Science Foundation of China (61702433, 61661146002), the Fundamental Research Funds for the Central Universities, VISTA AR project (funded by the Interreg France (Channel) England, ERDF), the China Scholarship Council and Bournemouth University.

M. L. Gavrilova et al. (Eds.): Trans. on Comput. Sci. XXXVII, LNCS 12230, pp. 91–108, 2020.
https://doi.org/10.1007/978-3-662-61983-4_6

application in visual effects industry. Scenes involving elastoplastic deformation are very common and varied, for example, clothes moving with wind, rubber toys bouncing on the floor, flowing honey, or the broken plastic board. In order to model such realistic behaviors under different circumstances, the robust simulation method needs to be capable of handling complex topological changes and various contact responses, such as collision and cohesion. To find the simulation method that can naturally model elastoplastic material along with complex topological changes is the current focus of the field.

Meshless simulation methods are powerful in dealing with complicated topological changes since it does not require high quality mesh and efforts to overcome the issues from severe mesh distortion. The MPM [29, 30] is an extension of the particle-in-cell (PIC) method. It combines the Eulerian Cartesian grids and Lagrangian particles: a continuum body is discretized into a set of particles, also referred to as material points that are free to move on top of the background Eulerian grid [16]. The grid uses partial derivatives of particles' displacement to solve the governing equations. The MPM can naturally process material point distribution and self-collisions. It also has been proved to be especially suitable for animating materials that undergo large deformations [11]. Despite its physical realism and geometrical convenience, the traditional MPM solver has several disadvantages: 1) Due to the governing equation based on spatial derivatives of displacements, the results are sensitive to the underlying particle distribution [7]. Also it has difficulty in solving singularity along discontinuities. 2) To observe boundary details, MPM has to maintain a fine resolution grid which brings high computational costs for particle-grid transfer, particularly throughout the whole simulation domain. While researchers have extensively studied refining regions of particular interest by using an adaptive grid [5], the ability to simulate detailed discontinuities dynamics, such as crack propagation, is still limited.

Recently, peridynamics has gained its popularity in meshless simulation for discontinuous deformation, originally proposed by Silling [20]. Peridynamics theory defines that a point in a continuum interacts directly with other points separated from it within a finite distance. The advantage of the peridynamics is that its way of treating the discontinuous parts, which may appear in the continuum body as a result of the strain or stress, is exactly the same as continuous part. The linear peridynamics treats the deformation more generally by processing the small deformation based on the referenced configuration, which provides some possibilities to simulate the materials with both solid and fluid properties. Due to its particle-based nature, peridynamics needs the additional efforts to handle complex physical contacts. Furthermore, the peridynamics originates from the solid mechanics, focusing on mechanical experiments. Currently there are only a few mature models and experiments in continuum mechanics being adopted by peridynamics methods for animating elastoplastic material [34].

A preliminary version of this work has been reported which created the innovative MPM with peridynamics truss particle structure for modeling several kinds of elastoplastic objects [15]. This work continues to investigate the concept of integrating the deformation displacement and simulation the response, while introducing the linearized peridynamics theory to create more general effects, such as viscoelastic solids and fluids. We present four main contributions:

Elasticity. We equip material point with virtual bonds and family points. The elastic energy density function is redefined in an integral way with this truss structure. Varied stiffness of elastic materials can be simulated with high realism and stability.

Plasticity. The virtual bond structure makes our model trivial to model plastic behaviors. We use a novel method to extract plasticity from the deviatoric part of constitutive model and accumulate plastic increment permanently at particle-grid transfer step.

Viscoelasticity. We incorporate a general peridynamics model to process the dynamics of viscoelastic materials using the modulus state. The force density is determined by the incremental deformation of bonds in the horizon which is suitable for the situation undergoing large deformation.

Fracture. We handle crack definition and propagation through deactivating the virtual bonds. The fracture criterion of each bond involves the deformation status of the connected material points and the grid cell it stays. We update fracture surfaces and fracture inner parts in different time integration methods. Our method avoids the difficulty of duplicating grids and large computation cost brought by multiple particle-grid transfer processes.

After discussing related work in Sect. 2, we outline the methodology and explain the hybrid particle-grid structure in Sect. 3. Section 4 describes the constitutive model for modeling elastoplastic material in details. The governing equation and the constitutive model of viscoelastic materials are explained in Sect. 5. Crack definition and propagation are discussed in Sect. 6. Experimental examples for evaluating our method and discussion of results are given in Sect. 7. In Sect. 7 we conclude the method and explain our future work.

2   Related Work

Elastoplastic Modeling. Terzopoulos and Fleischer [32, 33] pioneered the elastic and plastic simulation methods in computer graphics. O'Brien and colleagues [17] incorporated the finite element method (FEM) with multiplicative plasticity model and obtained realistic motion for a much wider range of materials. Later, Gerszewski et al. [6] adopted the deformation gradient for animating elastic behaviors based on point method. Levin [12] rediscretized elasticity on a Eulerian grid, which is similar to MPM grid. Based on previous hybrid grids and particle modeling methods, Stomakhin [27] incorporated energetically consistent invertible elasticity models into MPM for modeling snow, varying phase effects. Daniel and his colleagues [18] avoided computating the SVD in Stomakhin's work and used semi-implicit MPM discretization of viscoelasticity allowing for high spatial resolution simulations. They achieved a wide range of viscoelastic, complex fluid effects. Recently, Chen [4] presented a novel elastoplastic constitutive model to handle brittle fracture and ductile fracture in the peridynamics-based framework. At the same time, many researchers focused on developing the real time and haptic simulator for the elastic materials, such as garments. For example, Salsedo et al. [19] designed the HAPTEX system using dynamically variable spatial resolution to reduce the computational burden during rendering the fabrics, which Bottcher [1,2] extended by implementing separated computation threads for different simulation scales.

Material Point Method. MPM is a hybrid grid-particle method using the Cartesian grid to resolve topology changes, treat self-collisions and fracture naturally. It tracked mass, momentum dynamics and particle deformation through combining the Lagrangian theory without the inherent need for Lagrangian mesh connectivity, devised by Sulsky [29,30] for engineering applications. Stomakhin et al. [27] introduced MPM into computer graphics. They tracked the deformation gradient on particles and transformed the deformation back to grid nodes. This work obtained a wide variety of snow phenomenon. Later, Jiang and his colleagues proved that MPM is a useful method for granular materials by animating sand [10]. Based on previous work of granular materials, Tampubolon extended the MPM to simulate multi-phase behaviors through using multiple grids, such as porous sand and water interactions [31]. A majority of elastoplastic MPM works for computer graphics [9,28] focus on resolving intensive collision scenarios on the surface or the curve with millions degrees of freedom. Unlike above studies, our method incorporates the integral-based constitutive model to replace the typical partial derivative based model. This helps us alleviate the instability and difficulty issues from particle distribution of arbitrary elastoplastic deformation. For MPM, the final resolution highly depends on the grid resolution which means high quality simulation results in increased computation. This is remedied by our particle truss construction and the bond structure. With virtual bonds, the constitutive model can demonstrate detailed topological changes smaller than the grid cell.

Peridynamics. The peridynamics is an extension of solid mechanics method in which points in a continuum interact with nearby points. Different from Smoothed Particle Hydrodynamics (SPH), peridynamics is a non-local method. Instead of using spatial differential formulations, it uses spatial integral equations as the governing equations. Silling proposed the peridynamics theory [20] for efficiently and uniformly solving problems involving both continuities and discontinuities [4,7,24]. Its application sparked the engineering applications, such as multiscale material modeling [25] and crack dynamics [23]. Levine [13] introduced the peridynamics theory to computer graphics. He revisited brittle fracture studies by characterizing peridynamics as spring-mass systems with two specific parameters, strain metric and interaction horizon. Silling [21] proposes the linear version of peridynamics theory to simulate more general materials, such as linear fluid and viscoelastic objects. This method provided the possibility of multi-scale application using peridynamics [22]. Currently, most research

[4,7] is focused on how to reformulate elastic constitutive models and produce persuasive effects. However, the theoretical equivalence of peridynamics compared to continuum mechanics remains unclear [34]. A lot of mature theories and experiments in continuum mechanics have not been adopted for peridynamics in computer graphics. This motivates us to define the integral-based constitutive model equipped with the peridynamics structure within the MPM framework for simulating versatile elastoplastic materials.

3   Method

The governing equation of MPM arises from basic conservation of mass and momentum [27]. Weak formulation is obtained by multiplying the balance of momentum and integrating the governing equation over initial volume, we therefore propose an integral force density function $F^s(x_p)$ to replace spatial derivatives of displacement and redefine the weak formulation as:

$$\int_\Omega \rho a_p \delta u_p d\Omega + \int_\Omega \rho F^s(x_p) \delta u_p d\Omega = \int_\Omega \rho b_p \delta u_p d\Omega + \int_{\Gamma_\tau} \rho \delta u_p \overline{\tau_p} d\Gamma \quad (1)$$

where Ω denotes the integrating region in the current configuration, ρ is density, a_p is the acceleration of particle p, δu_p is the virtual displacement (infinitesimal feasible changes where constraints remain satisfied). b_p is the body force, for example, gravity. τ_p is the surface traction on part of the boundary Γ_τ.

This paper adopts the grid-particle transfer procedure of the MPM, however, with different way of collecting the deformation of particles. In our MPM framework, the material domain at t^n is discretised with particles at x_p^n. Each particle has volume V, mass m_p, velocity v_p^n, and other physical quantities, such as deformation matrix F_p, $Lam\acute{e}$ parameters μ_p and λ_p, plastic yield parameters ψ_p. In each time step, a new grid is generated. Grid node I is used to store nodal parameters, such as position x_I, mass m_I, velocity v_I, force f_I. Our framework adopts dyadic products of one-dimensional cubic B-splines as a basic weight function in [27] during the particle-grid transfer process. Here we outline the full update procedure:

1) **Particle-to-grid transfer** Transfer material point mass m_p and momentum $(mv)_p$ to the grid nodes as m_I and $(mv)_I$.
2) **Compute internal forces** The internal force of grid node I is calculated based on the stress tensor of each point, presented as $f_I^{INT} = \sum_{Np} m_p N_I(x_p) F^s(x_p) V$. This equation is derived from our integral-based energy density function. The detailed description of the update rule for $F^s(x_p)$ is given in Sect. 4.
3) **Update Grid Momentum** Nodal velocities at the timestep $n + 1$ are updated by $\hat{v}_I^{n+1} = v_I^n + \Delta t f_I / m_I^n$ for explicit time integration. f_I is the total force.
4) **Grid-based body collisions** Grid velocity v_I^{n+1} is updated by the collision field and friction parameter from [27].

5) **Grid-to-particle transfer** Transfers updated nodal velocity v_I^{n+1} and momentum $(mv)_I^{n+1}$ to particles.

6) **Particle collisions** Modify v_p^{n+1} by collision field on particle level to obtain detailed deformation behaviors, especially on the boundary.

7) **Fracture** Based on the current particle distribution and the deformation status of the grid cell, we remove the virtual bond that intersects with the fracture plane. The fracture model is discussed in Sect. 6.

4   Elastoplastic Models

In contrast to the partial differential equations used in the classical formulations, here we describe the internal force density function using an integral formulation of pairwise bond forces, inspired by Silling's constitutive model [24]:

$$F^s(x_p) = \int_{H_{x_p}} [T < x_p, x_p' > - T < x_p', x_p >]/\rho dH_{x_p} \qquad (2)$$

x_p' is the neighbor point of point x_p. Our work is motivated by the peridynamics theory in which a virtual bond is built between each family point pair. It is called as truss structure: each neighbor material point x_p' of material point x_p are referred to as its family members H_{x_p}. x_p has interaction with all its family members at same time. Each interaction is operated by a virtual bond. $T < x_p, x_p' >$ represents the interaction force between x_p and x_p'. The $F^s(x_p)$ collects the particle deformation in an integral way, avoiding the use of using the spatial derivatives of displacements $\frac{\delta u_{x_p}}{\delta x_p}$.

4.1   Elastic Model

When the elasticity is the only consideration, the energy density function is defined in [26] as:

$$E^s = \mu \|F_e - R_e\|^2 + \frac{\lambda}{2}(J_e - 1)^2 \qquad (3)$$

where F_e is the deformation gradient tensor, R_e is the rotation matrix and $J_e = det(F_e)$. In view of different contributions to topological changes, the energy density function can be decomposed into two parts: $\mu\|F_e - R_e\|^2$ as deviatoric part and $\frac{\lambda}{2}(J_e - 1)^2$ as isotropic part. However, F_e is based on the spatial derivatives of displacement which leads to the inability of the constitutive model to compute singularity issues, such as discontinuities. We can adopt the concept of integral deformation matrix $\overline{F_p}$ in [7] to describe the local deformation which has a similar meaning to F_e but is represented by the integration of displacement states and peridynamics truss structure. When the initial bond state and deformed bond between material point x_p and x_p' are $X = x_p - x_p'$ and $Y = y_p - y_p'$, the deformation matrix $\overline{F_p}$ shown in Eq. 4 represents the average deformation status of point x_p. H_{x_p} represents all family members. $w(Y)$ is the linear weight function. $\otimes$ is the dyadic product operator defined by Silling [20]. Thus an average deformed bond is calculated as $\overline{Y} = \overline{F_i}X$.

$$\overline{F_p} = [\sum_{H_{x_p}} w(Y)Y \otimes X][\sum_{H_{x_p}} w(Y) \otimes X]^{-1} \tag{4}$$

With these concepts, Eq. 3 is reformulated as the combination of the deviatoric and isotropic components:

$$E^s = \sum_{H_{x_p}} w(Y)(\mu E^{dev} + \frac{\lambda}{2}E^{iso}) \tag{5}$$

$E^{dev} = (\frac{|\overline{Y}|}{|X|} - 1)^2$ describes deformed energy similar to a mass spring system but removes the influence from differing bond lengths in order to simulate material with the same stiffness. It involves the weighed deformed bond length. Similarly, $E^{iso} = (\frac{|Y|}{|X|} - 1)^2$ represents single bond deformation energy.

Then the elastic force density function $T < x_p, x_p' >$ for the material point pair of x_p and x_p' is obtained through $\frac{\partial \psi}{\partial y_p}$, as:

$$T < x_p, x_p' >= \frac{2\mu w}{|X|^2}(\overline{Y} - |X|dir\overline{Y}) + \frac{\lambda w}{|X|^2}(Y - |X|dirY) \tag{6}$$

where $\frac{2\mu w}{|X|^2}(|\overline{Y}| - |X|)dir\overline{Y}$ involves the deformed bonds in the whole neighbor, similar to sheer stress effects. $\frac{\lambda w}{|X|^2}(|Y| - |X|)dirY$ is equalled to the spring force between by x_p and x_p'. The direction follows the current deformed bond. Using Eq. 2 and Eq. 6, the internal force of grid node I for updating nodal momentum is:

$$f_I^{INT} = \sum m_p N_I(x_p)[\sum_{H_{x_p}} w(Y)(T < x_p, x_p' > -T < x_p', x_p >)V] \tag{7}$$

Compared to many existing MPM methods, our method avoids the singular value decomposition (SVD) which is used to extract the elastic deformation gradient. We only involve the current virtual bond state Y for processing nodal internal forces, so the local step is fast. The standard SVD implementations can have a dramatic impact on performance [3]. Thus although it is not essential for performance to avoid the SVD, it is preferable not to implement the SVD. Also, as with our model, the advantages of avoiding SVD are obvious: we obtain a better stability for simulation with large time steps as in [7]; and reduce the complexity of the plasticity definition in the MPM framework.

4.2 Plastic Model

Many methods [27,35] take out part of the elastic deformation gradient tensor that exceeds the yield function and push it into the plastic deformation gradient calculation. Thanks to the construction of virtual bonds, the plasticity can be regarded as part of the bond's elastic extension and extracted within the yield criterion simply.

The plastic model is purely from deviatoric plastic flow theory [4]. Firstly, we reformulate our elastic model in Eq. 6 in order to adapt it for modeling plasticity. $|\overline{Y}| - |X|$ and $|Y| - |X|$ are average and single bond extension. When the deformation is smooth enough under small neighbor horizon, we predict $|\overline{Y}| - |X| \approx |Y| - |X|$. Then we have:

$$T < x_p, x_p' >= \frac{2\mu w}{|X|^2}(|Y| - |X|)dir\overline{Y} + \frac{\lambda w}{|X|^2}(|Y| - |X|)dirY \qquad (8)$$

Based on the plastic flow theory, the unified displacement is decomposed into isotropic and deviatoric parts, $e = (|Y| - |X|)/|X| = e^{iso} + e^{dev}$. Plastic deformation e^p is extracted from e^{dev}. Incorporate the plastic extension e^p into Eq. 8:

$$T < x_p, x_p' >= \frac{2\mu w}{|X|}(e^{iso} + e^{dev} - e^p)dir\overline{Y} + \frac{\lambda w}{|X|}(e^{iso} + e^{dev} - e^p)dirY \quad (9)$$

The bond concept helps divide the deformation into elasticity and plasticity with the yield function as $f(E_{dev})$:

$$E_{dev} = (\frac{2\mu w}{|X|} + \frac{\lambda w}{|X|})(e^{dev} - e^p), f(E_{dev}) = \frac{(E_{dev})^2}{2} - \psi_p \qquad (10)$$

where ψ_p is a controllable plastic material parameter. We use $f(E_{dev})$ to decide if the current configuration enters the plastic regime. If $f(E_{dev}) < 0$, the deformation is still within the elastic domain. If $f(E_{dev}) > 0$, part of deformation occurred as plasticity. We project the deformation back to the yield surface and add a plastic increment Δe^p to e^p permanently as Eq. 11.

$$\Delta e^p = \frac{|X|}{(\lambda)}[E_{dev} - \sqrt{2\psi_p}sign(E_{dev})] \qquad (11)$$

This model is still valid for elastic when e^p varnishes in above equations. With the appropriate plastic material parameter, the plastic model can be a user-controllable constitutive model for simulating elasticity and elastoplasticity simultaneously under the MPM framework.

5   Linear Viscoelastic Models

Viscoelastic materials behave with elastic resistance to deformation similarly to elastic objects, while undergoing large strains and complex non-Newtonian fluid characteristics. Here the Eulerian background grid in MPM is still suitable for implicit integration, while the particle dynamics is represented by the modulus state which is arising from the linearized peridynamics theory by Silling [21]. Through superposing the small deformation on an existing large deformation in the configuration of last step, the internal force density function takes the small incremental bond extension to update the response of viscoelastic material step by step. In Silling's linearized peridynamics theory [21], to calculate the internal force density function at the next step, the deformed bond state at current step is regarded as the reference configuration. With this prerequisite, the elastic force density in Eq. 6 needs to involve the information of the reference configuration.

Let u be the small displacement field superposed on the current deformation field. Linearizing the function $T < x_p, x_p' >$ near current deformation field leads to:

$$T < x_p, x_p' > = T^0 < x_p, x_p' > + K < x_p > \cdot U < x_p > \tag{12}$$

where $T^0 < x_p, x_p' >$ is the deformed bond force density at the previous time step, $U < x_p > = \sum_{H_{x_p}} w(Y)(Y - X)$ is the average displacement near the point x_p. $K < x_p > = \nabla T(x_p, x_p')$, is called the modulus state. It is the *Fréchet* derivative of the force density function with respect to the bond Y' which is between x_p and one of its family particles x_p''. Y' may not be the same bond as current bond Y. K replaces the stress strain in the previous sections to represent the deformation of material particles in linearized constitutive models. Detailed explanation can be found in Silling's work [21,22].

Note the linearized equation, thus the internal force density function F^s is rewritten as:

$$F^s(x_p) = \int_\Omega \int_\Omega [T^0 < x_p, x_p' > + K < x_p > \cdot U < x_p >) \tag{13}$$
$$- (T^0 < x_p', x_p > + K < x_p' > \cdot U < x_p' >)]/\rho d H_{x_p}$$

Based on the assumption of the equilibrated deformation as in [21], the reference configuration is assumed as equilibrated which indicates $\int_{H_{x_p}} (T^0 < x_p, x_p' > - T^0 < x_p', x_p >)]/\rho d H_{x_p} + b(x_p) = 0$.

The energy density function therefore is arranged leading to:

$$F^s(x_p) = \int_{H_{x_p}} \int_{H_{x_p}} [K[x_p] < x_p' - x_p, x_p'' - x_p > (u(x_p'') - u(x_p))]/\rho d H_{x_p} d H_{x_p}$$
$$- \int_{H_{x_p}} \int_{H_{x_p'}} [K[x_p'] < x_p - x_p', x_q - x_p' > (u(x_q) - u(x_p'))]/\rho d H_{x_p'} d H_{x_p} \tag{14}$$

where x_p' and x_p'' are family particles of the point x_p, x_q is the family particle of the point x_p'. This function not only involves the family particles of point x_p, but also the family particles x_q of point x_p'. Thus the zone being influenced is fundamentally double than the horizon defined before. Figure 1 shows the indirect interaction between x_p and x_q.

This linearization of the internal force density function is operated in the sense of a limit, under suitable restrictions on the smoothness of the deformation, motivated by Silling's work [21]. Through the linearization, the governing

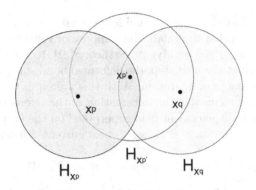

Fig. 1. Point x_p interacts with x_q even though they are outside each other's horizon because they are both within the horizon of intermediate points such as $x_p{'}$

equation requires the current displacement and the modulus state, which are irrelevant to the original object shape, leading to structureless material effects. Therefore, the linear theory is naturally appropriate for colloidal materials, such as foam, cream and sponge because it is able to keep the response of elastic material properties by utilizing the truss particle structures and to investigate the large topological changes experienced by processing the small incremental deformation based on the current large deformation field. Also, similar to classic peridynamics theory, the linear theory doesn't involve the deformation gradient, in other words, the crack propagation can be defined spontaneously by bond deactivation.

The viscoelastic model defined in [21] and [24] achieves the viscous elastic effects. It combines the strain energy density of the integral fluid constitutive models with the one energy density component which involves the deviatoric part of the deformation state (in the term $e - \frac{\vartheta}{3}$). Then energy density function is defined as:

$$E^s = \frac{\lambda \vartheta^2}{2} + \frac{\mu}{2} \sum_H w(|Y|)(e - \frac{\vartheta}{3})^2 V \tag{15}$$

$$\vartheta = \frac{3}{M} \sum_H w(|Y|)|Y| e V \tag{16}$$

$$M = \sum_H w(|Y|)|Y|^2 V \tag{17}$$

e is the extension of the bond, as defined in last section. ϑ represents the dilatation part of the bond extension. Thus the deviatoric part means the bond extension subtracts an isotropic expansion of the family particles. It includes not only shear, but also any deformation from the family particles other than isotropic expansion. Then the viscoelastic force density function $T < x_p, x_p{'} >$ is written as:

$$T < x_p, x_p{'} > = (\frac{3\lambda}{M} - \frac{\mu}{3})w(|Y|)|Y|\vartheta M + \mu w(|Y|)edirY \tag{18}$$

Here we define two bonds, $Y_1 = x'_p - x_p$ and $Y_2 = x''_p - x_p$ which are incorporated in the modulus state K. Thus K is written as:

$$K < x'_p - x_p, x''_p - x_p > = (\frac{9\lambda}{M^2} - \frac{\mu}{M})w(|Y_1|)w(|Y_2|)Y_1 \otimes Y_2 + \gamma(Y_1)\Delta(Y_2 - Y_1)$$

(19)

$$\gamma(Y) = \lambda w(|Y|)(dirY \otimes dirY) \tag{20}$$

Δ denotes the Dirac delta function in the simulation field. With the modulus state and current deformation field, the force density function is obtained.

6. Fracture

Crack simulation is a bottleneck of the MPM [14]. To processing the discontinuities at the interfaces, special treatments for creating cracks and partitioning fracture fragments into multigrid and multiple velocity fields are approaches [8]. When an excessive number of cracking interfaces are involved, the computation of multiple grid transferring can be very expensive. Additionally, the strategy to duplicate a grid is limited because during simulation small fragments are numerous and randomly generated so it is hard to duplicate a grid for each crack interface.

The dynamics with discontinuities is straightforward to compute in our MPM framework. If we simply remove over-deformed bonds like [4], it leads to numerous small fragments in the deformed area rather than several crack lines after collision happens. We now propose generating a crack cut by the fracture plane based on analyses of single point and global deformation status in the gird cell.

Firstly, we define the fracture criterion by removing the plastic displacement as:

$$l = \frac{e - e^p}{|X|(1 + p_{inactive})} \tag{21}$$

where $p_{inactive}$ is the percentage of broken bonds in total bonds in one grid cell where the material point stays.

After screening the material points whose l exceeds the threshold, we use cluster method to sort these points into several deformed areas based on position and normal. For each area, we calculate the central point and the largest deformed bond. The next step is to use the central point position and the bond direction as normal to construct the fracture plane for each area. Any bond intersected by the fracture plane will be removed. That is how crack line occurs. With $p_{inactive}$, this method can effectively reduce the number of small fracture pieces. Because if one grid has too many broken bonds, the active bonds in this grid cell are less likely to be removed.

In the MPM, grid cell size decides the resolution of whole simulation. This also works for crack dynamics. In experiments, we transfer particle velocity to three grid cells (illustrated in Fig. 2) in any direction to get stable, smooth results. When two sides of crack line are within this range, they will share additional fragment information through transfer. Therefore the using of one grid

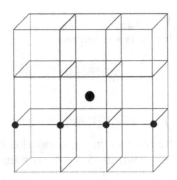

Fig. 2. For MPM transfer process, the information of one particle is transferred to neighbor 9 cell in 2D dimension.

leads to "fractures sticking to each other" effects. We alleviate this problem by applying two-time integration methods: material points on the crack surface are updated by its own bond forces; other material points which don't have any broken bonds (in the fragmented inner parts) are updated by grids as normal. Thus we avoid the mixing of altered crack fragments.

7   Result and Discussion

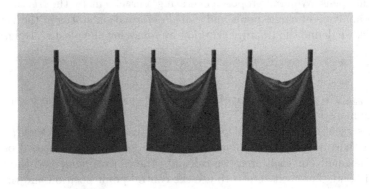

Fig. 3. The moving cloth with different material parameters show differing bending stiffness. From left to right: $\mu = 2 \times 10^4$, $\mu = 1.5 \times 10^5$, $\mu = 1 \times 10^6$.

We implemented the proposed methods and tested examples in this section. All examples are produced in Houdini software, including the material point discretization, dynamics processing, vorinoi fracture generation and rendering of the simulation. The Houdini Development Kit (HDK) tool is utilized to create customized dynamic nodes for the constitutive models.

Fig. 4. Throwing a ball against elastic and plastic boards shows visibly different results. In the first row, the elastic board can recover to the initial shape after the collision. The second row shows that plastic board keeps the deformed topology.

Fig. 5. The collision between two identical rabbits with different materials. This example demonstrates the different deformation of elastic rabbits (in the first row) and plastic rabbits (in the second row). Collision happens in (a) and (c). The elastic rabbits are able to recover as in (b). The plastic rabbits deformed afterwards in (d).

Implementation. In this paper, three different modeling geometry types are used.

Mesh based geometry: With the given input surface, we construct mesh as the surface and initialize several layers of particles underneath the surface.

Particle based geometry: For specific examples, such as the viscous elastic material, we represent the initial object shape with the unstructured particle, due to its simplicity.

Fig. 6. Simulation of a plastic wall when collided by a sphere.

Fig. 7. Stretch beams with different material parameters. From left to right, bending stiffness μ are: 0, 50, 500.

Fig. 8. Linear peridynamics theory is used for modeling viscoelastic fluids, such as honey.

Voronoi cell geometry: Houdini designs the voronoi cell particularly for fracture or cracks scenes. Each voronoi cell is a random polygon and its center point is used as the material points. The bond represents the connection between neighboring voronoi cells.

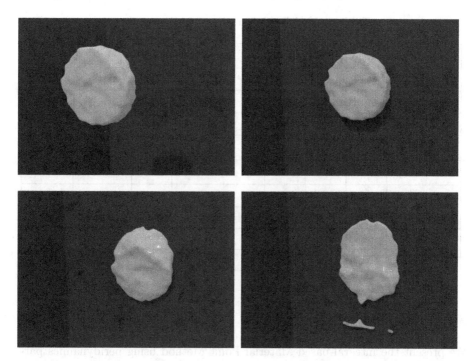

Fig. 9. A pie of whipped cream is thrown to the wall to show the effects of viscoelasticity.

Table 1 lists the modeling types, parameter settings and the performance data for all the examples presented in the paper. Ghost particles are added out of the object surface to guarantee that each material point has similar family density in the initial steps.

Model Validation. We use several examples with different material properties to evaluate our method. Figure 3 shows the examples of garment anchored by clothes pegs. With varied bending and stiffness parameters μ, the experiments present the realistic and fine wrinkles. Figure 4 shows the comparison of elastic board and plastic board collided by a ball. Our model can create correct behaviors. With complex topology objects, this method still works as in Fig. 5. Figure 6 shows the simulation of ductile plastic fracture. Figure 7 demonstrates the stretching beams deformation with different material stiffness. Figure 8 shows that honey flows from a glass bottle and drops on the floor. Linear peridynamics model is able to represent the viscoelastic fluids situation. Figure 9 shows that when whipped cream is thrown to the wall, it flows like dense fluid, whilst slightly retaining the original shape.

Table 1. Modeling information for all examples

	Type	Grid cell size	λ(MPa)	μ(MPa)	ϕ_p	Fracture threshold	Δt (ms)
Cloth	Mesh	0.005	1×10^6	2×10^4,1×10^5,1.5×10^5	1×10^{25}	1×10^{25}	0. 1
Elastic board	Mesh	0.02	3×10^6	1.5×10^5	1×10^{25}	1×10^{25}	0.02
Plastic board	Mesh	0.02	5×10^6	1.5×10^5	100	1×10^{25}	0.0001
Elastic bunny	Particles	0.01	1×10^5	1×10^5	1×10^{25}	1×10^{25}	0.1
Plastic bunny	Particles	0.01	1×10^6	3×10^5	30	1×10^{25}	0.01
Broken board	Voronoi	0.005	1×10^6	5×10^4	500	0.05	0.001
Stretching beam	Mesh	0.05	500	0,50,500	1×10^{25}	1×10^{25}	100
Honey	Particles	0.05	500	1×10^2	-	0.0304	10
Cream pie	Particles	0.04	5×10^3	5×10^2	-	0.035	10

8   Conclusion

We present the integral-based Material Point Method using peridynamics particle structure. This method integrates the deformation displacement of particles to compute the internal forces for grid nodes, which avoids the instability and complex implementation issues existing in the current MPM. This paper demonstrates various elastic deformation and plastic deformation scenarios. The linearized peridynamics theory is introduced in the paper to simulate general materials. Fracture can be modeled robustly without any singularity issues. Additionally, our method presents a novel integral-based view for multi-scale multi-material modeling and fractures modeling, which has potential to inspire future research in the field.

Limitations and Future Work. This paper presents numerous examples with elastic and plastic material. However, there is still much work to be achieved. Firstly, we represent fracture with Houdini voronoi structure which is represented by polygon with random number of vertexes. It is unable to generate the arbitrary fracture shape. The resolution is limited to the number and size of voronoi cells. Incorporating tetrahedron structure for a embedded geometry modeling is the future option for cooking detailed cracking interfaces. Secondly, the linearized peridynamics exhibits potential to simulate multi-scale materials using the similar viscoelastic models, such foam which is the combination of bubble and solids. We will explore more applications in future. Finally, we use explicit integration for its straightforwardness in HDK. It requires very small substeps for dealing with huge displacement. Additionally, the current study implements projective dynamics implicit integration method for fast simulation. It can obtain stable and robust results under large substeps. Our future work will focus on addressing above limitations and obtaining versatile and realistic elastoplastic performance.

References

1. Böttcher, G.: Haptic Interaction with Deformable Objects: Modelling VR Systems for Textiles. Springer, London (2011). https://doi.org/10.1007/978-0-85729-935-2
2. Bottcher, G., Allerkamp, D., Wolter, F.E.: Virtual reality systems modelling haptic two-finger contact with deformable physical surfaces. In: 2007 International Conference on Cyberworlds (CW 2007), pp. 292–299. IEEE (2007)
3. Chao, I., Pinkall, U., Sanan, P., Schröder, P.: A simple geometric model for elastic deformations. ACM Trans. Graph. (TOG) **29**(4), 38 (2010)
4. Chen, W., Zhu, F., Zhao, J., Li, S., Wang, G.: Peridynamics-based fracture animation for elastoplastic solids. In: Computer Graphics Forum, vol. 37, pp. 112–124. Wiley Online Library (2018)
5. Gao, M., Tampubolon, A.P., Jiang, C., Sifakis, E.: An adaptive generalized interpolation material point method for simulating elastoplastic materials. ACM Trans. Graph. (TOG) **36**(6), 223 (2017)
6. Gerszewski, D., Bhattacharya, H., Bargteil, A.W.: A point-based method for animating elastoplastic solids. In: Proceedings of the 2009 ACM SIGGRAPH/Eurographics Symposium on Computer Animation, pp. 133–138. ACM (2009)
7. He, X., Wang, H., Wu, E.: Projective peridynamics for modeling versatile elastoplastic materials. IEEE Trans. Visual Comput. Graphics **24**(9), 2589–2599 (2018)
8. Homel, M.A., Herbold, E.B.: Field-gradient partitioning for fracture and frictional contact in the material point method. Int. J. Numer. Meth. Eng. **109**(7), 1013–1044 (2017)
9. Jiang, C., Gast, T., Teran, J.: Anisotropic elastoplasticity for cloth, knit and hair frictional contact. ACM Trans. Graph. (TOG) **36**(4), 152 (2017)
10. Jiang, C., Schroeder, C., Selle, A., Teran, J., Stomakhin, A.: The affine particle-in-cell method. ACM Trans. Graph. (TOG) **34**(4), 51 (2015)
11. Jiang, C., Schroeder, C., Teran, J., Stomakhin, A., Selle, A.: The material point method for simulating continuum materials. In: ACM SIGGRAPH 2016 Courses, p. 24. ACM (2016)
12. Levin, D.I., Litven, J., Jones, G.L., Sueda, S., Pai, D.K.: Eulerian solid simulation with contact. ACM Trans. Graph. (TOG) **30**(4), 36 (2011)
13. Levine, J.A., Bargteil, A.W., Corsi, C., Tessendorf, J., Geist, R.: A peridynamic perspective on spring-mass fracture. In: Proceedings of the ACM SIGGRAPH/Eurographics Symposium on Computer Animation, pp. 47–55. Eurographics Association (2014)
14. Liang, Y., Benedek, T., Zhang, X., Liu, Y.: Material point method with enriched shape function for crack problems. Comput. Methods Appl. Mech. Eng. **322**, 541–562 (2017)
15. Lyu, Y., Zhang, J., Chang, J., Guo, S., Zhang, J.J.: Integrating peridynamics with material point method for elastoplastic material modeling. In: Gavrilova, M., Chang, J., Thalmann, N.M., Hitzer, E., Ishikawa, H. (eds.) CGI 2019. LNCS, vol. 11542, pp. 228–239. Springer, Cham (2019). https://doi.org/10.1007/978-3-030-22514-8_19
16. Moutsanidis, G., Kamensky, D., Zhang, D.Z., Bazilevs, Y., Long, C.C.: Modeling strong discontinuities in the material point method using a single velocity field. Comput. Methods Appl. Mech. Eng. **345**, 584–601 (2019)
17. O'brien, J.F., Bargteil, A.W., Hodgins, J.K.: Graphical modeling and animation of ductile fracture. In: ACM Transactions on Graphics (TOG), vol. 21, pp. 291–294. ACM (2002)

18. Ram, D., et al.: A material point method for viscoelastic fluids, foams and sponges. In: Proceedings of the 14th ACM SIGGRAPH/Eurographics Symposium on Computer Animation, pp. 157–163. ACM (2015)
19. Salsedo, F., et al.: Architectural design of the haptex system. In: Submitted to the Proceedings of this Conference (2005)
20. Silling, S.A.: Reformulation of elasticity theory for discontinuities and long-range forces. J. Mech. Phys. Solids **48**(1), 175–209 (2000)
21. Silling, S.A.: Linearized theory of peridynamic states. J. Elast. **99**(1), 85–111 (2010)
22. Silling, S.A.: A coarsening method for linear peridynamics. Int. J. Multiscale Comput. Eng. **9**(6), 609–622 (2011)
23. Silling, S.A., Askari, A.: Peridynamic model for fatigue cracking. SAND2014-18590. Sandia National Laboratories, Albuquerque (2014)
24. Silling, S.A., Epton, M., Weckner, O., Xu, J., Askari, E.: Peridynamic states and constitutive modeling. J. Elast. **88**(2), 151–184 (2007)
25. Silling, S.A., Askari, A.: Practical peridynamics. Technical report, Sandia National Laboratories (SNL-NM), Albuquerque, NM (United States) (2014)
26. Stomakhin, A., Howes, R., Schroeder, C., Teran, J.M.: Energetically consistent invertible elasticity. In: Proceedings of the ACM SIGGRAPH/Eurographics Symposium on Computer Animation, pp. 25–32. Eurographics Association (2012)
27. Stomakhin, A., Schroeder, C., Chai, L., Teran, J., Selle, A.: A material point method for snow simulation. ACM Trans. Graph. (TOG) **32**(4), 102 (2013)
28. Stomakhin, A., Teran, J., Selle, A.: Augmented material point method for simulating phase changes and varied materials. US Patent App. 14/323,798, 2 July 2015
29. Sulsky, D., Chen, Z., Schreyer, H.L.: A particle method for history-dependent materials. Comput. Methods Appl. Mech. Eng. **118**(1–2), 179–196 (1994)
30. Sulsky, D., Zhou, S.J., Schreyer, H.L.: Application of a particle-in-cell method to solid mechanics. Comput. Phys. Commun. **87**(1–2), 236–252 (1995)
31. Tampubolon, A.P., et al.: Multi-species simulation of porous sand and water mixtures. ACM Trans. Graph. (TOG) **36**(4), 105 (2017)
32. Terzopoulos, D., Fleischer, K.: Modeling inelastic deformation: viscolelasticity, plasticity, fracture. In: ACM Siggraph Computer Graphics, vol. 22, pp. 269–278. ACM (1988)
33. Terzopoulos, D., Platt, J., Barr, A., Fleischer, K.: Elastically deformable models. ACM Siggraph Comput. Graph. **21**(4), 205–214 (1987)
34. Xu, L., He, X., Chen, W., Li, S., Wang, G.: Reformulating hyperelastic materials with peridynamic modeling. In: Computer Graphics Forum, vol. 37, pp. 121–130. Wiley Online Library (2018)
35. Zhu, B., Lee, M., Quigley, E., Fedkiw, R.: Codimensional non-newtonian fluids. ACM Trans. Graph. (TOG) **34**(4), 115 (2015)

A Perceptually Coherent TMO
for Visualization of 360° HDR Images
on HMD

Ific Goudé[1(✉)], Rémi Cozot[2], and Olivier Le Meur[1]

[1] Univ Rennes, CNRS, IRISA, Rennes, France
`ific.goude@irisa.fr`
[2] Littoral Opal Coast University, Calais, France

Abstract. We propose a new Tone Mapping Operator dedicated to the
visualization of 360° High Dynamic Range images on Head-Mounted
Displays. Previous work around this topic has shown that the existing
Tone Mapping Operators for classic 2D images are not adapted to 360°
High Dynamic Range images. Consequently, several dedicated operators
have been proposed. Instead of operating on the entire 360° image, they
only consider the part of the image currently viewed by the user. Tone
mapping a part of the 360° image is less challenging as it does not preserve globally the dynamic range of the luminance of the scene. To cope
with this problem, we propose a novel Tone Mapping Operator which
takes advantage of 1) a view-dependant tone mapping that enhances the
contrast, and 2) a Tone Mapping Operator applied to the entire 360°
image that preserves the global coherency. Furthermore, the proposed
Tone Mapping Operator is adapted to the human eye perception of the
luminance on Head-Mounted Displays. We present two subjective studies
to model the lightness perception on such Head-Mounted Displays.

Keywords: High dynamic range · Tone mapping operator ·
Head-mounted display · 360° image

1 Introduction

Due to the growth of Virtual Reality (VR) technologies over the last years,
the visualization of 360° images has become common. Moreover, High Dynamic
Range (HDR) cameras are now used to capture the whole dynamic of a scene
with much more details in brightest and darkest areas, thereby providing realistic
panoramas.

Nonetheless, all manufactured Head-Mounted Displays (HMDs) still have
Standard Dynamic Range (SDR) screens, which prevent them from displaying
all the dynamic range of HDR images. To appreciate HDR contents through
standard displays, the well known process of tone mapping is used to get a limited

Supported by the ANR project ANR-17-CE23-0020.

M. L. Gavrilova et al. (Eds.): Trans. on Comput. Sci. XXXVII, LNCS 12230, pp. 109–128, 2020.
https://doi.org/10.1007/978-3-662-61983-4_7

range corresponding to that of SDR displays. Many Tone Mapping Operators (TMOs) exist [1,16] and can be divided into two main groups (global and local) and are often based on how the human perceives lightness and colors. In order to adapt existing TMOs to HMD visualization, we conducted two subjective evaluations to investigate how the Human Visual System (HVS) perceives images on HMDs.

Beyond perception, different approaches to address the problem of 360° image tone mapping on HMD can be considered. One solution is to apply the TMO to the whole 360° image, considering its entire dynamic range. The obtained result is globally coherent but, when considering only a viewport, the contrast can be unpleasantly reduced. As the user can only watch a limited part of the 360° image at a time, a TMO may be applied to the current viewport. Thus, the viewport contrast is enhanced while the global coherency is lost.

To overcome this problem, we propose a method that takes into account the results of two TMOs: one applied to the entire 360° image, and the other to the current viewport. As will be explained later, the viewport TMO provides a better contrast, while the global TMO preserves the spatial coherency. A preliminary version of this work has been reported [8]. The main contributions of this extended paper are: (1) a thorough work about lightness and colors perception on HMD that includes two subjective evaluations; (2) an improved TMO for 360° HDR images that ensures a spatial coherency and enhances contrasts while being perceptually coherent with the lightness perception of the human eye on HMD.

The paper in organised as follows. Section 2 introduces related work on perception models and TMOs dedicated to 360° images visualization on HMD. Then, we present the subjective evaluations we conducted to model lightness and colors perception in Sect. 3. As a result, we show that the perception model on a classic 2D display is slightly different than the one on an HMD. Then, we describe in detail our HMD-TMO in Sect. 4. In Sect. 5, we comment on our results and discuss the efficiency of our approach. Finally, Sect. 6 concludes the paper and presents some research avenues for future work. All acronyms and definitions are referred in the glossary Table 1.

2   Related Work

Understanding the HVS and how it reacts to stimuli is essential to ensure an efficient tone mapping. Color Appearance Models (CAMs) seek to describe how a stimulus is perceived depending on viewing conditions, such as the luminance of the background and the surround. Existing TMOs are often based on CAMs [1,16] to ensure the image processing to be coherent with the way we will perceive the tone mapped result. As the viewing conditions change on a HMD, the perception is different and CAMs have to be adapted to those conditions.

Table 1. Glossary of definitions and acronyms.

Luminance	Physical quantity of light emitted by an area in $[cd/m^2]$
Brightness	Attribute of a visual sensation according to which an area appears to emit more or less light [5]
Lightness	The brightness of an area judged relative to the brightness of a similarly illuminated area that appears to be white or highly transmitting [5]
HDR/SDR	High Dynamic Range/Standard Dynamic Range
HMD	Head-Mounted Display
TMO	Tone Mapping Operator
VR	Virtual Reality
HVS	Human Visual System
JND	Just Noticeable Difference
CAM	Color Appearance Model
FoV	Field of View
CDF	Cumulative Distribution Function

2.1 Lightness Perception Model

The basis of psycho-physical studies about lightness perception comes from the seminal work of Weber. He showed that the human capacity to distinguish a stimulus from a background is linearly proportional to the background luminance. In other words, the lighter the background L, the higher the difference ΔL (between stimulus and background) should be to perceive the stimulus. This ratio is commonly known as the Just Noticeable Difference (JND):

$$JND = \frac{\Delta L}{L} = k, \tag{1}$$

with ΔL the luminance difference between the stimulus and the background (in cd/m^2), L the background luminance (in cd/m^2) and k a constant (around 0.01 for traditional visualization condition on a 2D display [16]). Fechner integrated Weber's result to obtain the response of the visual system [6]:

$$R(L) = \int_0^L \frac{1}{kL(l)} dl = \frac{1}{k}ln(L), \tag{2}$$

where R is the lightness response for a given luminance L. Accordingly, the subjective perception of luminance, called lightness, is assumed to be the logarithm response to the physical luminance.

More recently, Stevens showed limits of the Fechner's model and proposed to use a power function to model the lightness perception [19]. Stevens psychophysical studies have led to the lightness perception equal to the physical luminance raised to the power of one third. Both of those models are still used and

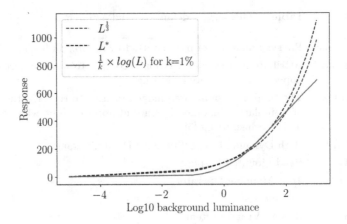

Fig. 1. Lightness functions comparison.

seem to give similar results in comparable conditions (see Fig. 1). The debate to know which representation of the lightness perception is the best one, i.e more accurate, is still open and research continue on this topic [2]. Decades later, Whittle conducted a subjective evaluation of lightness perception following a different protocol [21]. He measured the JND between two stimuli (respectively the reference and the test) in front of a unique background. The obtained results are similar to Weber's ones, luminance discrimination is equal to a constant k:

$$\frac{\Delta W}{W} = k, \qquad (3) \qquad\qquad W = \frac{\Delta L}{L_{min}}, \qquad (4)$$

with ΔL the luminance difference between the stimulus and the background, L_{min} the minimum luminance between the reference stimulus and the background. ΔW is the difference between the values of W for the two stimuli (reference and test).

This kind of representation is sufficient as a simple model of lightness perception, but current CAMs take into account more parameters of the HVS, such as the chrominance and the viewing conditions. First proposed by the CIE in 1997 (CIECAM97), this model has been reviewed several times. The most recent version (CAM16) has been proposed by Li *et al.* [12], it is a modified version of CIECAM02 written by Fairchild [5]. In his work, the perceived lightness J of a stimulus depends on the luminance stimulus, the luminance background and the lighting conditions of the surround. It can be expressed as:

$$J = 100 \times \left(\frac{A}{A_w}\right)^{c.z}, \qquad (5)$$

$$z = 1.48 \times \sqrt{\frac{Y_b}{Y_w}}, \qquad (6)$$

where A and A_w are the achromatic response of stimulus and the achromatic response of white reference respectively. z is defined as the base exponential nonlinearity with Y_b and Y_w the background luminance and the white reference luminance respectively. c is a nonlinearity factor of brightness function depending on the viewing condition (surround enlightening as illustrated in Fig. 2a) that can be Dark, Diminish or Average. The enlightening condition of the surround (expressed as c) has a direct effect on the degree of adaptation of the human eye denoted F. On a HMD, the viewing conditions are not well defined. As described later in Sect. 3, we suppose that the surround component is a function of the background and the background luminance influences much more the lightness perception than on classic 2D display. That why we need a complex perception model that takes into account the background luminance as a function. The influence of the background size and complex enlightening environment has been studied in [7,11]. Some adjustments have been proposed by Lee and Kyu-Ik [11] to express the adaptation degree F depending on the background luminance L_b instead of the three original viewing conditions (Dark, Dim, Avg):

$$
F = \begin{cases} 0.7379 + 0.392\big(1 - exp(0.0221.L_b)\big), & \text{if } L_b < 50cd/m^2 \\ 1, & \text{otherwise} \end{cases} \tag{7}
$$

where the adaptation degree F is only a function of the background luminance. Then the new nonlinearity factor, called now c_L, is computed depending on an adaptation luminance L_a:

$$
L_a = F.L_b + 0.2(1 - F)L_{d_{max}}, \tag{8}
$$

with $L_{d_{max}}$ the maximum luminance of the display and L_a the luminance of adaptation (20% of $L_{d_{max}}$ in traditional viewing condition). Finally, the adapted nonlinearity factor c_L is:

$$
c_L = \frac{c.\Delta L_{a|L_a=50}}{\Delta L_a}, \tag{9}
$$

$$
\Delta L_a = 1.88 L_a^{0.23} - 7.24 L_a^{0.11} + 8.26, \tag{10}
$$

where the nonlinearity factor of brightness c is equal to 0.69. $L_a = 50$ is a limit defined by the authors where $\Delta L_{a|L_a=50}$ is equal to 1.75.

This complex model allows us to express the nonlinearity adaptation factor c_L and the adaptation degree F as a function of the background luminance. Nevertheless, the nonlinearity factor c_L (Eq. 9) has to be adapted to fit with the particular viewing conditions encounter on HMDs. We ran subjective evaluations to compare perception on HMD with known models and found that the lightness perception is halved on a HMD compared with a 2D display (see Sect. 3).

2.2   Tone Mapping on HMD

Assuming that perception is the same for HMDs and 2D displays, two user studies performed a subjective comparison of several TMOs applied to many 360° HDR images in order to find the most appropriated one. The first evaluation ran by Perrin *et al.* [15] consists in applying existing TMOs to the entire 360° HDR image and display the obtained result on the HMD. However, none of the evaluated TMOs shows a clear improvement of perceived quality. The year after, Melo *et al.* [13] ran another user study to compare four TMOs on five 360° HDR images and found similar results. These results suggest that existing TMOs should be adapted to meet the requirements of 360° HDR images displayed on HMDs.

A few attempts to propose a TMO dedicated to HMD are presented right after. Yu [22] adapted the Photographic Tone Reproduction operator [17] applied to the viewport. The main contribution was first to take into account the fact that a user only looks at a limited part of the 360° image at a time. A second aimed to simulate light and dark adaption of human vision to provide smooth transitions between successive viewports. Indeed, the key value (log-luminance average) can significantly change from a view to another. To prevent flickering artifacts, Yu proposed to smooth the key value between successive views to coarsely reproduce the human eye adaptation behavior.

Cutchin and Li [3] proposed a method that performs a tone mapping on each viewport independently depending on its luminance histogram. The viewport histograms are divided into four groups corresponding to different TMOs. The authors noticed popping effects that happen when two successive views belong to different groups.

Both methods benefit from view dependency on an HMD and provide a better perceptible quality, but they still present some limits we want to overcome. Especially, these two methods do not tackle the spatial coherency as the TMO is applied to the viewport only. We propose a method that takes advantage of the viewport dependent operation with smooth transitions between successive views to ensure a good contrast while maintaining a global coherency considering the luminance of the entire 360° image. We will now present the subjective evaluations we conducted to model the lightness perception on HMD before detailing our method in Sect. 4.

3   Perception on HMD

Before delving into the proposed TMO dedicated to HMD, we describe two subjective experiments we conducted to study the HVS response on HMD. The first one focuses on lightness perception and measures the JND in the dynamic range of the HMD. Moreover, the protocol design follows CIECAM recommendations [5]. This experiment is helpful to validate the use of the logarithm of the luminance as a good representation of the perceived lightness. The second subjective evaluation is intended to be more general, regarding lightness and saturation. The experiment takes Whittle design [21] consisting in presenting two stimuli in front of a uniform background. Its usefulness is twofold. First it confirms results of the previous experiment about lightness. Second, it allows an evaluation of the perception of the chrominance on HMD. Resulting from these two evaluations, we propose to adapt a CAM that is coherent with the perception on HMDs and used in our TMO as describes later in Sect. 4.

3.1   First Experiment: Lightness as a Function of Luminance

The classic Weber's experiment seeks to determine the minimum perceptible difference value of luminance between a stimulus and a background. A fixed background is presented to participants while the stimulus is imperceptibly lighter. Then the stimulus luminance is increased until participants notice a difference between the stimulus and the background. This relative difference is the JND. More recently, the CIECAM [5] suggests to consider the surround relative luminance as a parameter because the perception acts differently depending on the environment enlightening. Furthermore, the stimulus should have a radius ranging from 2° to 4° in the visual field (corresponding to the foveal vision), a radius of 20° for the background (peripheral vision) and the surround encompasses the rest of the vision field (see Fig. 2a).   These recommendations are well defined

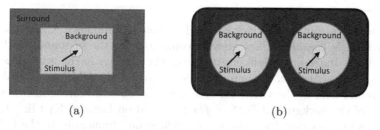

(a)   (b)

Fig. 2. (a) CIECAM02 recommendations for visualization conditions on 2D display. (b) Visualization conditions on HMD.

in case of visualization on a classic 2D display. New constraints are met when considering visualization on HMD. First, the surround field is not considered anymore because the black plastic structure of the HMD encompasses the whole visual field. Second, while the CIECAM model has been designed for distant display visualization that covers vision of about 20°, this angle corresponds to all of the Field of View (FoV) of the HMD (about 100°). To sum up, in our experiment on HMD, we consider a 4° stimulus, the background covers all the Fov of the HMD (100°), and the surround field is ignored (see Fig. 2b). The JND has been determined for ten background luminance levels covering all the dynamic range of the HMD. The test lasted about 15 min and the panel consisted of 20 participants (13 men and 7 women) with normal vision, from 20 to 57 years of age, with various socio-cultural backgrounds. After data fitting using robust estimators and classical regressions, we found the JND is linear and the slope is equal to 2.2% (±0.3%) as illustrated in Fig. 3. The sensitivity is still linear (ΔL as a function of L), resulting in a logarithmic response when using the Fechner's integration (Eq. 2). This evaluation emphasizes that the logarithmic lightness function is valid to model the human perception on an HMD.

However, this JND approximated to 2% is interpreted as a loss of contrast (two times less) for visualization on HMD compared with visualization on classic 2D display where the JND is usually around 1% (see Fig. 1). We suppose this

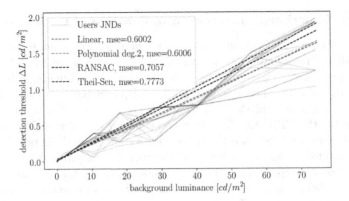

Fig. 3. ΔL as a function of L given the JND on an HMD.

phenomenon is due to the lack of fixed surround luminance. CAM proposed by Fairchild [5] considers three viewing conditions for the surround: Dark, Dim and Average. Indeed, the light emitted from the displays in the headset scatters on the plastic structure. Assuming the structure of the HMD is equivalent to the surround field in the CIECAM recommendations, the surround S is then a function of the background B $(S = f(B))$. Based on Lee and Kyu-Ik [11] work that takes into account the influence of background luminance in the lightness equations, we also adjusted the viewing-dependent component c_L to fit with our results.

$$c_L = \frac{c.r.\Delta L_{a|L_a=50}}{\Delta L_a}, \tag{11}$$

$$r = \frac{0.01}{k}, \tag{12}$$

where r is the ratio between the classic viewing condition constant at 1% and the found constant $k = 2.2\%$ on HMD. c is still equal to 0.69. We scaled the parameter c_L depending on the perception on HMD, which is almost halved.

We simulate the difference in lightness perception between two stimuli for a solid background in Fig. 4. The perceived lightness is strongly attenuated by the background luminance in case of HMD visualization compared with the three viewing conditions proposed in CIECAM02. These two factors (F and c_L Eqs. 7 and 11) are used in the next evaluation and confirm the validity of the lightness model.

3.2   Second Experiment: Chrominance Response Function

In order to validate our HMDCAM proposed above, we conducted a second experiment that includes the evaluation of the chrominance perception. This design is inspired by Whittle's experiment on luminance discrimination [21]. Instead of measuring the difference between a stimulus and a background, we compare two stimuli over a uniform grey background. We adapted this evaluation

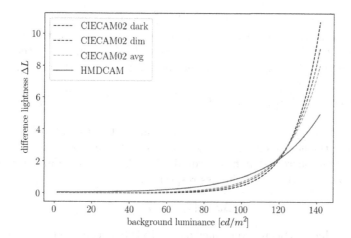

Fig. 4. Proposed HMDCAM compared with the three viewing conditions of CIECAM02.

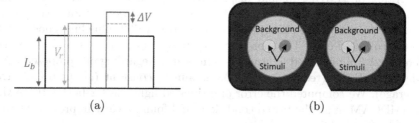

Fig. 5. (a) Schematic experiment with the background luminance L_b, the reference stimulus V_r and the difference ΔV between the two stimuli. (b) Schematic values represented on the HMD (binocular).

to determine JNDs of luminance and saturation for a set of different stimuli (see Fig. 5). The background L_b is an achromatic luminance in the range of the display. V_r is the chromatic or achromatic reference stimulus. Finally, ΔV is the difference between the reference and the test stimulus. ΔV can be either a difference in luminance L, in chroma C or in hue H. In this study, both the background and the reference stimulus are fixed while the test stimulus increases in luminance or saturation until participants notice a difference between the two stimuli. The two stimuli have a radius of 2° each and are separated by 8° of vision field. The background still covers the entire FoV of the HMD (100°). The panel consisted of 18 participants, from 20 to 57 years of age, with normal vision and various socio-cultural background. The test lasted about 45 min and was split into two parts. First, 8 luminance values are evaluated for 8 different backgrounds, that gives 32 discrimination luminance values. Then saturation has been evaluated for a unique background equal to 20% of the maximum luminance of the HMD (about 30 cd/m^2). The second part of the experiment consists of 8 saturation values for 4 colors: red, yellow, green and blue (32 values in total). The aim of this experiment is to confirm the HMDCAM that has been proposed after the first subjective study. To that end, for the evaluation of the lightness, we compute the CIECAM02 lightness response of both stimuli: J_{ref} the reference, and J_{test} the test average over all values determined by participants.

$$J_{ref} = 100\left(\frac{A_{ref}}{A_w}\right)^{c.z}, \qquad (13) \qquad J_{test} = 100\left(\frac{A_{test}}{A_w}\right)^{c.z}, \qquad (14)$$

where A_{ref} and A_{test} are respectively the achromatic response of the reference stimulus and the achromatic response of the test stimulus. c is defined according to the Average surround lighting condition. Then, we compute the absolute difference between the two lightness responses:

$$\Delta J = |J_{ref} - J_{test}| \qquad (15)$$

As the test value has been determined as the JND between itself and the reference stimulus, ΔJ should be almost constant for any of the 32 conditions. We compute ΔJ for all the tested values (in case of lightness evaluation) using either CIECAM02 or HMDCAM and display resulting curves on Fig. 6. We finally compute a linear regression over the two curves in each of the four background luminance condition. We clearly see that the CIECAM02 (blue lines) does not fit with the collected data. The more the stimuli luminance increases, the more the difference ΔJ of perceived lightness is significant. Regarding our proposed CAM modeled for HMD (red lines), the ΔJ is almost constant (about 6% of error in average). We computed the error of estimated lightness for both CIECAM02 and HMDCAM in all the tested conditions and found a clear improvement with our model (see Table 2).

Table 2. Error of estimated perception for lightness and saturation (CIECAM02 [5] compared with our proposed HMDCAM).

Background luminance [cd/m^2]	15	50	90	125
CIECAM02 lightness error [%]	13.1	18.8	17.3	9.7
HMDCAM lightness error [%]	3.8	7.1	8.2	5.2
Color	Red	Green	Blue	Yellow
CIECAM02 saturation error [%]	1.3	0.6	3.2	5.3
HMDCAM saturation error [%]	0.7	0.5	1.7	2.8

We reproduced exactly the same protocol for the evaluation of perceived saturation. Δs is the absolute difference between the perceived saturation of the reference stimulus and the test stimulus. The proposed HMDCAM slightly improves the results of the perception of saturation (see Table 2). Nevertheless, the error does not differ so much between classic viewing condition and on a HMD because the error of CIECAM02 stays low. To sum up, we have seen that the perception on HMD differs from classical perception on 2D display. Our

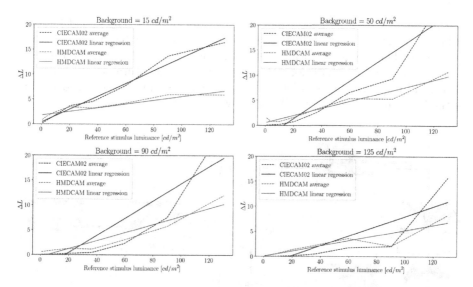

Fig. 6. CIECAM02 compared with our HMDCAM model for the collected subjective data on lightness perception.

two experiments showed that the perception of a difference between two levels of luminance is halved. We then proposed a HMDCAM that better describes the perception on HMD. Further experiments could lead to a more accurate HMDCAM as the current one does not fit perfectly with the data; but we can afford to rely on it for our purpose. In the next section, we present our TMO that uses the HMDCAM to improve the quality of the tone mapped images.

4 A New TMO for HMD

In this section we present the HMD-TMO proposed in [8] and we bring some major revisions that improve significantly the global framework. The framework is presented in Fig. 7. Red blocks indicate the proposed improvements. Recall that the input is a 360° HDR image and the output is a tone mapped image of the current viewport visualized on an HMD. The upper branch performs a tone mapping on the entire 360° image and thus preserves the spatial coherency. This operator is based on the log-luminance histogram of the image. We will see that computing a naive histogram of the equirectangular projection of the 360° image leads to an unrepresentative distribution of the luminance. We propose a correction that improves the result of the global TMO. Concurrently, the lower branch performs a tone mapping on the viewport image to enhance the contrast. This operator is based on the Photographic Tone Mapping Operator [17]. It has not been changed compared with the original method [8] as it produces the expected result. In our original version [8], the combination of the resulting luminances of these two TMOs was based on a geometric mean. We relax this combination and propose to use a weighted sum in logarithmic domain. The weight factor α is in the range (0, 1) and gives more emphasize on the global or the viewport luminance. The geometric mean is reached when $\alpha = 0.5$. Finally, the resulting tone mapped viewport is colorized using the classic desaturated color method proposed by Schlick [18]. We detail the three operations with the improvements in the following section (global TMO, viewport TMO and combination).

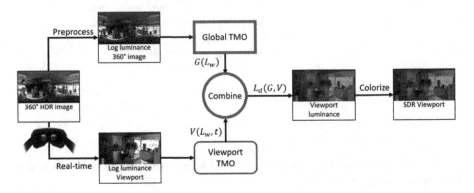

Fig. 7. Our operator combines a Global TMO $G(L_w)$ and a Viewport TMO $V(L_w, t)$. The Global TMO (upper branch) preserves the global coherency of the scene while the Viewport TMO (lower branch) enhances contrast. The combination of both produces our final HMD-TMO $L_d(G, V)$. (Color figure online)

4.1   Global TMO

The global TMO is based on the Visibility Matching Tone Reproduction Operator proposed by Ward *et al.* [9]. It consists of a log-luminance histogram equalization scaled into the display dynamic range. To avoid artifacts due to a too high contrast in the tone mapped image, the authors add a pass of histogram adjustment that matches with the HVS luminance response. We adapted this step using the perception model on HMD. Thus, the log-luminance distribution is needed to compute the TMO, but a naive histogram of the equirectangular projection of the 360° image results in a wrong distribution. Actually, the projection gives more significance to the poles (top and bottom) of the 360° image than to the equatorial area as illustrated by Fig. 8. To avoid this over-represented contribution in the histogram, we apply a weight to the pixels depending on the elevation in the equirectangular image to obtain a right distribution [4, 20]:

$$w_{x,y} = cos\left(\pi \times \left(\frac{y}{H} - 0.5 \right) \right), \tag{16}$$

where $w_{x,y}$ is the weight of the pixel (x, y) (instead of 1), and H is the image height in number of pixels. The histogram is computed in floating numbers, it is

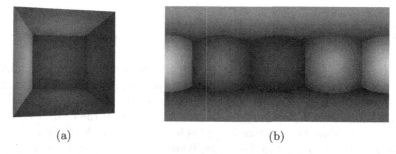

(a)   (b)

Fig. 8. (a) Inside of a cube, each wall has the same dimension. (b) 360° image (equirect-angular projection), the poles (green and red areas) take half of the image. (Color figure online)

then cumulative and normalized to give the Cumulative Distribution Function (CDF). This correction is especially needed given that, in general cases, the pod of the 360° camera that captures the HDR image lets a black area in the bottom, which produces an offset in black level as illustrated in Fig. 9. Finally, the weighted log-luminance CDF is given by

$$P(b) = \frac{\sum_{b_i < b} f(b_i)}{\sum_{b_i} f(b_i)}, \tag{17}$$

$$f(b_i) = \sum_{x,y} w_{x,y} \times log\big(L_w(x,y)\big), \tag{18}$$

where $f(b_i)$ is the log-luminance weighted sum of all pixels (x,y) that fall into bin b_i. The number of bins is at least equal to 100 as proposed by the authors to avoid banding artifacts due to quantization.   The tone curve G proposed by

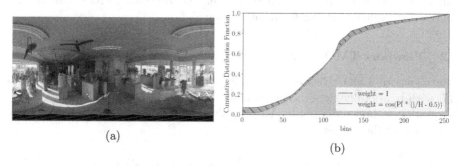

(a)
(b)

Fig. 9. (a) Equirectangular projection of Florist 360° image. The camera pod (hatched in red) is over-represented. (b) Comparison of CDF without weights (blue curve), and with weights (orange curve). The offset in low luminances (bin 0) is generated by the camera pod. (Color figure online)

Ward *et al.* is a scaled version of $P(b)$:

$$G(x, y) = exp\big(ln(L_{dmin}) + \big(ln(L_{dmax}) - ln(L_{dmin})\big) \times P\big(L_w(x, y)\big)\big), \quad (19)$$

where L_{dmin} and L_{dmax} are respectively the minimum and maximum luminance of the display, $L_w(x, y)$ is the world luminance of the pixel (x, y). $P(L_w(x, y))$ is the CDF defined in Eq. 17, and $G(x, y)$ the resulting luminance of the pixel. The last step is a pass of histogram adjustment. If the slope of the CDF is too steep, the contrast produced by the tone mapping is too high. In order to preserve a perceptually coherent contrast in the image, Ward *et al.* [9] proposed to trimming the histogram based on the human perception. If the contrast between two levels of displayed luminance is perceptually higher than it is with the corresponding levels of world luminance, then we have to trim the histogram. It can be written thus:

$$\frac{dL_d}{dL_w} \leq \frac{J_d}{J_w}, \quad (20)$$

where L_d and L_w are respectively the display and the world luminance while J_d and J_w are the corresponding perceived lightness. We use the iterative process proposed by Ward *et al.* for the ceiling [9].

At the end, we obtain a CDF with a right distribution while the ceiling histogram is perceptually coherent with the HMDCAM. We remind that the human eye is less sensitive on HMD than on classic display (about halved sensitive as seen in Sect. 3). This phenomenon is notable on tone curves in Fig. 10, a gentler slope is allowed for luminances that are sparingly present when the ceiling follows the HMDCAM.   While the CDF without any ceiling produces a too high contrast, trimming the histogram with a classic perception model flatten the image. The ceiling based on our HMDCAM better preserves contrast and stays perceptually coherent when visualized on HMD.

The global TMO preserves the coherency of the scene and is perceptually coherent on an HMD. However, the contrast in the viewport can be improved when not considering the entire 360° image. The viewport TMO enhances the contrast as explained in the following section.

4.2   Viewport TMO

The viewport TMO relies on the Photographic Tone Reproduction operator [17] with temporally smoothed parameters to avoid flickering and simulate eye adaptation as first proposed by Yu [22]. This TMO is based on the log-average luminance of the image:

$$\bar{L}_w\big(V(t)\big) = \frac{1}{N} exp\Big(\sum_{x,y} log\big(\delta + L_w(x, y)\big)\Big), \quad (21)$$

where $\bar{L}_w(V(t))$ is the viewport key value at a given time, $L_w(x, y)$ the pixel luminance, δ a small value to avoid singularity in case the image contains black pixels, and N the number of pixels in the viewport. Here, time t corresponds to an orientation of the camera due to the head movement. To ensure a smooth

(a) Without ceiling (yellow curve).   (b) HMDCAM ceiling (red curve).

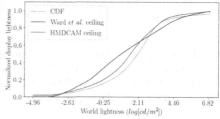

(c) Ward ceiling (blue curve).   (d) Tone curves comparison.

Fig. 10. (a) Histogram adjustment without ceiling, the contrast is too high. (b) With HMDCAM ceiling, the contrast is coherent with the perception on HMD. (c) With Ward ceiling, the contrast is too low. (d) Comparison of corresponding tone curves. (Color figure online)

transition between two successive viewports, the key and the white values are interpolated as:

$$\bar{L}'_w(t) = \tau\bar{L}_w\big(V(t)\big) + (1-\tau)\bar{L}'_w(t-1), \tag{22}$$

$$L'_{white}(t) = \tau L_{white}\big(V(t)\big) + (1-\tau)L'_{white}(t-1), \tag{23}$$

where $\bar{L}'_w(t)$ and $L'_{white}(t)$ are respectively the smoothed key and white values between two successive views and τ is a time dependent interpolation variable. The value of τ determines the adaptation time. For $\tau = 1$, there is no adaptation, while for $\tau = 0$, the luminance is never updated. Based on TMOs that use models of eye adaptation [10,14], we decided to fix τ value corresponding to one second of adaptation (for both light and dark): $\tau = \Delta t$ where Δt is the time spent between the previous and the current frame in second. Finally, the luminance is scaled and high values are attenuated to avoid clipping:

$$L(x,y,t) = \frac{a}{\bar{L}'_w(t)} L_w(x,y), \tag{24}$$

$$V(x,y,t) = \frac{L(x,y,t)\left(1 + \frac{L(x,y,t)}{L'^2_{white}(t)}\right)}{1 + L(x,y,t)}, \tag{25}$$

where a is a user defined variable which scales the luminance (commonly 0.18) and $L(x,y,t)$ the time dependent scaled luminance. Our Viewport TMO is the

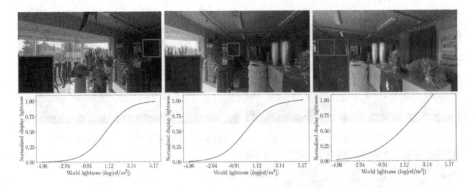

Fig. 11. Photographic Tone Reproduction operator [17] applied to a viewport sequence with smooth transitions. As the key value and the white value evolve from a view to another, the tone curve is modified and a same zone in the scene (red inset) becomes brighter or darker. (Color figure online)

displayed luminance $V\big(L_w(x,y),t\big)$ as illustrated in Fig. 11. In his operator, Yu actually uses Eq. (24) that does not avoid clipping in high luminances. We have now the global coherency assured by the 360° image CDF $(G(L_w))$ and the viewport contrast $(V(L_w,t))$ that we want to combine to obtain our final tone mapped image.

4.3   TMOs Combination

Combination of global and viewport luminances ensures the global coherency to be preserved and the viewport contrast to be enhanced. To obtain a resulting perceptually uniform luminance, the combination has to be done in the perceptual domain (the logarithm is a good representation as seen in Sect. 3):

$$L_d(x,y,t) = e^{\alpha.ln\big(G(x,y)\big)+(1-\alpha).ln\big(V(x,y,t)\big)}, \tag{26}$$

$$L_d(x,y,t) = e^{\alpha.ln\big(G(x,y)\big)} \times e^{(1-\alpha).ln\big(V(x,y,t)\big)}, \tag{27}$$

$$L_d(x,y,t) = \left(e^{ln\big(G(x,y)\big)}\right)^{\alpha} \times \left(e^{ln\big(V(x,y,t)\big)}\right)^{1-\alpha}, \tag{28}$$

$$L_d(x,y,t) = G(x,y)^{\alpha} \times V(x,y,t)^{1-\alpha}, \tag{29}$$

where $G(x,y)$ and $V(x,y,t)$ are our global and viewport TMOs respectively, α is the weight in range $(0,1)$ that gives more emphasize on the global or the viewport result, and finally L_d is the display luminance. The effect of the α value is showed by Fig. 12. As expected, the viewport TMO (left) enhances the contrast by exploiting all its dynamic range. Contrarily, the global TMO (right) brightens the image because this area is bright compared with the rest of the 360° image. The value of α can change depending on the processed scene. More results are shown in the following section.

Fig. 12. α varies linearly from 0 to 1, given more emphasize on the viewport TMO (left), then more and more on the global TMO (right).

4.4 Color Saturation

Once our TMO has calculated the tone mapped luminance, we compute the color of all the pixels of the tone mapped image using the Schlick's approach [18]:

$$C' = \left(\frac{C}{L_w}\right)^s L_d, \tag{30}$$

where C and C' are respectively the input and output trichromatic values (RGB), L_w the world luminance and L_d the tone mapped luminance. The saturation parameter s is set to 0.7 for our results.

5 Results

We implemented our HMD-TMO using Unity3D because of its friendly interface for managing VR and its capacity to handle HDR. We used the HTC Vive Pro[1] as a HMD. We benefited from GPU programming with shaders to compute 360° image histograms on the 2048 × 1024 equirectangular projection, and the 1440 × 1600 viewports (left and right views for the binocular vision) key values in real time. Rendering (computation of the colored tone mapped image) is achieved with an image effect shader applied to the HDR viewport. The global TMO is computed once for all and takes less than one second. The navigation (calculation and display of successive viewport images) is performed in real-time: 90 frames are computed per second (Intel Core i7 vPro 7th Gen, NVidia Quadro M2200). The efficiency of our TMO is clearly showed in the example presented in Fig. 13. The two images on the left (Fig. 13a) result from the viewport TMO. A little movement of the camera produces a significant change in displayed luminance, especially for the blue strip behind "Student Service". The middle images (Fig. 13b) result from the global TMO. The spatial coherency is preserved, the blue color stays the same. Nevertheless, some details are lost due to clipping in the right of top image. The two lasts images (Fig. 13c) result from the linear combination of both TMOs. The spatial coherency and details are well preserved, the blue strip does not change significantly and light reflects on the wall are visible. Figure 14 presents some additional results of our HMD-TMO. In all of our results, we fixed $\alpha = 0.5$.

---

[1] https://www.vive.com/fr/product/vive-pro/.

(a)   (b)   (c)

Fig. 13. (a) Viewport TMO: The blue strip change significantly. (b) Global TMO: Some details are lost due to clipping. (c) TMOs combination: the spatial coherency and the details are preserved. (Color figure online)

(a)   (b)   (c)

Fig. 14. (a) Viewport TMO: the local contrast is enhanced. (b) Global TMO: the coherency is preserved. (c) TMOs combination: the spatial coherency is preserved while the local contrast is enhanced.

6   Conclusion

HDR imaging enables to capture the whole dynamic of a 360° scene. Previous subjective studies have shown that naive tone mapping of the entire 360° image or tone mapping of a viewport does not provide convincing results. To overcome these limitations, we have proposed a new HMD-TMO. More precisely, our contribution is twofold: (1) a CAM that describes well the perception on HMD; (2) a perceptually coherent TMO that combines both global and viewport TMOs. The linear combination allows the TMO to be adaptive depending on the encountered scene. This new TMO does not tackle the limits of a viewport tone mapping but ensures a spatial coherency while navigating through the 360° HDR content. Our future work heads toward HDR video tone mapping for visualization on HMD. The main challenge will consist in accounting for: temporal coherency, sudden change in luminance range through time, naturalness of time adaptation, etc. An automatic tuning of the α parameter used in the combination could tackle those limits.

Acknowledgments. All 360° HDR images come from free SYNS, LizardQ and HDRI Haven datasets. This work has been supported by the ANR project ANR-17-CE23-0020. We would like to thank Kadi Bouatouch for his help and proofreading. Thanks to reviewers for their constructive commentaries. Thanks to all experiment participants for their contributions.

References

1. Banterle, F., Artusi, A., Debattista, K., Chalmers, A.: Advanced High Dynamic Range Imaging. AK Peters/CRC Press, Boca Raton (2017)
2. Brill, M.H., Carter, R.C.: Does lightness obey a log or a power law? Or is that the right question? Color Res. Appl. **39**(1), 99–101 (2014)
3. Cutchin, S., Li, Y.: View dependent tone mapping of HDR panoramas for head mounted displays. In: Proceedings of the 26th International Conference on Artificial Reality and Telexistence and the 21st Eurographics Symposium on Virtual Environments, pp. 29–36. Eurographics Association (2016)
4. De Abreu, A., Ozcinar, C., Smolic, A.: Look around you: saliency maps for omnidirectional images in VR applications. In: 2017 Ninth International Conference on Quality of Multimedia Experience (QoMEX), pp. 1–6. IEEE (2017)
5. Fairchild, M.D.: Color Appearance Models. Wiley, Hoboken (2013)
6. Fechner, G.T., Howes, D.H., Boring, E.G.: Elements of Psychophysics, vol. 1. Holt, Rinehart and Winston, New York (1966)
7. Gloriani, A.H., et al.: Influence of background size, luminance and eccentricity on different adaptation mechanisms. Vision. Res. **125**, 12–22 (2016)
8. Goudé, I., Cozot, R., Banterle, F.: HMD-TMO: a tone mapping operator for 360° HDR images visualization for head mounted displays. In: Gavrilova, M., Chang, J., Thalmann, N.M., Hitzer, E., Ishikawa, H. (eds.) CGI 2019. LNCS, vol. 11542, pp. 216–227. Springer, Cham (2019). https://doi.org/10.1007/978-3-030-22514-8_18
9. Larson, G.W., Rushmeier, H., Piatko, C.: A visibility matching tone reproduction operator for high dynamic range scenes. IEEE Trans. Vis. Comput. Graph. **3**(4), 291–306 (1997)

10. Ledda, P., Santos, L.P., Chalmers, A.: A local model of eye adaptation for high dynamic range images. In: Proceedings of the 3rd International Conference on Computer Graphics, Virtual Reality, Visualisation and Interaction in Africa, pp. 151–160. ACM (2004)
11. Lee, S.H., Sohng, K.I.: A model of luminance-adaptation for quantifying brightness in mixed visual adapting conditions. IEICE Trans. Electron. **94**(11), 1768–1772 (2011)
12. Li, C., et al.: Comprehensive color solutions: CAM16, CAT16, and CAM16-UCS. Color Res. Appl. **42**(6), 703–718 (2017)
13. Melo, M., Bouatouch, K., Bessa, M., Coelho, H., Cozot, R., Chalmers, A.: Tone mapping HDR panoramas for viewing in head mounted displays. In: VISIGRAPP (1: GRAPP), pp. 232–239 (2018)
14. Pattanaik, S.N., Tumblin, J., Yee, H., Greenberg, D.P.: Time-dependent visual adaptation for fast realistic image display. In: Proceedings of the 27th Annual Conference on Computer Graphics and Interactive Techniques, pp. 47–54. ACM Press/Addison-Wesley Publishing Co. (2000)
15. Perrin, A.F., Bist, C., Cozot, R., Ebrahimi, T.: Measuring quality of omnidirectional high dynamic range content. In: Applications of Digital Image Processing XL, vol. 10396, p. 1039613. International Society for Optics and Photonics (2017)
16. Reinhard, E., Heidrich, W., Debevec, P., Pattanaik, S., Ward, G., Myszkowski, K.: High Dynamic Range Imaging: Acquisition, Display, and Image-Based Lighting. Morgan Kaufmann, Burlington (2010)
17. Reinhard, E., Stark, M., Shirley, P., Ferwerda, J.: Photographic tone reproduction for digital images. ACM Trans. Graph. (TOG) **21**, 267–276 (2002)
18. Schlick, C.: Quantization techniques for visualization of high dynamic range pictures. In: Sakas, G., Müller, S., Shirley, P. (eds.) Photorealistic Rendering Techniques. Focus on Computer Graphics (Tutorials and Perspectives in Computer Graphics), pp. 7–20. Springer, Heidelberg (1995). https://doi.org/10.1007/978-3-642-87825-1_2
19. Stevens, S.S.: To honor fechner and repeal his law. Science **133**(3446), 80–86 (1961)
20. Upenik, E., Ebrahimi, T.: A simple method to obtain visual attention data in head mounted virtual reality. In: 2017 IEEE International Conference on Multimedia & Expo Workshops (ICMEW), pp. 73–78. IEEE (2017)
21. Whittle, P.: Increments and decrements: luminance discrimination. Vision. Res. **26**(10), 1677–1691 (1986)
22. Yu, M.: Dynamic tone mapping with head-mounted displays. Standford Univ. Rep. **5** (2015)

Simulating Crowds and Autonomous Vehicles

John Charlton(✉) , Luis Rene Montana Gonzalez , Steve Maddock ,
and Paul Richmond

University of Sheffield, Sheffield S10 2TN, UK
{j.a.charlton,lrmontanagonzalez1,s.maddock,p.richmond}@sheffield.ac.uk

Abstract. Understanding how people view and interact with
autonomous vehicles is important to guide future directions of research.
One such way of aiding understanding is through simulations of virtual
environments involving people and autonomous vehicles. We present a
simulation model that incorporates people and autonomous vehicles in
a shared urban space. The model is able to simulate many thousands of
people and vehicles in real-time. This is achieved by use of GPU hardware, and through a novel linear program solver optimized for large numbers of problems on the GPU. The model is up to 30 times faster than
the equivalent multi-core CPU model.

Keywords: Pedestrian simulation · Real-time rendering ·
GPU-computing · Autonomous vehicles

1 Introduction

Self-driving vehicles are an important area of current research and industry.
There is a lot of work examining how best to implement this developing technology. One guiding factor of this is an understanding of how people feel about
the use of autonomous vehicles, since they will be users, as passengers, and will
also interact with the vehicles as pedestrians. One way of gaining such understanding is through the use of visualizations of virtual simulations of pedestrian
crowds and autonomous vehicles. Creating simulations that combine people and
autonomous vehicles demonstrates potential phenomena that may arise from this
novel situation. It also provides outreach opportunities to gauge public opinion,
and increase confidence of sharing the same area. Of special interest is the use
of autonomous vehicles that share the same space as pedestrians. This type of
transportation increases the area available for both the vehicles and people to
move around in. It also allows the autonomous vehicles to reach any location,
resulting in true door-to-door transportation. This could potentially allow many
more people and vehicles to be able to use the same space compared to segregat-
ing them, resulting in larger overall accessible areas, potentially reducing traffic
and densities.

© Springer-Verlag GmbH Germany, part of Springer Nature 2020
M. L. Gavrilova et al. (Eds.): Trans. on Comput. Sci. XXXVII, LNCS 12230, pp. 129–143, 2020.
https://doi.org/10.1007/978-3-662-61983-4_8

Part of the requirement for such simulations is the ability to simulate many people and vehicles. This allows for large public spaces containing many thousands of people to be visualized, such as areas surrounding busy transport hubs or city centers. Another requirement is to run in real-time. This allows for user interactivity, particularly for applications such as virtual reality. The choice of simulation model tends to be one in which the more computationally complex it is, the more realistic the motion it produces tends to be. By using particular agent-based simulation models with inherent parallelism, it is possible to create simulations with greater numbers of people and agents, running at faster speeds. This is achieved by running such simulations on GPU hardware, due to the larger throughput available for GPUs compared to CPUs. This has been seen in other pedestrian models previously [1, 2].

The work presented here builds on previous work by Charlton et al. [3], which presented an efficient pedestrian steering model for GPU hardware using the ORCA steering model. That work shows speed increases of up to 30 times compared to the original multi-core CPU model. The speedup is achieved by parallelizing as much of the data and computation as possible, choosing data parallel algorithms and spatial partitioning to allow communication between people to provide speedup. It makes use of a low-dimensional linear program solver that efficiently solves numerous problems simultaneously on the GPU [4], and adapts the solver to optimize for a position close to a point in 2D space, rather than a linear function as described in the paper. This model also uses a grid-based spatial partitioning scheme to efficiently communicate data within the GPU [5].

The work presented in this paper expands upon the work of Charlton et al. [3] by including autonomous vehicles in the simulation. The model has been extended with rules to explain interaction between people and vehicle and between vehicle and vehicle. It allows high performance simulations involving both people and autonomous vehicles interacting in the same space. The resulting model has been incorporated into a visualization to demonstrate the effects of simulations involving people and autonomous vehicles in the same shared space.

The organization of the paper is as follows. Section 2 covers background information and related work. Section 3 explains in detail the implementation of the ORCA model on the GPU and extensions to allow for autonomous vehicles. Section 4 presents results of the visualization of the autonomous vehicles and people simulation, and discussion of the multi-core CPU and GPU ORCA models. Finally, Sect. 5 gives conclusions.

2   Background

Many types of models have been proposed to generate local pedestrian motion and collision avoidance [6–8]. The simplest separation of steering models is between continuum models and microscopic models. Continuum models attempt to treat the whole crowd in a similar way to a fluid, allowing for fast simulation of larger numbers of people, but are lacking in accuracy at the individual person scale [9]. Moving part of the calculation to the GPU has shown performance improvements [10]. Overall, however, the model is not ideal for solving on the GPU due to the large sparse data structures. In comparison, microscopic models tend to be paired with a global path planner to give people goal locations and trajectories. Such models specify rules at the individual person scale, with crowd-scale dynamics being an emergent effect of the rules and interactions, and easily allow for non-homogeneous agents and behavior.

Popular microscopic models are cellular automata (CA), social forces [11] and velocity obstacles (VO) [12]. CA are popular due to the ability to reproduce observable phenomena [13,14], but a downside is the inability to reproduce other behaviors due to using discrete space. CA models are computationally lightweight and lend themselves well to specify certain complex behavior. However, CA pedestrian models tend to use discrete spatial rules, where the order of agent movements are sequential, which does not lend itself to parallelism and GPU implementations [15]. Social force models use a computationally lightweight set of rules that allows for crowd-scale observables such as lane formation. They are well suited to parallelizing on the GPU since all agents can be updated simultaneously, with good performance for many simulated people [16,17]. However, generated simulations can result in unrealistic looking motion and produce undesirable behavior at large densities.

Velocity obstacles (VO) work by examining the velocity and position of nearby moving objects to compute a collision-free trajectory. Velocity-space is analyzed to determine what velocities can be taken which do not cause collisions. VO models lend themselves to parallelization since agents are updated simultaneously and navigate independently of one another with minimal explicit communication. It tends to be more computational and memory intensive than social forces models, but the large throughput capability of the GPU for such parallel tasks make it a very suitable technique for GPU implementation. Early models assumed that each person would take full responsibility for avoiding other people. Several variations include the reactive behavior of other models [18–20]. One example is reciprocal velocity obstacles (RVO), where the assumption is that all other people will take half the responsibility for avoiding collisions [21,22]. This model has been implemented on the GPU [2] and has shown credible speedup over the multi-core CPU implementation through use of hashing instead of naive nearest neighbor search. Group behavior has also been included in VO models [23,24] allowing people to be joined into groups. Such people attempt to remain close to other members of the group and aim for the same goal location. 25There are many further extentions to VOs to specialize movement and behaviors to account for a variety of agent and robot types, such as elliptical agents [25], holonomic movement [26], and non-holonomic movement [27,28]. A further extension of particular interest is optimal reciprocal collision avoidance (ORCA). It provides sufficient conditions for collision-free motion. It works by solving low-dimension linear programs. Freely available code libraries have been implemented for both single- and multi-core CPU [29].

VO techniques are very suitable candidates for GPU implementation. The RVO model and implementation by Bleiweiss [2] show notable performance gains against multi-core CPU equivalent models. However, these methods must perform expensive calculations to find a suitable velocity. They tend to perform slower and are not guaranteed to find the best velocity. ORCA is deemed more suitable because of its performance relative to other VO models and collision-free motion, theoretically providing "better" motion (i.e. less collisions). A critical analysis of common VO approaches is presented by Douthwaite et al. [30]. In their analysis they find the ORCA model to scale the best out of the tested VO models, and also find ORCA provides the smoothest trajectories.

Linear programming is a way of maximizing an objective function subject to a set of constraints. For ORCA, linear programming is used to find the closest velocity to a person's desired velocity which does not result in collisions. It is important to choose a solver that is efficient on the GPU at low dimensions. A popular solver type is the Simplex method. This is best suited for large dimension problems and struggles at lower dimensions. The incremental solver [31] is efficient at low dimensions but suffers on the GPU due to load balance: not all GPU threads have the same amount of computation, which reduces the performance on such parallel architecture. The batch GPU two-dimension linear solver [4] is an efficient way to solve the numerous linear problems simultaneously. We make use of this approach, demonstrating its use for large-scale simulations.

There is a lot of work examining the ethics and safety of autonomous vehicles [32–36]. There is also examination into understanding how users respond to autonomous vehicles, and therefore how such vehicles should be programmed. A recent survey and overview of this is provided by Rasouli and Tsotsos [37]. Schwarting et al. use a variety of psycological metrics which model the altruism and selfishness of people to predict their interactions towards autonomous vehicles [38]. Bonnefon et al. examined the idea of pedestrian-first safely compared to passenger-first safety of autonomous vehicles. That is, given a scenario which will cause harm to either the pedestrians or passengers, whose safety will be prioritized. They found people would prefer others to buy pedestrian-first safe vehicles, but would prefer to ride in passenger-first safe vehicles, which provides a moral, ethical, and utilitarian dilemma as to the choice of algorithms used in autonomous vehicles [39]. Pettersson and Karlsson [40] find that different ways of presenting information on the same subject can yield different types of data. This means that the larger variety of methods of presenting and interacting with information about autonomous vehicles, the more understanding of the users can be found. Work into simulating autonomous vehicles has been carried out with agent-based models. Boesch and Ciari [41] present an agent-based simulation model for autonomous vehicles, called MATsim, with the aim of it being simple enough for usage for those interested. This tool is used in a variety of applications, such as examining an autonomous taxi service [42], providing a theoretical examination in which to target future experimental research. Zhang et al. [43] try to predict the effect autonomous vehicle will have on city parking through use of an agent based model, and estimate that up to 90% of parking demand could be eliminated.

3   The Algorithm

This section provides an overview of the algorithm as well as important changes to allow simulating of autonomous vehicles. For more in-depth description of the original ORCA algorithm, see the work of van den Berg et al. [44], or for more detail on the GPU implementation, see the work of Charlton et al. [3]. The main changes are changes to the avoidance rules determining how much people and vehicles should avoid each other.

As an overview to the ORCA model, each agent in the model has a start location and an end location they want to reach as quickly as possible, subject to an average speed and capped maximum speed. For each simulation iteration, each agent "observes" properties of other nearby agents, namely radius, the current position and velocity. For each nearby agent a half-plane of restricted velocities is calculated (Fig. 1). By selecting a velocity not restricted by this half-plane, the two agents are guaranteed to not collide within time τ, where τ is the *lookahead time*, the amount of forward time planning people make to avoid collisions. By considering all nearby agents, the set of half-planes creates a set of velocities that, if taken, do not collide with any nearby agents in time τ. The agent then selects from the permissible velocities the one closest to its desired velocity and goal. Figure 1d shows the resulting half-planes caused by neighboring agents on an example setup, and the optimal velocity that most closely matches the person's desired velocity.

It is possible that the generated set of half-planes does not contain any possible velocities. Such situations are caused by large densities of people. The solution is to select a velocity that least penetrates the set of half-planes induced by the other agents. In this case, there is no guarantee of collision-free motion.

The computation of velocity subject to the set of half-planes is done using linear programming. The problem for the linear program is defined with the constraints corresponding to the half-plane $ORCA_{a|b}$ of velocities, attempting to minimize the difference of the suitable velocity from the desired velocity. Since each agent needs to find a new velocity, there is a linear problem corresponding to each agent, each iteration. The algorithm used to solve this is the batch-GPU-LP algorithm [4]. It is an algorithm designed for solving multiple low-dimensional linear programs on the GPU, based on the randomized incremental linear program solver of Seidel [31].

This batch-LP solver works by initially assigning each thread to a problem (i.e. one pedestrian). Each thread must solve a set of half-plane constraints, subject to an optimization function. Respectively, these are that the person should not choose a velocity that collides with other people, and the person wants to travel as close to their desired velocity as possible.

Each half-plane constraint is considered incrementally. If the current velocity is not satisfied by the currently considered constraint a new valid velocity is

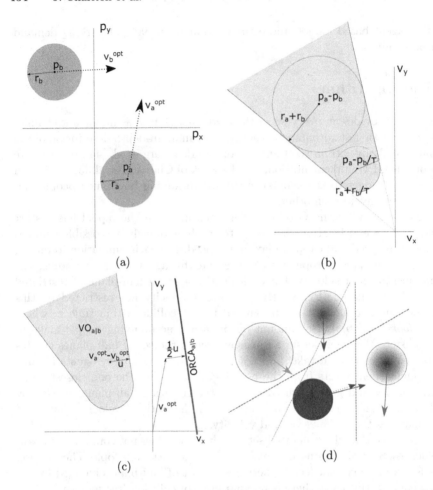

Fig. 1. (a) A system of 2 people a and b with corresponding radius r_a and r_b. (b) The associated velocity obstacle $VO_{a|b}$ in velocity space for a look-ahead period of time τ caused by the neighbor b for a. (c) The vector of velocities $v_a^{opt} - v_b^{opt}$ lies within the velocity obstacle $VO_{a|b}$. The vector u is the shortest vector to the edge of the obstacle from the vector of velocities. The corresponding half-plane $ORCA_{a|b}$ is in the direction of u, and intersects the point $v_a^{opt} + \frac{1}{2} u$. (d) A view of a blue agent and its neighbors, as well as the generated half-planes caused by the neighbors interacting with the blue agent. The solid blue arrow shows the desired velocity of the blue agent. The dotted blue arrow is the resulting calculated velocity that does not collide with any neighbor in time τ. (Color figure online)

calculated. The calculation of a new velocity is one of the most computationally expensive operations. It is also very branched, as only only some of the solvers require a new valid velocity and others can maintain their current value. This branching calculation causes the threads that do no need to perform a calcu-lation to remain idle while the other threads perform the operation. This is an unbalanced workload on the GPU device and can vastly reduce the throughput as many threads do not perform any calculations, exacerbated by the fact that those threads performing the operation must take a lot of time to complete the operation.

The implementation of this calculation uses ideas from cooperative thread arrays [45] to subdivide the calculation into *"work units"*, blocks of equal size computation. These work units can be transferred to and computed by different threads, allowing for a balanced work load and good performance. If the thread does not need to compute a new velocity, then it can aid in another problem's calculation. This algorithm shows performance improvements over state-of-the-art CPU LP solvers and other GPU LP solvers [4].

3.1   Extension

This section presents the changes made to the ORCA model to allow for simulating both people and autonomous vehicles. ORCA is a version of an RVO model. In this model, people will take 50% of the responsibility to avoid colliding. This is reflected in the calculation of the half plan $ORCA_{A|B}$ being shifted by $\frac{1}{2}\,u$, explained in Fig. 1c. Because the agent takes (at least) half of the responsibility for avoidance, it will assume the other agent will take the remaining half, and hence collision will be avoided between the two agents.

We include a variable parameter $f_{A|B}$, that represents the fractional responsibility that agent A will take to avoid agent B. This variable is used when calculating the position of the half-plane $ORCA_{A|B} = v_{opt} + f_{A|B}u$. For the standard case of people-people interaction, $f = \frac{1}{2}$.

Because of the different nature of movement of people and vehicles, the avoidance taken between vehicles and people will not be reciprocal. As such, the weighting of u in Fig. 1 will be different. Since colliding with an autonomous vehicle could provide greater risk of health and damage, we assume people will tend to naturally take more responsibility in avoiding collisions with vehicles (the amount of avoidance is $f_{person|car} > \frac{1}{2}$).

The vehicles themselves could move in a variety of ways. In order to maintain the parallelism of the ORCA model, we let autonomous vehicles follow the same sets of steering rules as people, i.e. they also follow the ORCA algorithm. By ensuring the executing code path is equivalent for all agents, regardless of size or how much they should contribute to avoiding others, there is no performance loss by varying the number of vehicles in the simulation, compared to simulating only people. When a vehicle must avoid colliding with another car, they will reciprocally avoid each other and each take half the responsibility, much as people do when interacting with people, i.e. $f_{car|car} = \frac{1}{2}$.

To ensure guaranteed collision-free motion, $f_{A|B} + f_{B|A} >= 1$. If an agent knows how much another will avoid collisions, they can know how much they should avoid collision. If a person knows that vehicles will not attempt to avoid collisions (i.e. $f_{car|person} = 0$), then people know they are entirely responsible for getting out of the way ($f_{person|car} = 1$).

Regarding the code itself, it has been rewritten to minimize branching code paths which ensures GPU performance is maintained, regardless of the proportion of people and autonomous vehicles in the simulation. The GPU is composed of many threads, much like multicore CPUs, though with many more threads. These threads are grouped into execution units called warps. A warp usually consists of 32 threads. If threads in a warp execute different code the other threads, some are masked out and remain idle while the branching code is executed, and hence reduce the performance of the code. The code is written to ensure both people and autonomous vehicles follow the same code path, and so no threads are idle for this reason, and performance is not affected by the inclusion, or proportion of autonomous vehicles.

4   Results

This section presents the results of two experiments. The first experiment is composed of two test cases to demonstrate the appearance and correctness of the model. The first test case is a 2-way crossing and the second test case is an 4-way crossing. The second experiment demonstrates the performance compared to the equivalent multi-core CPU version [29,44].

For the first experiment, all the test cases are set up in a similar way. Multiple associated start and end regions are chosen, such that people and vehicles are spawned in a start region with a target in an associated end region. Random spawn locations are chosen so that there is no overlap with other people within a certain time period based on person size and speed. Within a simulation, each agent has a goal location to aim for. The agent's velocity is in the direction of the goal location, scaled to the walking speed. Once an agent reaches the goal location they are removed from the simulation. Once all agents have reached their goal the simulation is ended. The avoidance responsibility values are set such that people are entirely responsible for avoiding collisions with the autonomous vehicles. This is mathematically represented as $f_{person|car} = 1$, $f_{car|person} = 0$.

The first test case was a 2-way crossing, with the two crowds attempting to pass amongst each other to reach their destination. Figure 2 shows the result of this. The second test case was a 4-way crossing, visualized in Fig. 3. Each crowd must navigate directly across the environment, causing avoidance of not only head-on agents, but also side-on. The 3D model of the vehicle is that of the "Pod", used by the Transport Systems Catapult [46].

The second experiment was designed to test the performance of the GPU implementation in comparison to the multi-core CPU implementation. Figure 4 shows the results that varying numbers of agents have on the frame time. Various test cases (e.g. 2-way and 4-way crossings) with different agent parameters were run, and the timings averaged between them. In this experiment no visualization was used so as to ensure the timings were due to the algorithm only. The GPU solution gives speed increases of up to 30 times compared to the multi-core CPU implementation. Results for the single-core CPU version are not given as for any sizeable number of agents the multi-core CPU implementation always outperforms the single-core CPU implementation. This is due to better utilization

Fig. 2. Visualization of 2,500 agents in Unreal. Two crowds navigate past each other, one heading from left to right and the other heading from right to left. Inset: an eye-level view of the simulation, taken at the same time

of the CPU device. The colored bars of Fig. 4 correspond to the primary (left) vertical axis, which uses a logarithmic scale. The relative time taken between the charts corresponds to the secondary (right) vertical axis, with linear scale. This result is the same that was found when simulating only people, as in the previous work of Charlton et al., using the same hardware [3]. This occurs because there is no computational difference between agents representing people or vehicles. On the GPU this results in the same code being executed, which maintains parallelism across the device and results in consistent performance regardless of the proportions of people and autonomous cars. Hence, the same performance between the proposed model and the previous work is maintained.

The results show that the speed increases proportionally to the number of agents. Greater relative speed-up occurs for even larger numbers of agents, but the time taken per frame is below real time. The GPU simulations ran at close to 30 frames a second (33ms per frame) for up to 5×10^5 agents. The CPU version performs better for smaller number of agents, with a crossover occurring at approximately 2×10^3 agents. This is due to the GPU device not being fully utilized for smaller simulations and the reduced throughput being outperformed by the CPU. The experiments were run on an NVIDIA GTX 970 GPU card with 4 GB dedicated memory and a 4-core/8-thread Intel i7-4790K with 16 GB RAM. The GPU was connected by PCI-E 2.0. The GPU software was developed with NVIDIA CUDA 8.0 on Windows 10. On the GPU tested, there was a limit on the amount of usable memory of 4 GB, which corresponded to approximately 5×10^5 agents. It is expected that relative performance increases will continue to be obtained for larger numbers of agents for the GPU implementation for GPUs

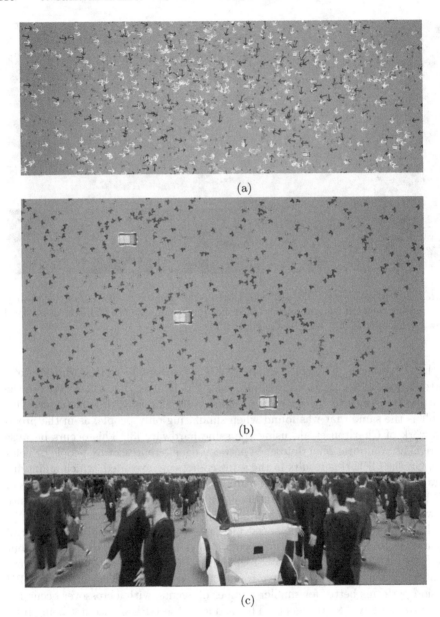

Fig. 3. Visualization of 2,500 agents in Unreal. Four crowds navigate past each other, two heading between left and right and two between top and bottom. a) Shows a zoomed-out view, with arrows showing the motion of each agent. b) shows a zoomed-in section of the above image. c) shows an eye-level view of the simulation

with larger memory capacity. For example a modern Tesla V100 with 32 GB of on-board RAM would support up to 4×10^6 agents.

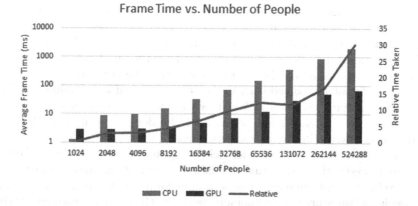

Fig. 4. Frame time (in ms) for multi-core CPU and GPU ORCA models with varying numbers of agents. Logarithmic scale on primary (left) vertical axis. Relative timing is given on the secondary (right) vertical axis, in linear scale. Simulation time only without visualization of the pedestrians.

5   Conclusions

We have introduced extensions to the previously presented GPU ORCA model [3] to allow for simulation of autonomous vehicles. The flexibility in being able to alter the amount of avoidance people and vehicles make with each other allows for simulating a wide variety of different cases. The experimental results shows were for agents taking full responsibility for avoiding colliding with vehicles, however the model contains the ability to alter this amount. This aids autonomous vehicle designers to assess the levels of responsibility to achieve safe operation within a crowded environment.

Our model is currently limited in the number of agents in the simulation size due to GPU memory. The models use large amounts of memory for storing the ORCA half-planes of each person. Memory usage could be reduced by considering fewer people. This would reduce the memory of each person but may result in less realistic motion with greater chance of collisions. A solution to the lack of memory is with Maxwell and later architectures, which can use managed memory [47] to page information from CPU to GPU on demand. This would allow for many more people to be simulated, up to the computer's system RAM capacity. It is expected that greater relative speedups between multi-core CPU and GPU will continue to be obtained for even larger amounts of simulated people.

It is expected that the more computationally expensive steering models would include more realistic motion such as side-stepping for pedestrians, more realistic densities, and less probability of collisions. In comparison, it is expected that the model in this paper would have greater performance and larger numbers of simulated people. An interesting extension would be to account for non-holonomic motion, such as the work of Alonso-Mora et al. [48] or acceleration, Berg et al. [44]. These models create extra linear constraints that arise due to the limitation in motion of the agent, and further constrain the possible motions. The simulation would then be composed of the ORCA model for pedestrians, and one of these extended models for vehicles, interacting and avoiding each other.

The current work involves writing the data from the simulation to a file before visualization using Unreal. The data is copied from the GPU to the CPU, then loaded into Unreal and copied back to the GPU in Unreal for visualization. This is expensive. Future work will look at how to use the Unreal engine to visualize a simulation as it is calculated, which could be done by sharing GPU buffer information between the simulation program and the Unreal Engine.

A further extension to this model includes the use of virtual reality hardware. Users are placed within the virtual simulation to navigate around simulated people and vehicles. This could function as training for people to become accustomed to being in the same area as autonomous vehicles. The use of a treadmill or other walking device that combines with virtual reality would also provide benefits. By physically walking, it would create stronger immersion in the simulation.

Acknowledgements. This research was supported by EPSRC grant "Accelerating Scientific Discovery with Accelerated Computing" (grant number EP/N018869/1), and by the Transport Systems Catapult, and the National Council of Science and Technology in Mexico (Consejo Nacional de Ciencia y Tecnología, CONACYT).

References

1. Barut, O., Haciomeroglu, M., Sezer, E.A.: Combining GPU-generated linear trajectory segments to create collision-free paths for real-time ambient crowds. Graph. Models **99**, 31–45 (2018)
2. Bleiweiss, A.: Multi agent navigation on the GPU. White paper, GDC, vol. 9 (2009)
3. Charlton, J., Gonzalez, L.R.M., Maddock, S., Richmond, P.: Fast simulation of crowd collision avoidance. In: Gavrilova, M., Chang, J., Thalmann, N.M., Hitzer, E., Ishikawa, H. (eds.) CGI 2019. LNCS, vol. 11542, pp. 266–277. Springer, Cham (2019). https://doi.org/10.1007/978-3-030-22514-8_22
4. Charlton, J., Maddock, S., Richmond, P.: Two-dimensional batch linear programming on the GPU. J. Parallel Distrib. Comput. **126**, 152–160 (2019)
5. Richmond, P.: Flame GPU technical report and user guide. Department of Computer Science Technical Report CS-11-03, University of Sheffield (2011)
6. Pettré, J., Kallmann, M., Lin, M.C.: Motion planning and autonomy for virtual humans. In: ACM SIGGRAPH 2008 Classes, SIGGRAPH 2008, New York, NY, USA, pp. 42:1–42:31. ACM (2008)
7. Pettré, J., Pelechano, N.: Introduction to Crowd Simulation. In: Bousseau, A., Gutierrez, D. (eds.) EG 2017 - Tutorials. The Eurographics Association (2017)
8. Thalmann, D.: Populating virtual environments with crowds. In: Proceedings of the 2006 ACM International Conference on Virtual Reality Continuum and Its Applications, VRCIA 2006, New York, NY, USA, p. 11. ACM (2006). Event-place: Hong Kong, China
9. Narain, R., Golas, A., Curtis, S., Lin, M.C.: Aggregate dynamics for dense crowd simulation. In: ACM SIGGRAPH Asia 2009 Papers, SIGGRAPH Asia 2009, New York, NY, USA, pp. 122:1–122:8. ACM (2009)

10. Fickett, M., Zarko, L.: GPU continuum crowds. CIS Final Project Final report, University of Pennsylvania (2007)
11. Helbing, D., Molnár, P.: Social force model for pedestrian dynamics. Phys. Rev. E **51**, 4282–4286 (1995)
12. Fiorini, P., Shiller, Z.: Motion planning in dynamic environments using velocity obstacles. Int. J. Robot. Res. **17**, 760–772 (1998)
13. Blue, V., Adler, J.: Emergent fundamental pedestrian flows from cellular automata microsimulation | request PDF. Transp. Res. Rec.: J. Transp. Res. Board **1644**, 29–36 (1998)
14. Blue, V., Adler, J.: Cellular automata microsimulation of bidirectional pedestrian flows. Transp. Res. Rec.: J. Transp. Res. Board **1678**, 135–141 (1999)
15. Schönfisch, B., de Roos, A.: Synchronous and asynchronous updating in cellular automata. Biosystems **51**, 123–143 (1999)
16. Karmakharm, T., Richmond, P.: Agent-based large scale simulation of pedestrians with adaptive realistic navigation vector fields. EG UK Theory Pract. Comput. Graph. **10**, 67–74 (2010)
17. Richmond, P., Romano, D.M.: A high performance framework for agent based pedestrian dynamics on GPU hardware. In: Proceedings of EUROSIS ESM, vol. 2008 (2008)
18. Abe,Y., Yoshiki, M.: Collision avoidance method for multiple autonomous mobile agents by implicit cooperation. In: Proceedings 2001 IEEE/RSJ International Conference on Intelligent Robots and Systems. Expanding the Societal Role of Robotics in the the Next Millennium (Cat. No.01CH37180), vol. 3, pp. 1207–1212, October 2001
19. Kluge, B., Prassler, E.: Recursive probabilistic velocity obstacles for reflective navigation. In: Yuta, S., Asama, H., Prassler, E., Tsubouchi, T., Thrun, S. (eds.) Field and Service Robotics: Recent Advances in Reserch and Applications. Springer Tracts in Advanced Robotics, pp. 71–79. Springer, Heidelberg (2006). https://doi.org/10.1007/10991459_8
20. Fulgenzi, C., Spalanzani, A., Laugier, C.: Dynamic obstacle avoidance in uncertain environment combining PVOs and occupancy grid. In: Proceedings 2007 IEEE International Conference on Robotics and Automation, Rome, Italy, pp. 1610–1616, IEEE, April 2007
21. Berg, J.V.D., Lin, M., Manocha, D.: Reciprocal Velocity Obstacles for real-time multi-agent navigation. In: IEEE International Conference on Robotics and Automation, ICRA 2008, pp. 1928–1935, May 2008
22. Guy, S.J., et al.: ClearPath: highly parallel collision avoidance for multi-agent simulation. In: Proceedings of the 2009 ACM SIGGRAPH/Eurographics Symposium on Computer Animation, SCA 2009, New York, NY, USA, pp. 177–187. ACM (2009)
23. He, L., Pan, J., Narang, S., Wang, W., Manocha, D.: Dynamic group behaviors for interactive crowd simulation. arXiv:1602.03623 [cs], February 2016
24. Yang, Z., Pan, J., Wang, W., Manocha, D.: Proxemic group behaviors using reciprocal multi-agent navigation. In: 2016 IEEE International Conference on Robotics and Automation (ICRA), pp. 292–297 (2016)
25. Best, A., Narang, S., Manocha, D.: Real-time reciprocal collision avoidance with elliptical agents. In: 2016 IEEE International Conference on Robotics and Automation (ICRA), pp. 298–305, IEEE (2016)

26. Hughes, R., Ondřej, J., Dingliana, J.: Holonomic collision avoidance for virtual crowds. In: Proceedings of the ACM SIGGRAPH/Eurographics Symposium on Computer Animation, SCA 2014, Aire-la-Ville, Switzerland, Switzerland, pp. 103–111, Eurographics Association (2014)

27. Wang, L., Li, Z., Wen, C., He, R., Guo, F.: Reciprocal collision avoidance for nonholonomic mobile robots. In: 2018 15th International Conference on Control, Automation, Robotics and Vision (ICARCV), pp. 371–376. IEEE (2018)

28. Huang, X., Zhou, L., Guan, Z., Li, Z., Wen, C., He, R.: Generalized reciprocal collision avoidance for non-holonomic robots. In: 2019 14th IEEE conference on industrial electronics and applications (ICIEA), pp. 1623–1628. IEEE (2019)

29. Snape, J.: Optimal Reciprocal Collision Avoidance (C++), March 2019. github.com/snape/RVO2. Original-date: 2013–06–25T03:11:32Z

30. Douthwaite, J.A., Zhao, S., Mihaylova, L.S.: Velocity obstacle approaches for multi-agent collision avoidance. Unmanned Syst. **7**(01), 55–64 (2019)

31. Seidel, R.: Small-dimensional linear programming and convex hulls made easy. Discrete Comput. Geomet. **6**(3), 423–434 (1991). https://doi.org/10.1007/BF02574699

32. Gogoll, J., Müller, J.F.: Autonomous cars: in favor of a mandatory ethics setting. Sci. Eng. Ethics **23**(3), 681–700 (2017)

33. Lin, P.: Why ethics matters for autonomous cars. In: Maurer, M., Gerdes, J., Lenz, B., Winner, H. (eds.) Autonomous Driving, pp. 69–85. Springer, Heidelberg (2016). https://doi.org/10.1007/978-3-662-45854-9_4

34. McBride, N.: The ethics of driverless cars. SIGCAS Comput. Soc. **45**, 179–184 (2016)

35. Althoff, M., Mergel, A.: Comparison of Markov chain abstraction and Monte Carlo simulation for the safety assessment of autonomous cars. IEEE Trans. Intell. Transp. Syst. **12**(4), 1237–1247 (2011)

36. Guo, J., Kurup, U., Shah, M.: Is it safe to drive? An overview of factors, metrics, and datasets for driveability assessment in autonomous driving. IEEE Trans. Intell. Transp. Syst. (2019)

37. Rasouli, A., Tsotsos, J.K.: Autonomous vehicles that interact with pedestrians: a survey of theory and practice. IEEE Trans. Intell. Transp. Syst. **21**, 900–918 (2019)

38. Schwarting, W., Pierson, A., Alonso-Mora, J., Karaman, S., Rus, D.: Social behavior for autonomous vehicles. Proc. Natl. Acad. Sci. **116**(50), 24972–24978 (2019)

39. Bonnefon, J.-F., Shariff, A., Rahwan, I.: The social dilemma of autonomous vehicles. Science **352**(6293), 1573–1576 (2016)

40. Pettersson, I., Karlsson, I.C.M.: Setting the stage for autonomous cars: a pilot study of future autonomous driving experiences. IET Intell. Transp. Syst. **9**, 694–701 (2015)

41. Boesch, P.M., Ciari, F.: Agent-based simulation of autonomous cars. In: 2015 American Control Conference (ACC), pp. 2588–2592. IEEE (2015)

42. Hörl, S.: Agent-based simulation of autonomous taxi services with dynamic demand responses. Proc. Comput. Sci. **109**, 899–904 (2017)

43. Zhang, W., Guhathakurta, S., Fang, J., Zhang, G.: Exploring the impact of shared autonomous vehicles on urban parking demand: An agent-based simulation approach. Sustain. Cities Soc. **19**, 34–45 (2015)

44. Berg, J.V.D., Snape, J., Guy, S.J., Manocha, D.: Reciprocal collision avoidance with acceleration-velocity obstacles. In: 2011 IEEE International Conference on Robotics and Automation, pp. 3475–3482, May 2011

45. Wang, Y., Davidson, A., Pan, Y., Wu, Y., Riffel, A., Owens, J.D.: Gunrock: a high-performance graph processing library on the GPU. arXiv:1501.05387 [cs], pp. 1–12 (2016)
46. Catapult, T.S.: Driverless Pods
47. Nvidia: Tuning CUDA Applications for Maxwell (2018)
48. Alonso-Mora, J., Breitenmoser, A., Beardsley, P., Siegwart, R.: Reciprocal collision avoidance for multiple car-like robots. In: 2012 IEEE International Conference on Robotics and Automation, pp. 360–366, May 2012

MagiPlay: An Augmented Reality Serious Game Allowing Children to Program Intelligent Environments

Evropi Stefanidi[1], Dimitrios Arampatzis[1], Asterios Leonidis[1(✉)],
Maria Korozi[1], Margherita Antona[1], and George Papagiannakis[1,2]

[1] Institute of Computer Science (ICS),
Foundation for Research and Technology – Hellas (FORTH), Heraklion, Greece
{evropi,arabatzis,leonidis,korozi,antona,
papagian}@ics.forth.gr
[2] Department of Computer Science, University of Crete, Heraklion, Greece

Abstract. A basic understanding of problem-solving and computational thinking is undoubtedly a benefit for all ages. At the same time, the proliferation of Intelligent Environments has raised the need for configuring their behaviors to address their users' needs. This configuration can take the form of programming, and coupled with advances in Augmented Reality and Conversational Agents, can enable users to take control of their intelligent surroundings in an efficient and natural manner. Focusing on children, who can greatly benefit by being immersed in programming from an early age, this paper presents an authoring framework in the form of an Augmented Reality serious game, named MagiPlay, allowing children to manipulate and program their Intelligent Environment. This is achieved through a handheld device, which children can use to capture smart objects via its camera and subsequently create rules dictating their behavior. An intuitive user interface permits players to combine LEGO-like 3D bricks as a part of the rule-based creation process, aiming to make the experience more natural. Additionally, children can communicate with the system via natural language through a Conversational Agent, in order to configure the rules by talking with a human-like agent, while the agent also serves as a guide/helper for the player, providing context-sensitive tips for every part of the rule creation process. Finally, MagiPlay enables networked collaboration, to allow parental and teacher guidance and support. The main objective of this research work is to provide young learners with a fun and engaging way to program their intelligent surroundings. This paper describes the game logic of MagiPlay, its implementation details, and discusses the results of a statistically significant evaluation conducted with end-users, i.e. a group of children of seven to twelve years old.

Keywords: Augmented Reality · Intelligent Environments · Chatbot
conversational agent · End user programming · Gamification

© Springer-Verlag GmbH Germany, part of Springer Nature 2020
M. L. Gavrilova et al. (Eds.): Trans. on Comput. Sci. XXXVII, LNCS 12230, pp. 144–169, 2020.
https://doi.org/10.1007/978-3-662-61983-4_9

1   Introduction

Children are immersed in the world of Mathematics upon entering school, beginning from simple additions and subtractions, and gradually but constantly adding to that knowledge. Hence, by the time they graduate, they already have years of training in mathematical thinking and problem-solving techniques, thus being able to absorb new related knowledge more efficiently. But what about programming? Is it not as important for children to be educated in programming techniques, and get acquainted with algorithmic thinking from a young age? With the spread of technology and its adoption in various aspects of everyday life, the understanding of computational thinking and problem solving is a benefit for all ages [1].

While some claim that it is never too late to start coding, even at an older age [2], it is argued that the earlier an individual learns programming and starts to develop algorithmic-like thinking, the better [3]. Having programming skills does not only refer to the actual act of coding, e.g. using textual tools and information, but also to having a basic understanding of a language's underlying computational logic, one of the most valued skills nowadays. At the same time, no age is too early to learn programming, as even younger children can utilize other means, such as symbols and blocks, to grasp the logic of coding [3]. For example, younger coders can use blocks depicting arrows to compose a sequence that will make an animal move towards a particular destination.

However, the coding learning aspect is not the only objective or benefit of computational thinking. Programming is becoming increasingly necessary in various aspects of life, not only in the sense that more people are learning how to program, but also in that new technologies require people to possess programming skills to control and configure them. However, the range of programming skills can vary greatly, thus restricting the capabilities of those with zero or limited knowledge to enjoy the benefits and be able to manipulate these new technologies without an expert's assistance; for example the expensiveness and complexity of Smart homes technologies [4] has limited their embrace by users who are not technically proficient [5]. Especially regarding intelligent spaces, which contain smart objects, the need to manage their behavior by everyone, and not just by programming experts, is becoming more and more apparent, as by 2020 their installed base is forecast to grow to almost 31 billion worldwide[1]. To that end, intuitive End-user Development (EUD) interfaces are necessary to allow everyone -not just programming experts- to manage intelligent spaces [5, 6], including residents, who must be able to configure their own technologically-enhanced houses [7]. Thus, a new type of programming environment is emerging, allowing non-technical users to specify their own logic over the simple, yet effective trigger-action model [8–14]. In particular, EUD has attracted the interest of many researchers, especially in the domain of domestic life, where smart homes [15] have become the most popular testbed for creating automated tasks based on the inhabitants' preferences, needs and daily routines. Nevertheless, very few approaches exist to-date allowing children to effectively program their surroundings.

---

[1] https://www.statista.com/statistics/471264/iot-number-of-connected-devices-worldwide.

Advances in the fields of Augmented Reality (AR), Conversational Interfaces and Agents could be coupled with the aforementioned popular "if *trigger*, then *action*" programming paradigm [16], along with tangible programming (which utilizes physical blocks) for constructing programs [17], to allow children to control digital "everyday objects", in a fun and engaging manner. As studies have shown [18–20], enabling children to program their physical surroundings constitutes an important subject, since the negotiation with the physical world plays a critical role in children's early cognitive development; children can learn from building with blocks, drawing on paper, and even building make-believe worlds from boxes and bags [21]. Beyond world understanding, children can be also implicitly introduced to the concept and principles of programming, while applying gamification principles increases their motivation to remain engaged and overall performance [22].

At the same time, collaboration can bring in numerous benefits. In particular, online collaboration provides the opportunity for sharing of resources, accessibility of multilevel interaction, and higher order thinking activities [23]. Moreover, according to Lev Vygotsky's theory of the Zone of Proximal Development, there is a difference between what a learner can achieve without help, and what they can achieve with guidance and encouragement from a skilled partner [24].

In [25] we presented BricklAyeR, a platform that allows non-programmers to collaborate and configure IEs. It fuses uniquely the concepts of AR and interactive virtual characters [26, 27] with situated 3D programming, as users create rules dictating the behavior of smart devices by connecting 3D virtual programming bricks (using the metaphor of tangible blocks). With the exploitation of tangible programing, the rule creation process becomes more direct and less abstract, and thus more appealing in the eyes of children [28] (e.g. easier to understand, remember, explain). Transferring the metaphor of tangible programming into the virtual world (through AR) further enhances its benefits (e.g. ease of use, expressiveness), while minimizing (or eliminating) many of its drawbacks; for example, smaller parts of large brick compositions can be represented as single blocks in order to save space and can be expanded on demand [17].

BricklAyeR [25], reports a preliminary version of this work; in the context of this paper MagiPlay was developed, focusing on children, education, and gamification. Built on top of BricklAyeR, it allows children to define the behavior of smart artifacts in their surrounding IE using a portable device, e.g. a tablet. This is achieved via a novel a hybrid approach that enables rule-based programming with the use of 3D LEGO-like bricks and spatial computing. Rather than connecting the bricks in the physical world, this is done in AR on top of a virtual baseplate. This approach presents an innovative interaction paradigm, providing solutions to various challenges of previous 3D and tangible programming approaches (e.g. 3D bricks can easily be moved, scaled and reused to overcome physical space requirements since the entire augmented "world" is the user's canvas). Moreover, via AR, the artifact collection task is simplified, by enabling children to easily explore their physical environment and directly select the object they need -instead of having to browse through extensive lists. The latter becomes especially important in emerging intelligent spatial computing environments that include a plethora of IoT devices. Moreover, by being immersed, children can get a better understanding of all the available smart artifacts, their actions, and their locations. Finally, MagiPlay inherently supports networked collaboration, so that parents, teachers, or any skilled user can assist the child by means of remote help, while a Conversational Agent makes the experience more natural by enabling interaction via natural language.

The main contribution of this paper is the description of this novel serious game that permits children to program Intelligent Environments. The characterization as novel, stems from the fact that very few research approaches (as described in the Related Work section) equip children with appropriate tools enabling end-user development. In more detail, the paper provides information regarding (i) **the gameplay** that enables the creation of IF-THEN rules dictating the behavior of smart artifacts, and subsequently fosters the cultivation of algorithmic thinking, (ii) **the interaction paradigm** that fuses interaction in AR, tangible interaction and touchscreen interaction, (iii) **the implementation** that employs state-of-the-art technologies, and (iv) the results of a **user-based evaluation** with the participation of 10 children.

The following sections present: a discussion of background theory and related work, the high-level requirements of MagiPlay, a description of the game logic and the interaction paradigm, the implementation details, the findings of the user-based evaluation, and a discussion regarding future work.

2 Background Theory and Related Work

End-User development has already been applied in various domains, including commercial software where users can incorporate their own functionality (e.g. recording macros in word processors, defining e-mail filters). Moreover, the proliferation of web-enabled devices and services in domains such as the smart home [15], has led to the application of various programming principles that enable non-technical users to create complex automation scenarios using sequence-based approaches [10] or if-this-then-that rules (e.g. IFTTT[2], Zapier[3]). The idea of providing end-users with suitable tools to be able to program and configure their surroundings, has already been discussed in literature [5–7, 9, 29], and the programming technique of "if trigger, then action" is a step towards that direction. This technique can express most desired behaviors, while at the same time permit inexperienced users to quickly learn to program and average users to successfully create rules with multiple triggers and actions [16]. Recently, this type of programming has been applied in the domain of Ambient Intelligence (AmI), where users can create simple "if trigger, then action" rules to specify the behavior of intelligent spaces [30] and classrooms [31].

From an interaction perspective, AR is extensively used in EUD systems to increase task-related intuitiveness [32] by providing a more natural interface [33] that enables users to interact straightforwardly with spatial information [34]. For example, the Reality Editor [35] and Smarter Objects [36] allow programming and operating physical objects by associating them with virtual ones, while Hammer [37] and RPAR

---

[2] https://ifttt.com/discover.

[3] https://zapier.com.

[38] enable intuitive robot programming by non-skilled operators. Additionally, the integration of AR in collaborative settings, establishes a common location awareness [39] for all participants.

Addressing the subject of gamification, the number of games that have been developed with the aim to facilitate the learning of programming is anything but small; from creating graphics with Logo [20] to interactive stories with Alice [40] and games with Scratch [41]. The task of learning how to program includes the acquisition and development of several complex skills, which underlines the importance of high motivation of learners in the process [42]. Games may allow interactive entertained and creative experiences, and have therefore been used as motivational strategies in introductory programming teaching [43].

Regarding Conversational Agents (CAs) and the use of Natural Language Programming, recent technological advances have made it possible for users to interact with smart devices using spoken language in a natural way, like engaging in a conversation with a person [44]. Chatbot technology can be used to create Conversational Interfaces, where the user's input is interpreted using pattern matching, and the system's output is provided by templates. Recently, Chatbot technology has been extended by incorporating methods for interpreting commands to a device. A CA would be appropriate to support a player during a game, in a seamless and natural manner by simply talking to them. The need for such support is outlined in [42], where in their analysis and categorization of games, the authors state that no games were found that support learning during the gameplay experience, only some that give feedback after the mission ends. They mention that if the game provides support while the learner is engaged in the task, it will help the student reflect about their errors in the context they happen [45].

There are several works published about games developed to support computer programming learning [42]. By using games as an educational mean, the aim is to motivate students towards learning activities, shorten the time of transition between theory and practice, and bring together abstract concepts and concrete activities. Focusing on children programming, in [21] a wizard-of-Oz prototype was used in order to empower children to program their own Story Room, while storytelling was already explored in the beginning of the last decade, in [46]. Moreover, [47] presents an educational programming application for smart home programming, addressed to older children (12–13 years old). Utilizing Google's Blockly [48], it provides its users with a block-based, visual programming interface, effectively allowing them to program by themselves.

A plethora of other educational games exist, neatly categorized in [42], which classifies them by type, and highlights the programming skills and topics supported by them. Though noteworthy, these approaches do not provide children with a comprehensive game-like environment, allowing them to build rules to program Intelligent Environments in a playful and engaging manner. Therefore, with respect to the related work, our approach delivers MagiPlay, a novel serious game, enabling children to effectively program in AR their surrounding objects and Intelligent Environments, in a playful manner. MagiPlay uniquely fuses the concepts of interacting in AR, 3D block-based and tangible programming, and programming of smart artifacts, so as to deliver an intuitive user interface, which is engaging and fun for children to use. Moreover, it promotes creativity by actively engaging children in building their own interactive stories [21, 46], rather than being passive participants.

3 High Level Requirements of Our AR Spatial Computing Authoring Framework

This section presents the high-level functional requirements that MagiPlay satisfies, which have been solidified through an extensive literature review and an iterative requirements elicitation process, based on multiple collection methods such as brainstorming, focus groups, observation, and scenario building.

FR-1. The rule-creation process should be intuitive and easy to follow by young children (7 to 12 years old).

FR-2. In terms of interaction, the rule-creation process should follow the metaphor of tangible programming, while at the same time employ Augmented Reality to enhance user experience.

FR-3. Players should be able to discover and collect smart artifacts from their physical Intelligent Environment. Not all smart artifacts in the IE should be available for manipulation through MagiPlay for safety reasons (e.g., young children should not be allowed to program the oven).

FR-4. Players should be able to browse the collected artifacts and use them in the rule creation process in order to dictate the behavior of the Intelligent Environment. Children should have the ability to save a rule and later continue where they left off.

FR-5. MagiPlay should notify the players of any syntactic errors in their rule, so as to allow them to easily correct them.

FR-6. Upon the creation of a rule, players should be able to simulate it (either in the virtual or in the physical world), in order to experience its effects. During simulation, users should be able to view which part of the rule is taking effect at a given moment, as well as the smart artifact whose behavior is subsequently being influenced.

FR-7. MagiPlay should permit players to deploy the created rules into the Intelligent Environment. During deployment, children should specify the execution details of a rule; for example, schedule its recurrence (i.e. always, every night, on Mondays).

FR-8. Players should be able to collaborate (if they wish to) in every step of the rule creation process. In more details, they should be able to connect with other players and work together to collect artifacts in the IE, build the rule and simulate it.

4 AR Serious Game Dynamics, Mechanics, Components

MagiPlay is an AR serious game that allows children to use their handheld devices (e.g. tablets) to manipulate the behavior of the smart artifacts inside their Intelligent Environment. The goal of the game is to help children program their surroundings by creating simple IF-THEN rules and cultivate their algorithmic thinking at the same time in a fun and engaging way. Algorithmic thinking refers to logical, sequenced processes that together create a desired result, having its origins in mathematics [49]. In its simplest form, an algorithm is a method for solving a problem in a step-by-step manner. Thus, children can learn about algorithmic problem solving whenever they discover a set of steps that can be completed to achieve a task. In addition, these steps should integrate unusual contingencies (using conditional, or "if" statements) and repetitions (using loops, or "while" statements) [50]. Endorsing those principles, MagiPlay promotes computational thinking as will be later presented in this section, in the description of the different modes the game offers.

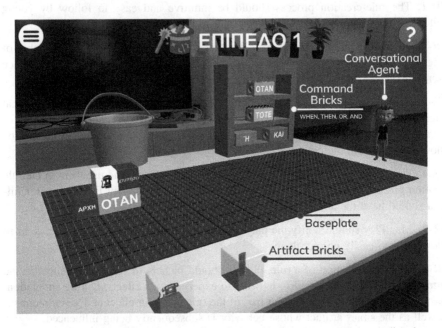

Fig. 1. Snapshot of our AR spatial computing rule-based creation process (in-game literals were in Greek to accommodate evaluation purposes with children)

MagiPlay is actively deployed in the "Intelligent Home" simulation space located at the Ambient Intelligence Facility (http://ami.ics.forth.gr/) within the FORTH-ICS campus. Inside this environment, everyday activities are enhanced with the use of innovative interaction techniques, Artificial Intelligence, sophisticated middleware, commercial equipment and technologically augmented custom-made artifacts [30, 51]. In its current version, MagiPlay supports the manipulation of several artifacts residing in the living room of the "Intelligent Home": i.e. (i) smart tabletop lamps, (ii) a smart TV, (iii) a smart door, (iv) an IP phone, and (v) a smart speaker.

MagiPlay follows the trigger-action paradigm [16], enabling children to connect services, devices and artifacts by creating simple IF-THEN rules. However, not all smart artifacts in the IE can be manipulated by children, e.g. a smart oven, for safety reasons. Every rule is composed of one or multiple triggers and one or multiple actions (e.g. when TRIGGER then ACTION). In more detail, the trigger refers to an event that occurs, e.g. the door opens, while the action is the subsequent response that should happen in that case, e.g. the light turns on. Despite the limitations stemming from using simple IF-THEN rules, which seem to hinder the expressivity of the programs that can be created, according to [52], "a task specific language with appropriate tool support provides an ideal environment for users to create their own applications".

The rule creation process takes place over a designated, LEGO-like, brick building baseplate (Fig. 1), which is superimposed -via Augmented Reality- on any flat surface of the physical environment (e.g. a coffee table). On top of that baseplate players can combine 3D virtual blocks (i.e. bricks), in order to create the desired rules and define how several smart artifacts respond to contextual stimuli (e.g. user actions, time-based conditions, environmental factors). Espousing that the metaphor of building blocks can be beneficial for novice programmers, and in particular children, who in their majority are familiar with LEGO-like structures, such a visualization was selected so as to resemble the process of connecting physical bricks while building concrete three dimensional structures; moreover, such visualization offers easy access to the entire programming vocabulary as well as a graphical overview of the control flow [53]. For example, it allows the player to view at a glance all the available bricks (e.g. WHEN, THEN), while giving them the ability to have a holistic view of what they are building (i.e. alternative execution paths across different axes).

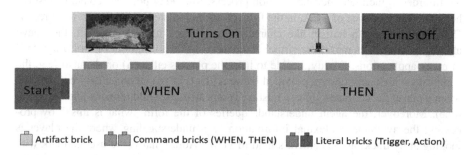

Fig. 2. Diagram depicting the creation of the rule "WHEN the TV *turns on*, THEN the LAMP turns off" mechanic

On the right side of the baseplate a 3D bookcase resides, containing the available command bricks (i.e. WHEN, THEN, OR, AND), which are at the player's disposal at any time. The front side of the baseplate is reserved to host the 3D glass bricks that enclose the smart artifacts that players can manipulate and use in the rule under-creation (i.e. artifact bricks). When building a rule, 3D command bricks can be placed next to each other, while the connection between a command and an artifact brick is carried out by stacking the artifact on top of the command brick. Consider the following rule: WHEN the TV turns on, THEN turn off the lights (Fig. 2). In this case, a WHEN command brick is connected with a THEN command brick, while the artifact brick representing the TV is placed on top of one of these command bricks. A rule can entail multiple triggers and multiple actions, e.g. WHEN the living room door opens OR WHEN the kitchen door opens, THEN dim the bedroom lights AND THEN turn off the bedroom speakers (Fig. 3). Namely, in the trigger part of the rule, OR/AND command bricks can be used by placing a WHEN command brick next to each one, while in the action part, AND bricks are followed by adjacent THEN bricks (OR bricks are not supported in the action part of the rule, since this does not make sense in our context).

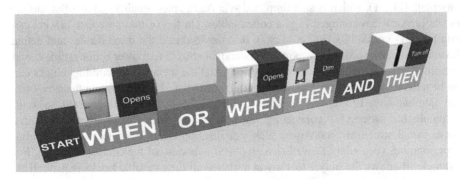

Fig. 3. Representation in 3D of a rule containing both multiple triggers and multiple actions.

In order to facilitate the rule creation process, MagiPlay provides context-sensitive help with the guidance of a CA, in the form of a 3D animated character, named Freddy. Communicating with human-like characters feels more natural; after all, they have already been used as narrators, virtual audiences and demonstrators of tool usage [54] in many applications. Freddy, is able to help the players either (i) on demand (e.g. the child asks which services are provided by an artifact) or (ii) automatically by inferring when a player is "confused" (e.g. a mistake is repeated, the child remains idle for a long time). Moreover, the agent understands queries of the form "what is this?" by processing the available contextual information (e.g. understanding where the player is looking at by tracking the camera's field of view). Additionally, the user can talk with Freddy in order to configure a rule; for instance, in the middle of the rule creation process, players can ask the agent to do something that they would otherwise have to do by interacting with the screen, like "select the turn on action for the living room lamp on the left".

MagiPlay offers four (4) gaming modes, which are described below:

Mode 1: Follow the Game Plot Mode
In this mode (Fig. 1), players have to complete a series of levels by carrying out simple programming tasks. In more detail, for each level, Freddy either dictates a specific rule that must by created (e.g. create the rule 'WHEN the phone rings THEN the speakers turn off'), or specifies an objective that the player must find out how to fulfill (e.g. create a rule to ensure that 'when you study in your bedroom major distractions are eliminated to keep you focused'). The latter in particular, promotes the cultivation of problem-solving skills by presenting an abstract form of the problem and expecting the child to find the solution. Thus, development of algorithmic thinking is achieved, since in both cases children are expected to discover a set of steps that need to be followed to complete the required task [50].

Levels increase in complexity as they advance, and require the collection of new (i.e. previously unavailable) artifacts. For example, the first level could require the creation of a simple trigger-action rule utilizing the smart TV and a smart lamp (i.e. WHEN the TV turns on, THEN turn off the lamp), while the second level could introduce the smart projector artifact, and require a rule including the "OR" operator in the trigger part (i.e. WHEN the TV turns on OR the projector turns on, THEN turn off the lamp).

The process of collecting an artifact (Fig. 4) requires the players to move freely about their surroundings, find the required physical artifact and capture an image of it, using the camera of their device. When directing the camera towards a real-world object, the respective software component recognizes it and creates a glass brick bearing an easily recognizable image of it. As soon as a player "collects" an artifact, it gets unlocked and placed into the game inventory and in front of the baseplate, so as to be within reach when needed. Artifacts "hidden" in the player's inventory can be accessed at any time; a player can get detailed information regarding their capabilities (i.e. triggering events, available actions) and use them as desired.

A level completes when the player has collected all the necessary artifacts and has appropriately combined them with command bricks on the baseplate to form the required rule. In case of errors, Freddy outlines the problem to the player (e.g. missing a THEN block), so that they can fix it. Given that the rule is syntactically correct, the player is awarded with the respective experience points (based on its difficulty) and can then choose to simulate and/or deploy the rule (mode 3).

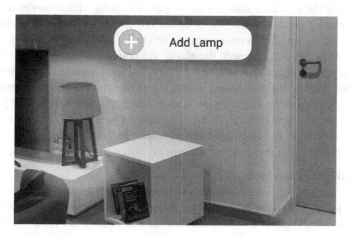

Fig. 4. Snapshot of the artifact collection process. The lamp and door artifacts are highlighted to inform the player that they can be collected.

Mode 2: Free Exploration Mode

In this mode, children can freely interact with all unlocked artifacts of the environment in order to build rules of their preference, and then simulate or deploy them (mode 3). While in this mode, players cannot unlock new artifacts, but they are rewarded with a limited amount of experience points for creating syntactically correct rules. This allows for a stress and goal-free environment, where children can experiment without the pressure of achieving a specific goal in order to advance the game. Nonetheless, given that MagiPlay aims to encourage algorithmic thinking, appropriate user guidance is provided via the Validity Checker (Sect. 5.2) to ensure that, even without the explicit moderation of the previous mode, children can create syntactically correct rules that exploit the unlocked artifacts.

Mode 3: Simulation and Deployment Mode

After the creation of a rule (via modes 1 or 2), players can simulate it in order to physically experience their effects, before actually deploying it. Simulation and debugging of rules have already been addressed in studies regarding trigger-action rules [55, 56], enabling end-users to understand whether their rules behave as desired and without conflicts. In the case of MagiPlay, simulation currently focuses on enabling children to see first-hand what they have accomplished so far in a sandboxed environment, without allowing the new rule to mingle with any other rules already installed in the target environment. MagiPlay enables simulation by interacting: (i) either with the physical objects of the environment (e.g. opening the door), (ii) or with the artificial objects of the virtual environment (e.g. open the virtual door through the tablet device), (iii) or with a combination of the two.

In more detail, the following combinations are available: (i) virtual-to-virtual: artificially trigger a rule and view its effects virtually through the screen, (ii) virtual-to-physical: virtually trigger a rule and view its effects on the physical environment or (iii) physical-to-virtual: physically manipulate devices to trigger a rule and view its effects virtually through their screen. Consider the following virtual-to-virtual example of a rule dictating that when the TV is turned on, the lights should be dimmed; the player, while in the simulation mode, can tap on the TV artifact and turn it on from the respective menu option. As a result, the player will notice that the lights in their virtual environment dim, without this affecting its physical surrounding environment. After verifying that the rule has the desired effect, the player can immediately deploy it.

Regarding deployment, players must decide whether a rule will run (i) just once, (ii) during a specific time period (e.g. for the next two hours), or (iii) always. As soon as a rule is deployed, the Intelligent Environment integrates it, and from that point onward, is able to adapt its behavior accordingly when the rule gets triggered.

Mode 4: Collaboration Mode

MagiPlay inherently supports collaboration, allowing for a multi-user experience. The importance for collaboration when playing educational games, especially in the home context [57], is highlighted by the research described in [58] and [59], which suggest that additional human support is always beneficial when someone plays a game, since teams achieve goals more effectively.

In the case of MagiPlay, parents, teachers, or other users can connect to the game (modes 1 & 2) and provide support to the child (i.e. remote pair programming). We call *session* an instance of the game, running on one or more tablets, in which one or more players are connected, and *workspace* the physical space (e.g. desk, coffee table, kitchen countertop, floor) on which the brick building baseplate is placed for the current session. Thus, adult players can connect to an active session and view the same workspace as the child-player, and actively help them when they require assistance. In more detail, the "external" users can view the baseplate in real-time, along with the available 3D programmable bricks, and make changes. For example, if an external player connects two programming bricks, the child will also view that composition in the baseplate, and vice versa.

5 MagiPlay Implementation

MagiPlay combines different technologies in order to deliver an immersive collaborative platform, where the player can interact with physical programmable artifacts in an AR environment in order to dictate the behavior of an IE. The implementation of the User Interface is based on Apple's ARKit[4] and Unity[5]. The first is an advanced AR platform that recognizes planes (e.g. tables) in the environment and allows to dock objects on the recognized areas. The latter is a cross-platform game engine, which supports ARKit, and simplifies the process of creating and handling 3D scenes.

5.1   The Infrastructure Behind MagiPlay

LECTOR
LECTOR [31] is a framework that takes advantage of the ambient facilities already existing in IEs in order to identify when the users need help or support and intervene to improve their quality of life. It observes either human- or artifact-oriented behaviors (SENSE), identifies whether they require actions (THINK), and intervenes (ACT) accordingly—when deemed necessary. It follows the trigger-action model [16, 60], which has been in the spotlight as a form of programming Intelligent Environments, using simple "if then" rules. LECTOR introduces a three (3) step process for connecting behaviors with interventions. The first step is to define a behavior, the next step is to describe the conditions under which the behavior becomes a trigger, and the last step is to connect it with an intervention (action).

Based on that framework, MagiPlay offers players five different types of bricks to create rules: a) command bricks: they represent the available coding commands that can be used within the trigger-action programming principle (i.e. WHEN, THEN, AND, OR, IF), b) artifact bricks: they represent the smart objects of the IE, c) behavior bricks: they represent half-formed rules containing only the trigger part (behavior), d) intervention bricks: they represent half-formed rules containing only the action part (intervention), e) complete rule bricks: they represent a complete rule, and f) literal bricks: they are generated when an artifact brick is connected to a command brick and they represent either the exact value that will trigger the condition of the rule (e.g. door opens) or the action that the artifact will take (e.g. turn the light on). Thus, users can create reusable trigger and action rules. These different types of bricks can be seen collectively in Fig. 5.

---

[4] https://developer.apple.com/arkit/.

[5] https://unity3d.com/.

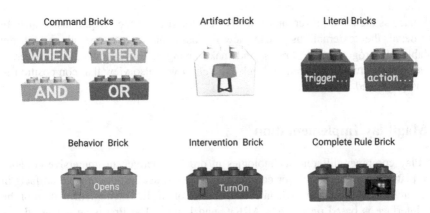

Fig. 5. The different types of programming bricks available in MagiPlay

ParlAmI

ParlAmI [30] is a multimodal conversational interface (CI) powered by LECTOR. It introduces a hybrid approach that combines natural language understanding (NLU) with semantic reasoning and service-oriented engineering so as to deliver a multimodal CI that assists its users in defining the behavior of Intelligent Environments. Particularly, it offers an alternative easy-to-use approach toward generating such rules (especially for novice users with little or no programming experience) through conversing in natural language with a context-aware intelligent virtual agent (i.e. chatbot). This is the framework based on which, Freddy was created.

AmI-Solertis

AmI-Solertis [61] is a framework allowing users to create behavior scenarios in the context of ambient intelligence, by delivering a scripting mechanism that can dynamically adapt the execution flow and govern the "high-level business logic" (i.e. behavior) of the Intelligent Environment, as well as a complete suite of tools allowing management, programming, testing, and monitoring of all the individual artifacts (i.e. services, hardware modules, software components). AmI-Solertis enables the creation of programs called AmI scripts, which constitute software agents who dictate how the technologically-enhanced environment will react in contextual stimuli (e.g. physical aspects, users, current activities) [62].

The main goal of MagiPlay is to allow children to program their environment, and this requires an infrastructure that is able to communicate with smart artifacts and manage them. Hence, the AmI-Solertis platform is appropriate for enabling the low-level management and configuration of the behavior of Intelligent Environments. It is used in multiple parts of MagiPlay; particularly the interaction with the programmable artifacts requires a lot of data (i.e. location, description, available triggers and actions and parameters, images of the actual artifact) and most of them are harvested from it. AmI-Solertis only provides the available triggers and actions of an artifact, while being agnostic about the physical artifact.

5.2   The Software Infrastructure of MagiPlay

This Section presents in detail the software infrastructure of MagiPlay, presented in Fig. 6 below.

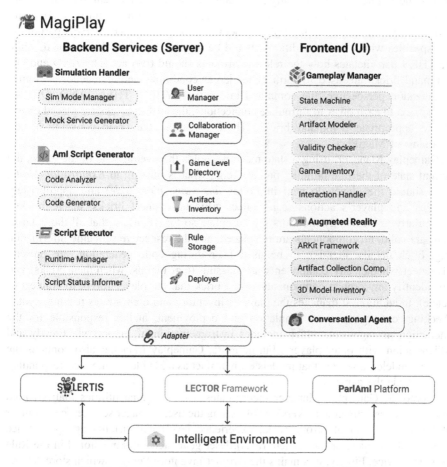

Fig. 6. Overview of the high-level architecture of MagiPlay

Artifact Collection Component

In order to detect the artifacts in the Intelligent Environment, MagiPlay uses a fusion of information regarding their position and physical form and appearance, collected from AmI-Solertis using the Artifact Inventory service. More specifically, images of objects are used to create a Machine Learning Model in the 3D Model Inventory in order to achieve object recognition through the handheld device's camera [63]. In addition to object recognition, we use the positional data from the device in order to identify where the player is looking at with their device, and in conjunction with the location data provided for each artifact through AmI-Solertis, MagiPlay determines if the player is possibly looking at a specific artifact.

Gameplay Manager

The actual game logic of MagiPlay is implemented by its Gameplay Manager (i.e. its main game engine). A rule in reality articulates a conditional statement in the following form: WHEN (trigger+) THEN (action+), represented by a pair of WHEN and THEN command bricks and multiple artifact bricks in between. The WHEN part of the rule specifies which exact conditions should be met for the rule to be executed, while the THEN part dictates how the relevant artifacts should (re-) act. The AND and OR command bricks are used to form either larger conditions and/or reactions. From a visualization perspective, the command bricks (i.e. WHEN, THEN, AND, OR) are placed next to each other to formulate connections; the artifact bricks are placed on top of the appropriate command bricks. These constitute the basic conventions and invariants of MagiPlay.

Gameplay Manager, using a state machine, holds the overall state of the game, the current state of the rule building process (e.g., what is missing in *Exploration Mode*, what should the player do next in *Follow the game plot mode*) and appropriately handles any player's actions (e.g. collect artifacts, connect bricks, delete bricks). Particularly, it constantly monitors the baseplate so to: (i) ensure that all the connections are valid, no components are misplaced, and the respective semantic information (e.g. brick details, literals), to be used later during code generation, are present, (ii) detect whether any components are missing (e.g. literals, when/then bricks) and (iii) identify any orphan components (e.g. a brick that the player forgot to connect or delete). In addition, it manages the player's inventory and orchestrates parsing, syntax checking, code generation, simulation and deployment, and is responsible for the interaction management, which includes instrumentation of support via Freddy and collaboration with other players. Furthermore, Gameplay Manager also contains the artifact modeler, a service that models each artifact as a 3D block with a corresponding image inside the game.

Moreover, Gameplay Manager incorporates a set of game utilities that: (i) hold information regarding the players' profile, using the user manager service, (e.g. number of hints asked and of errors made, experience level) and (ii) manage persistence (storage of complete or incomplete rules). User generated rules are stored in the Rule Storage Service. Finally, it contains the Artifact Inventory Service, which stores all the needed metadata for the artifacts, in order to be able to use them in game and generate valid AmI-Solertis behavioral scripts. For each artifact, the following data are obtained from AmI-Solertis: (i) the service name, (ii) the context and (iii) the function names for the events and triggers of each artifact, while data about an artifact's availability for each player (e.g. the oven may be available to older children and unavailable to the younger ones) is handled internally by MagiPlay itself.

Finally, Gameplay Manager contains the Validity Checker that actively: i) assesses how the user progresses with the creation process in conjunction with data received from the Game Level Directory which stores the rules for each level of the "Follow the game plot" mode, ii) validates that the rule generates well-formed executable code (i.e. without missing arguments) and iii) evaluates the components of the rule that is being created and warns the user for potential logical errors (e.g. use the same component in the trigger and action part of the rule) or conflicts (e.g. duplicate rules, rules with the same triggers, but different actions). For example, if the user creates the following rule "WHEN the lights are ON, THEN the lights should turn-off", then MagiPlay will warn about the use of the "lights" component in both part of the rule; currently, MagiPlay, only issues warnings, since its fully dynamic nature does not permit semantic validation or detection of logical inconsistencies (e.g. detect that the above rule will always turn-off the lights, as soon as another rule turns them on).

The AmI Script Generator

In order to be able to run the generated code from the 3D programming bricks, MagiPlay takes advantage of the AmI-Solertis ecosystem. Each rule is handled as an AmI-Solertis behavioral script, which, following the software-as-a-service model, constitutes a program that defines the high-level behavior of the Intelligent Environment. To do so, it uses any of the available intelligent services, while at the same time it is considered a new service that can be reused by other components. This module generates a behavioral script given a JSON file that depicts a rule (i.e., describes it by including the selected artifacts, actions, triggers and connections between those bricks. The code analyzer inspects and interprets the attributes of that file so as to generate a detailed intermediate description designating the actual services and their functions to be used. The code generator processes that intermediate definition and creates an executable script which adheres to the principles of an AmI-Script, allowing for usage of the AmI-Solertis platform and infrastructure. This simplifies a process that would otherwise be quite complicated. Upon successful generation, the script can either be used to simulate the rule or be deployed in the environment using the corresponding AmI-Solertis services.

The Execution Service

The Execution Service uses the deployment and execution monitor services of AmI-Solertis, which are responsible for deploying and executing behavioral scripts, in order to run the behavior script that corresponds to the created rule. MagiPlay oversees the execution process through the Runtime Manager. In addition, the execution service adds an artificial delay between each action to improve the user experience of the game, since otherwise the actions would run instantly by default, and the user would not experience the process of executing the rule. Moreover, whenever a function of a service is called or a response is received regarding an action, the Script Status Informer service sends a feedback message about the state of the execution to the running game session, which is used to visually present to the user the state of the execution.

Simulation Handler

The Simulation Handler is responsible for the simulation aspects of a created rule. The different simulation modes (e.g. virtual-to-virtual, virtual-to-physical, physical-to-virtual) are modeled in the Sim Model Manager service. In particular, depending on the simulation mode, the Mock Service Generator instantiates the necessary mock services (i.e. artificial services that impersonate smart artifacts or services and mimic their operation) using the appropriate utilities of AmI-Solertis and the AmITest framework [64] so as to allow MagiPlay to simulate an AmI Script (e.g. trigger events, interact with smart artifacts).

Deployer Service

The Deployer service is responsible for the deployment of a created rule. It takes advantage of the AmI-Solertis DevOps infrastructure (e.g. Software Packager, Deployer, Executor) and serves as a bridge to MagiPlay. MagiPlay uses this service as a black box that encapsulates the necessary logic to configure, deploy and execute an AmI Script in the Intelligent Environment.

Freddy the Conversational Agent

In order to create the virtual character (i.e. Freddy) that is used as the CA in our platform, and then import and use it in our Unity project, the Adobe Fuse[6] 3D modeling application was used. The 3D model was then uploaded to Mixamo[7], an online character animation service, for rigging, and for creating the desired animations for the character. Moreover, the model produced included some basic blendshapes, also known as morph target animations, which allowed us to animate the face of the character and achieve lip synchronization while speaking.

Regarding the infrastructure behind the character's ability to speak, the framework which enabled the ParlAmI platform is used. That is, the user's input is processed by the ParlAmI analysis pipeline [65], which then provides the output that controls what the CA should say or do at each moment. For example, if the user asks for help, the platform recognizes the intent of the user (i.e. ask for guidance), and the corresponding action script is activated for the character. Moreover, the use of ParlAmI facilitates the configuration, via the Agent, of certain parts of a rule, as was mentioned in the Game Description. Namely, if during rule creation the user asks the agent to "select the turn on action for the living room lamp on the left", the system understands the following intents: (i) configure part of a rule, (ii) set the action of the current rule being built, and finally that (iii) the action should be to "turn on the living room lamp on the left". This intent classification and extraction is made possible through RASA NLU[8], an open source Python library for building conversational software that is used to detect the entities in the input sentence as well as the intention behind it, which is used in ParlAmI for that purpose.

Collaboration Component

MagiPlay can be used by multiple users in real time who can collaborate and build rules together. This is achieved by following best practices when developing an application that allows communication across different devices and real time data exchanging. In more detail, a session synchronization service is used when a workspace is shared between two or more users and is responsible for their synchronization. From a technical perspective, it collects, in real time, any data needed for the workspace (i.e. programming blocks that are being used, real time position in the scene, status of each block) and then transmits that data to any other user that is in the same session, in order to get the same view of the shared workspace.

---

[6] https://www.adobe.com/gr_en/products/fuse.html.

[7] https://www.mixamo.com/.

[8] https://rasa.com/docs/rasa/nlu/about/.

6   User-Based Evaluation

A user-based evaluation experiment was conducted in order to assess the user experience and draw insights by observing potential end-users interacting with the system and noting their comments and general opinion. In more detail, ten children of ages between seven and twelve years participated in the experiment (four girls and six boys). Since the experiment involved the participation of children, their legal guardians/parents gave their informed consent for inclusion before they participated in the study[9]. The goal was to test the overall usability of MagiPlay and answer the following questions:

A. Do children enjoy playing the game?
B. Can children create rules without facing serious problems?

    The evaluation experiment was scheduled to last about one hour and took place in the simulation space of the "Intelligent Living Room" of the AmI Facility. Two evaluators conducted the study, one acting as moderator and the other as an observer. Both were keeping observation notes to ensure that nothing relevant was missed, since no video recording equipment was used.

    Since this was the first user-based study conducted for MagiPlay, it was decided to study Modes 1 and 3, and schedule a subsequent evaluation (with a different cohort of users) for the remaining modes. Moreover, in the context of this experiment Freddy acted merely as an assistant (and not as a CA), dictating the rules the children had to create in each level, and assisting them in the whole process. To this end, children were asked to play three levels of the "Follow the game plot mode" of MagiPlay, during which they were asked to create three rules defining the behavior of objects inside the "Intelligent Living Room":

R1. **WHEN** the PHONE *rings* **THEN** the SPEAKER *turns on*
R2. **WHEN** the DOOR closes **THEN** the LIGHTS *turn off*
R3. **WHEN** the DOOR closes **THEN** the LIGHTS *turn on* **AND** the TV *turns on*

    Given that this evaluation introduces many unknown concepts to the children, such as programming smart objects, creating IF-THEN rules and interacting in AR, we were quite precautious with the complexity of the rules that we requested the children to create. Our goal was to avoid extensive training courses that would teach children how to correctly use all available operators, but rather to observe and analyze their reactions to core concepts of the game.

    Regarding the pre-experiment specifics, the moderator explained the purpose of the experiment to the parents, asked them to sign the consent form, and requested that they remain silent during the experiment and not intervene, so as to not obstruct the whole process. Next, the moderator engaged in a short casual conversation with each child to make them feel comfortable, while it was communicated to them that the more problems they uncover, the more helpful they become since their mission was to help us understand *"if we have indeed created a good game for children"*.

---

[9] The study and its protocol were approved by the Ethics Committee of FORTH-ICS (Reference Number: 57/18-11-2019).

During the experiment itself, where the children had to perform three (3) tasks (i.e. R1–R3), the moderator was responsible for orchestrating the entire process, assisting the children when required, and managing any technical difficulties. With the use of a custom observation grid, the moderator and the observer could easily record a variety of metrics. In particular, verbal or non-verbal child behavior and emotions (e.g. focused, smiling, frowning) were monitored and recorded so as to perceive whether children enjoy playing the game or feel overwhelmed by it. Additionally, interaction errors (e.g. the child did not rotate tablet so as to find the baseplate with the camera) were noted, in order to understand if children exhibit any problems with the selected interaction modality, while errors related to the rule creation process (e.g. the child selected the wrong command brick) were recorded so as to reveal if children understand how to create a rule. Moreover, the hints/prompts given by the moderator were also documented, since we were interested to see whether children were able to overcome an issue without help, revealing the extent to which the interface adheres to the design for error principle [66]. Finally, the user success rate was calculated by marking tasks as partial success if a major interaction problem was observed, and if a major error occurred in the rule creation process, yet the task was accomplished successfully. Tasks were marked as a failure if they were not accomplished successfully (e.g. due to many errors, comprehension or other major problems encountered).

After completing the tasks, the children were asked a few questions (post-study questions) in order to infer their opinion on the system, what they liked or disliked the most, and whether they had any suggestions to make. Finally, the moderator thanked the children, commented on how helpful they were and offered them a small gift to express the gratitude of the entire team.

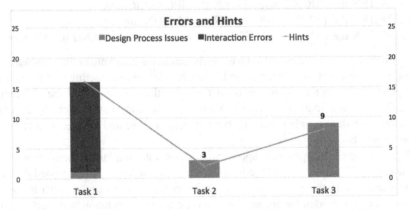

Fig. 7. Total number of issues during the design process, interaction errors, and hints per task

The evaluation results indicated that in general, the children did not encounter major problems, there were no failures and the overall user success rate was 82%, which showcases that children managed to complete the tasks without facing serious problems (Question B). However, two types of errors were observed in general, related to: (i) the adopted interaction techniques (AR, Touch), and (ii) the rule creation process. Regarding interaction in AR, almost all children had difficulties locating the artifact bricks, which were positioned in front of the baseplate, and in most of the cases, they were out of the camera's field of view. Similarly, the majority of children were not aware from the beginning that Freddy was "standing" on the right side of the baseplate; instead, they realized its existence later on during playing. Regarding touch interaction, all children tried to drag-n-drop the bricks on the mat, instead of just tapping on the desired location, revealing that such an interaction technique would be more intuitive for that target group. Additionally, in some cases placing a brick on a specific location on the mat was quite difficult to achieve accurately. Interestingly, the majority of the children instead of relocating or disposing the misplaced bricks, chose to bring new ones and add them to the rule.

Regarding the rule creation process, all children were able to create the first two rules without issues. However, during the creation of the third rule (that includes two actions, i.e. the LIGHTS *turn on* **AND** the TV *turns on*), eight (8) out of ten (10) children correctly placed the AND brick on the baseplate but did not understand that a THEN brick should follow. To tackle this issue, we plan to automatically put a WHEN or a THEN command brick next to a placed AND brick, by checking if a trigger or an action should follow.

Figure 7 displays the total number of errors related to the rule creation process (e.g. the child did not select the right artifact brick), erroneous interactions (e.g. the child tried to drag and drop the bricks on the baseplate which is not supported), and hints per task. As seen, during the first task (Task 1) there were several interaction errors, since this was the first encounter of the children with the game. Interestingly, these errors were eliminated in the subsequent tasks, which signifies that the players became familiar with the interaction paradigm very quickly, thus providing a partial answer to question B. On the contrary, only one error was recorded regarding the rule creation process for the first task. This is explained by the fact that it was an introductory task, where Freddy acted as an assistant trying to familiarize the children with the creation of IF-THEN rules. The increase in the amount of errors regarding Task 3, is explained by the fact that it involved the creation of a rule with two actions. As described before, eight (8) out of ten (10) children did not understand that a THEN brick should follow the AND brick. Additionally, as displayed in Fig. 8, the average number of errors (including erroneous interactions) decreased as the Tasks advanced, while the same pattern is observed regarding the average number of provided hints.

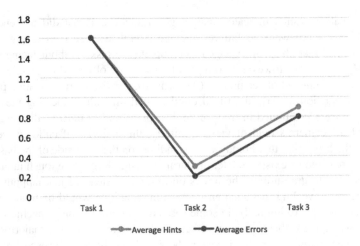

Fig. 8. Average errors (errors & interaction errors) and average hints

The notes by the observer revealed that all children (except one, a seven-year-old boy) exhibited positive signs of engagement (e.g. remained focused, did not give up due to mistakes) and seemed to enjoy playing, which answers question A. Observed behaviors include smiling, showing enthusiasm and surprise when simulating a rule. Despite the fact that the moderator and observer did not notice any direct or indirect signs of boredom, frustration, or indifference from the majority of the children, one of them -the younger (seven years old) of all the children who participated- seemed overwhelmed by the whole evaluation experience, mainly due to the fact that the child was inherently shy. Additionally, the children's answers to the post-study questions demonstrated that they particularly liked and enjoyed the game, which also provides an answer to question A.

Concluding, the evaluation study evinced that children enjoyed the game and liked the concept, as resulted from the analysis of the post-study questions and the interpretation of the children's feelings and behaviors while interacting with MagiPlay. At the same time, it was established that, despite some minor issues, children were able to successfully create IF-THEN rules and program the "Intelligent Living Room" using MagiPlay.

7   Conclusions and Future Work

This paper has presented MagiPlay, an Augmented Reality serious game allowing children to program their world and get immersed into computational thinking. It offers an intuitive, 3D-block programming interface, which enables the creation of simple if-then rules by connecting virtual LEGO-like bricks. Towards harnessing the benefits of collaboration and providing another layer of support for the children, MagiPlay inherently supports collaboration so that parents, teachers, or any skilled user can assist the child by means of remote help. Additionally, a Conversational Agent is available supporting interaction via natural language, and at the same time serving as a guide, and a "helper" for the child-user.

The findings of the user-based evaluation experiment revealed that children of ages between seven and twelve years were able to perform the required tasks without encountering major problems, whilst enjoying advancing the game levels. It is noteworthy that children expressed positive feelings in almost every part of the rule creation process, especially on the artifact collection and the simulation phases. The issues revealed through this experiment are going to be resolved for the next version of MagiPlay, while we are going to take into consideration several suggestions made by the children (e.g. skip helping tips provided by Freddy) so as to improve the overall user experience.

In terms of advanced functionality, we would like to explore ways to enable MagiPlay's simulation feature to be used as a debugging facility. To that end, we plan to further enhance understanding of code execution and algorithmic thinking, by visualizing the whyline of trigger action-rules [55], as well as to further address the issue of meaningless rules (e.g. never-ending loops). Moreover, future work includes the addition of appropriate components and logic to identify and resolve contradicting rules, which will determine which rule will apply in case of conflicts, as well as redundancy, as [56] presents, to eliminate duplicates. In particular, regarding inconsistencies and contradictions in rules, possible ways to achieve this could be introducing concepts such as a hierarchy, the existence of more authoritative users, or prioritizing recently created rules. Another solution could be to ask the user for conflict resolution, the moment that it is detected, after attempting to create a rule. These ideas are also discussed in [16], as possible fixes for rule conflicts, along with machine-learning approaches, which could mediate conflicts internally by interpolating between conflicting actions. We would therefore like to further investigate these approaches to see which one could provide the best results in our case.

Potential future improvements also include: (i) the addition of a map that displays the location of the available smart artifacts inside the environment in order to facilitate their discovery, (ii) the introduction of a supplementary textual representation of the rule in natural language, which will be dynamically updated as the creation process progresses, aiming to provide appropriate feedback regarding its current state in a user-friendly manner, (iii) support alternative themes (e.g. high-tech futuristic glowing spheres instead of bricks), (iv) detach the baseplate from a flat surface and convert it into an ambient floating platform and (v) further rely on AR to permit on-site smart artifact manipulation (e.g. virtually press the coffee maker button to start brewing coffee instead of selecting the same function from a list).

Acknowledgments. This work is supported by the FORTH-ICS internal RTD Programme 'Ambient Intelligence Environments'.

Author Contributions. Conceptualization: [ES, DA, AL, MK, GP]; Implementation: [ES, DA]; Evaluation experiment preparation and execution: [ES, DA, AL, MK]; Writing - original draft preparation: [ES, DA, AL, MK]; Writing - review and editing: [MA, GP]; Supervision: [AL, MA, GP].

Conflict of Interest Statement. The authors declare that the research was conducted in the absence of any commercial or financial relationships that could be construed as a potential conflict of interest.

References

1. Bransford, J., Sherwood, R., Vye, N., Rieser, J.: Teaching thinking and problem solving: research foundations. Am. Psychol. **41**, 1078 (1986)
2. Myth-Busting Reasons to Start Coding Even at an Older Age. https://www.makeuseof.com/tag/3-myth-busting-reasons-start-coding-even-older-age/. Accessed 20 Feb 2018
3. What's the Right Age for Kids to Learn to Code? https://people.howstuffworks.com/whats-the-right-age-kids-learn-code.htm. Accessed 20 Feb 2018
4. Brush, A.J., Lee, B., Mahajan, R., Agarwal, S., Saroiu, S., Dixon, C.: Home automation in the wild: challenges and opportunities. In: Proceedings of the SIGCHI Conference on Human Factors in Computing Systems, pp. 2115–2124. ACM (2011)
5. Dahl, Y., Svendsen, R.-M.: End-user composition interfaces for smart environments: a preliminary study of usability factors. In: Marcus, A. (ed.) DUXU 2011. LNCS, vol. 6770, pp. 118–127. Springer, Heidelberg (2011). https://doi.org/10.1007/978-3-642-21708-1_14
6. Dey, A.K., Sohn, T., Streng, S., Kodama, J.: iCAP: interactive prototyping of context-aware applications. In: Fishkin, K.P., Schiele, B., Nixon, P., Quigley, A. (eds.) Pervasive 2006. LNCS, vol. 3968, pp. 254–271. Springer, Heidelberg (2006). https://doi.org/10.1007/11748625_16
7. Truong, K.N., Huang, E.M., Abowd, G.D.: CAMP: a magnetic poetry interface for end-user programming of capture applications for the home. In: Davies, N., Mynatt, E.D., Siio, I. (eds.) UbiComp 2004. LNCS, vol. 3205, pp. 143–160. Springer, Heidelberg (2004). https://doi.org/10.1007/978-3-540-30119-6_9
8. IFTTT. https://ifttt.com/. Accessed 05 Oct 2017
9. Newman, M.W., Elliott, A., Smith, T.F.: Providing an integrated user experience of networked media, devices, and services through end-user composition. In: Indulska, J., Patterson, D.J., Rodden, T., Ott, M. (eds.) Pervasive 2008. LNCS, vol. 5013, pp. 213–227. Springer, Heidelberg (2008). https://doi.org/10.1007/978-3-540-79576-6_13
10. Walch, M., Rietzler, M., Greim, J., Schaub, F., Wiedersheim, B., Weber, M.: homeBLOX: making home automation usable. In: Proceedings of the 2013 ACM Conference on Pervasive and Ubiquitous Computing Adjunct Publication, pp. 295–298. ACM (2013)
11. De Russis, L., Corno, F.: HomeRules: A Tangible end-user programming interface for smart homes. In: Proceedings of the 33rd Annual ACM Conference Extended Abstracts on Human Factors in Computing Systems, pp. 2109–2114. ACM, New York (2015). https://doi.org/10.1145/2702613.2732795
12. Zipato. https://www.zipato.com/. Accessed 07 Oct 2017
13. Supermechanical: Twine. Listen to your world. Talk to the web. http://supermechanical.com/twine/technical.html. Accessed 06 Oct 2017
14. Zapier. https://zapier.com/. Accessed 07 Oct 2017
15. Stojkoska, B.L.R., Trivodaliev, K.V.: A review of internet of things for smart home: challenges and solutions. J. Clean. Prod. **140**, 1454–1464 (2017)
16. Ur, B., McManus, E., Pak Yong Ho, M., Littman, M.L.: Practical trigger-action programming in the smart home. In: Proceedings of the SIGCHI Conference on Human Factors in Computing Systems, pp. 803–812. ACM, New York (2014). https://doi.org/10.1145/2556288.2557420

17. McNerney, T.S.: Tangible programming bricks: an approach to making programming accessible to everyone (1999)
18. Brosterman, N.: Inventing Kindergarten. Harry N. Abrams. Inc., Publishers, New York (1997)
19. Bruner, J.S.: Toward a Theory of Instruction. Harvard University Press, Cambridge (1966)
20. Papert, S.: Mindstorms: Children, computers, and Powerful Ideas. Basic Books, Inc., New York (1980)
21. Montemayor, J., Druin, A., Farber, A., Simms, S., Churaman, W., D'Amour, A.: Physical programming: designing tools for children to create physical interactive environments. In: Proceedings of the SIGCHI Conference on Human Factors in Computing Systems, pp. 299–306. ACM (2002)
22. Wilson, K.A., et al.: Relationships between game attributes and learning outcomes: review and research proposals. Simul. Gaming 40, 217–266 (2009)
23. Oliveira, I., Tinoca, L., Pereira, A.: Online group work patterns: how to promote a successful collaboration. Comput. Educ. 57, 1348–1357 (2011)
24. Vygotsky, L.S.: Mind in Society. Harvard University Press, Cambridge (1978)
25. Stefanidi, E., Arampatzis, D., Leonidis, A., Papagiannakis, G.: BricklAyeR: a platform for building rules for AmI environments in AR. In: Gavrilova, M., Chang, J., Thalmann, N.M., Hitzer, E., Ishikawa, H. (eds.) CGI 2019. LNCS, vol. 11542, pp. 417–423. Springer, Cham (2019). https://doi.org/10.1007/978-3-030-22514-8_39
26. Vacchetti, L., et al.: A stable real-time AR framework for training and planning in industrial environments. In: Ong, S.K., Nee, A.Y.C. (eds.) Virtual and Augmented Reality Applications in Manufacturing, pp. 129–145. Springer, London (2004). https://doi.org/10.1007/978-1-4471-3873-0_8
27. Kateros, S., Georgiou, S., Papaefthymiou, M., Papagiannakis, G., Tsioumas, M.: A comparison of gamified, immersive VR curation methods for enhanced presence and human-computer interaction in digital humanities. Int. J. Herit. Digit. Era 4, 221–233 (2015)
28. Wang, D., Wang, T., Liu, Z.: A tangible programming tool for children to cultivate computational thinking. Sci. World J. 2014, 428080 (2014). https://doi.org/10.1155/2014/428080
29. Davidoff, S., Lee, M.K., Yiu, C., Zimmerman, J., Dey, Anind K.: Principles of smart home control. In: Dourish, P., Friday, A. (eds.) UbiComp 2006. LNCS, vol. 4206, pp. 19–34. Springer, Heidelberg (2006). https://doi.org/10.1007/11853565_2
30. Stefanidi, E., Foukarakis, M., Arampatzis, D., Korozi, M., Leonidis, A., Antona, M.: ParlAmI: a multimodal approach for programming intelligent environments. Technologies 7, 11 (2019)
31. Korozi, M., Leonidis, A., Antona, M., Stephanidis, C.: LECTOR: towards reengaging students in the educational process inside smart classrooms. In: Horain, P., Achard, C., Mallem, M. (eds.) IHCI 2017. LNCS, vol. 10688, pp. 137–149. Springer, Cham (2017). https://doi.org/10.1007/978-3-319-72038-8_11
32. Neumann, U., Majoros, A.: Cognitive, performance, and systems issues for augmented reality applications in manufacturing and maintenance. In: Proceedings of the Virtual Reality Annual International Symposium, IEEE 1998, pp. 4–11. IEEE (1998)
33. Kasahara, S., Niiyama, R., Heun, V., Ishii, H.: exTouch: spatially-aware embodied manipulation of actuated objects mediated by augmented reality. In: Proceedings of the 7th International Conference on Tangible, Embedded and Embodied Interaction, pp. 223–228. ACM (2013)
34. Zaeh, M.F., Vogl, W.: Interactive laser-projection for programming industrial robots. In: IEEE/ACM International Symposium on Mixed and Augmented Reality, ISMAR 2006, pp. 125–128. IEEE (2006)

35. Heun, V., Hobin, J., Maes, P.: Reality editor: programming smarter objects. In: Proceedings of the 2013 ACM Conference on Pervasive and Ubiquitous Computing Adjunct Publication, pp. 307–310. ACM, New York (2013). https://doi.org/10.1145/2494091.2494185
36. Heun, V., Kasahara, S., Maes, P.: Smarter objects: using AR technology to program physical objects and their interactions. In: CHI 2013 Extended Abstracts on Human Factors in Computing Systems, pp. 961–966. ACM (2013)
37. Mateo, C., Brunete, A., Gambao, E., Hernando, M.: Hammer: an android based application for end-user industrial robot programming. In: 2014 IEEE/ASME 10th International Conference on Mechatronic and Embedded Systems and Applications (MESA), pp. 1–6. IEEE (2014)
38. Chong, J.W.S., Ong, S.K., Nee, A.Y.C., Youcef-Youmi, K.: Robot programming using augmented reality: an interactive method for planning collision-free paths. Robot. Comput.-Integr. Manuf. **25**, 689–701 (2009). https://doi.org/10.1016/j.rcim.2008.05.002
39. Brown, B., MacColl, I., Chalmers, M., Galani, A., Randell, C., Steed, A.: Lessons from the lighthouse: collaboration in a shared mixed reality system. In: Proceedings of the SIGCHI Conference on Human Factors in Computing Systems, pp. 577–584. ACM, New York (2003). https://doi.org/10.1145/642611.642711
40. Kelleher, C., Pausch, R., Kiesler, S.: Storytelling alice motivates middle school girls to learn computer programming. In: Proceedings of the SIGCHI Conference on Human Factors in Computing Systems, pp. 1455–1464. ACM (2007)
41. Resnick, M., et al.: Scratch: programming for all. Commun. ACM **52**, 60–67 (2009)
42. Vahldick, A., Mendes, A.J., Marcelino, M.J.: A review of games designed to improve introductory computer programming competencies. In: 2014 IEEE Frontiers in Education Conference (FIE) Proceedings, pp. 1–7 (2014). https://doi.org/10.1109/FIE.2014.7044114
43. Aldrich, C.: Learning Online with Games, Simulations, and Virtual Worlds: Strategies for Online Instruction. Wiley, Hoboken (2009)
44. McTear, M., Callejas, Z., Griol, D.: Introducing the conversational interface. In: McTear, M., Callejas, Z., Griol, D. (eds.) the conversational interface, pp. 1–7. Springer, Cham (2016). https://doi.org/10.1007/978-3-319-32967-3_1
45. Van Merriënboer, J.J., Kirschner, P.A.: Ten Steps to Complex Learning: A Systematic Approach to Four-Component Instructional Design. Routledge, London (2017)
46. Alborzi, H., et al.: Designing StoryRooms: interactive storytelling spaces for children. In: Proceedings of the 3rd Conference on Designing Interactive Systems: Processes, Practices, Methods, and Techniques, pp. 95–104. ACM (2000)
47. Seraj, M., Große, C.S., Autexier, S., Drechsler, R.: Smart homes programming: development and evaluation of an educational programming application for young learners. In: Proceedings of the 18th ACM International Conference on Interaction Design and Children, pp. 146–152 (2019)
48. Blockly. https://developers.google.com/blockly. Accessed 16 Mar 2020
49. Blannin, J., Symons, D.: Algorithmic thinking in primary schools (2019). https://doi.org/10.1007/978-3-319-60013-0_128-1
50. Tucker, A., Deek, F., Jones, J., McCowan, D., Stephenson, C., Verno, A.: A model curriculum for K-12 computer science. Final Report of the ACM K-12 Task Force Curriculum Committee, CSTA (2003)
51. Leonidis, A., et al.: Ambient intelligence in the living room. Sensors **19**, 5011 (2019)
52. Newman, M.W.: Now we're cooking: Recipes for end-user service composition in the digital home (2006)
53. Weintrop, D., Wilensky, U.: To block or not to block, that is the question: students' perceptions of blocks-based programming. In: Proceedings of the 14th International Conference on Interaction Design and Children, pp. 199–208. ACM (2015)

54. Stefanidi, E., Partarakis, N., Zabulis, X., Zikas, P., Papagiannakis, G., Thalmann, N.M.: TooltY: An approach for the combination of motion capture and 3D reconstruction to present tool usage in 3D environments. In: Thalmann, N.M., Zheng, J. (eds.) Intelligent Scene Modelling and Human Computer Interaction. Springer, Basel (2020)

55. Manca, M., Paternò, F., Santoro, C., Corcella, L.: Supporting end-user debugging of trigger-action rules for IoT applications. Int. J. Hum Comput Stud. **123**, 56–69 (2019)

56. Corno, F., De Russis, L., Monge Roffarello, A.: My IoT Puzzle: debugging IF-THEN rules through the jigsaw metaphor. In: Malizia, A., Valtolina, S., Morch, A., Serrano, A., Stratton, A. (eds.) IS-EUD 2019. LNCS, vol. 11553, pp. 18–33. Springer, Cham (2019). https://doi.org/10.1007/978-3-030-24781-2_2

57. Laporte, L., Zaman, B.: A comparative analysis of programming games, looking through the lens of an instructional design model and a game attributes taxonomy. Entertain. Comput. **25**, 48–61 (2017)

58. Schmid, R.F., Miodrag, N., Francesco, N.D.: A human-computer partnership: The tutor/child/computer triangle promoting the acquisition of early literacy skills. J. Res. Technol. Educ. **41**, 63–84 (2008)

59. Greenlee, B.J., Karanxha, Z.: A study of group dynamics in educational leadership cohort and non-cohort groups. J. Res. Leadersh. Educ. **5**, 357–382 (2010)

60. Remagnino, P., Foresti, G.L.: Ambient intelligence: a new multidisciplinary paradigm. IEEE Trans. Syst. Man Cybern. - Part A: Syst. Hum. **35**, 1–6 (2005). https://doi.org/10.1109/TSMCA.2004.838456

61. Leonidis, A., Arampatzis, D., Louloudakis, N., Stephanidis, C.: The AmI-solertis system: creating user experiences in smart environments. In: Proceedings of the 13th IEEE International Conference on Wireless and Mobile Computing, Networking and Communications (2017)

62. Preuveneers, D., et al.: Towards an extensible context ontology for ambient intelligence. In: Markopoulos, P., Eggen, B., Aarts, E., Crowley, James L. (eds.) EUSAI 2004. LNCS, vol. 3295, pp. 148–159. Springer, Heidelberg (2004). https://doi.org/10.1007/978-3-540-30473-9_15

63. Core ML | Apple Developer Documentation. https://developer.apple.com/documentation/coreml. Accessed 31 Oct 2018

64. Louloudakis, N.: AmITest : a framework for semi - automated testing of Ambient Intelligence environments (2017). https://elocus.lib.uoc.gr/dlib/e/f/b/metadata-dlib-1499846119-176002-29371.tkl

65. Stefanidi, Z., Leonidis, A., Antona, M.: A multi-stage approach to facilitate interaction with intelligent environments via natural language. In: Stephanidis, C., Antona, M. (eds.) HCII 2019. CCIS, vol. 1088, pp. 67–77. Springer, Cham (2019). https://doi.org/10.1007/978-3-030-30712-7_9

66. Norman, D.: The Design of Everyday Things: Revised and Expanded Edition. Basic Books, New York (2013)

Author Index

Alhakamy, A'aeshah 19
Antona, Margherita 144
Arampatzis, Dimitrios 144
Arnaldi, Bruno 1, 57

Beham, Michael 39

Chang, Jian 91
Charlton, John 129
Cozot, Rémi 109

Gaugne, Ronan 57
Ginina, Elena 39
Gonzalez, Luis Rene Montana 129
Goudé, Ific 109
Gouranton, Valérie 1, 57
Gračanin, Denis 39
Guo, Shihui 91

Korozi, Maria 144

Lacoche, Jeremy 1
Le Meur, Olivier 109
Lécuyer, Flavien 57
Leonidis, Asterios 144
Li, Yanran 77
Lyu, Yao 91

Maddock, Steve 129
Martin, Nicolas 1
Matković, Krešimir 39
Meyer, Miriah 39

Papagiannakis, George 144

Reuzeau, Adrien 57
Richmond, Paul 129

Sarafopoulos, Ari 91
Splechtna, Rainer 39
Stefanidi, Evropi 144

Terrier, Romain 1
Tuceryan, Mihran 19

Wang, Shuangbu 77

Xia, Yu 77

Yang, Xiaosong 77
You, Lihua 77

Zhang, Jian Jun 77, 91
Zhang, Jinglu 91

Printed in the United States
By Bookmasters